Quod scriptura, non iubet vetat

The Latin translates, "What is not commanded in scripture, is forbidden:'

On the Cover: Baptists rejoice to hold in common with other evangelicals the main principles of the orthodox Christian faith. However, there are points of difference and these differences are significant. In fact, because these differences arise out of God's revealed will, they are of vital importance. Hence, the barriers of separation between Baptists and others can hardly be considered a trifling matter. To suppose that Baptists are kept apart solely by their views on Baptism or the Lord's Supper is a regrettable misunderstanding. Baptists hold views which distinguish them from Catholics, Congregationalists, Episcopalians, Lutherans, Methodists, Pentecostals, and Presbyterians, and the differences are so great as not only to justify, but to demand, the separate denominational existence of Baptists. Some people think Baptists ought not teach and emphasize their differences but as E.J. Forrester stated in 1893, "Any denomination that has views which justify its separate existence, is bound to promulgate those views. If those views are of sufficient importance to justify a separate existence, they are important enough to create a duty for their promulgation ... the very same reasons which justify the separate existence of any denomination make it the duty of that denomination to teach the distinctive doctrines upon which its separate existence rests." If Baptists have a right to a separate denominational life, it is their duty to propagate their distinctive principles, without which their separate life cannot be justified or maintained.

Many among today's professing Baptists have an agenda to revise the Baptist distinctives and redefine what it means to be a Baptist. Others don't understand why it even matters. The books being reproduced in the *Baptist Distinctives Series* are republished in order that Baptists from the past may state, explain and defend the primary Baptist distinctives as they understood them. It is hoped that this Series will provide a more thorough historical perspective on what it means to be distinctively Baptist.

The Lord Jesus Christ asked, *"And why call ye me, Lord, Lord, and do not the things which I say?"* (Luke 6:46). The immediate context surrounding this question explains what it means to be a true disciple of Christ. Addressing the same issue, Christ's question is meant to show that a confession of discipleship to the Lord Jesus Christ is inconsistent and untrue if it is not accompanied with a corresponding submission to His authoritative commands. Christ's question teaches us that a true recognition of His authority as Lord inevitably includes a submission to the authority of His Word. Hence, with this question Christ has made it forever impossible to separate His authority as King from the authority of His Word. These two principles—the authority of Christ as King and the authority of His Word—are the two most fundamental Baptist distinctives. The first gives rise to the second and out of these two all the other Baptist distinctives emanate. As F.M. Iams wrote in 1894, "Loyalty to Christ as King, manifesting itself in a constant and unswerving obedience to His will as revealed in His written Word, is the real source of all the Baptist distinctives:' In the search for the *primary* Baptist distinctive many have settled on the Lordship of Christ as the most basic distinctive. Strangely, in doing this, some have attempted to separate Christ's Lordship from the authority of Scripture, as if you could embrace Christ's authority without submitting to what He commanded. However, while Christ's Lordship and Kingly authority can be isolated and considered essentially for discussion's sake, we see from Christ's own words in Luke 6:46 that His Lordship is really inseparable from His Word and, with regard to real Christian discipleship, there can be no practical submission to the one without a practical submission to the other.

In the symbol above the Kingly Crown and the Open Bible represent the inseparable truths of Christ's Kingly and Biblical authority. The Crown and Bible graphics are supplemented by three Bible verses (Ecclesiastes 8:4, Matthew 28:18-20, and Luke 6:46) that reiterate and reinforce the inextricable connection between the authority of Christ as King and the authority of His Word. The truths symbolized by these components are further emphasized by the Latin quotation - *quod scriptura, non iubet vetat*— i.e., "What is not commanded in scripture, is forbidden:' This Latin quote has been considered historically as a summary statement of the regulative principle of Scripture. Together these various symbolic components converge to exhibit the two most foundational Baptist Distinctives out of which all the other Baptist Distinctives arise. Consequently, we have chosen this composite symbol as a logo to represent the primary truths set forth in the *Baptist Distinctives Series*.

MY CHURCH

ITS CHARACTERISTICS

&

PERPETUITY

J. B. MOODY
1838-1931

"MY CHURCH"

ITS CHARACTERISTICS & PERPETUITY

By

JOSEPH BURNLEY MOODY

With a Biographical Sketch of the Author by John Franklin Jones

- The Messengers of the N.T. Churches
- The N.T. Churches, the Stewards of the Faith
- N.T. Church Characteristics
- Loyalty to the N.T. Church
- N.T. Church Communion with Christ

Lectures delivered to the Theological Class
at Hall-Moody Institute, Martin, Tennessee

Printed by
The Baptist Book Concern,
Louisville, Kentucky
1908

he Baptist Standard Bearer, Inc.

NUMBER ONE IRON OAKS DRIVE • PARIS, ARKANSAS 72855

Thou hast given a *standard* to them that fear thee;
that it may be displayed because of the truth.
-- Psalm 60:4

Reprinted 2006

by

THE BAPTIST STANDARD BEARER, INC.
No. 1 Iron Oaks Drive
Paris, Arkansas 72855
(479) 963-3831

THE WALDENSIAN EMBLEM
lux lucet in tenebris
"The Light Shineth in the Darkness"

ISBN# 1579785239

PREFACE

Why another book on this subject? Why another on any subject? No two authors present any subject alike, nor do preachers. If all preachers should discuss the same subjects, why may not a few writers? Especially, since all have quit this special and important subject. The subject of this book has been so neglected by both writers and preachers, that a general skepticism, and disbelief, and antagonism possess the public mind. The overwhelming majority of the Christian world, with all public writers and speakers, misuse and abuse the right use of the word, church, and I believe it will go better with those who abused Christ, than with those who persistently abuse His church, "that He gave himself for." I would no more speak falsely of His church than I would of Him. If He has fulfilled the promise of His presence, power, protection and perpetuity to that executive body to which He committed His doctrines and ordinances, then all questions are settled in that one. The son of a preacher heard church perpetuity proved, and he decided at once, that the faith once for all delivered, must be found with Christ's organized and perpetuated church; so "he left all and followed him." No body of men is authorized to mix much error with a little truth, and that, with perverted ordinances, and claim to be *the* or *a* church of Christ. He never authorized but one church, and it is the one you find in the sacred and profane history of the first centuries.

I have books both larger and smaller than this on Baptist History. I hope many more will be written during this century, as each writer has his limit of influence. I have tried to avoid the details of the larger, and to add something to the smaller. The general histories are too large and costly for the common reader, and there is too much he does not want to know. So I have aimed to cull out what pertains to the Baptists, and to let each historian trace our history. The usual exerps have done good, and I hope these more connected ones will be better. I have complied with the divine rule to have "two or three witnesses" to establish the doctrine, and have combined the docrinal, practical and historical. I com mit it to God, and submit it to His people.

J. B. MOODY.

"MY CHURCH"

Upon this rock I will build my church, and the gates of Hades shall not prevail against it.—Matt. 16:18.

This is a great mystery; but I speak concerning Christ and the church.—Eph. 5:32.

The church of the living God, the pillar and ground of the truth.—1 Timothy 3:15.

Might be known by the church the manifold wisdom of God.—Eph. 3:10.

Unto him be glory in the church by Christ Jesus throughout all ages, world without end. Amen.—Eph. 3:21.

Feed the church of God, which he hath purchased with his own blood.—Acts 20:28.

He that hath an ear, let him hear what the Spirit saith unto the churches.—Rev. 2:17.

Despise ye the church of God.—1 Cor. 11:22.

Lectures by J. B. MOODY,
Dean Hall-Moody Institute, Martin, Tenn.

INDEX

	PAGE
The Messengers of the Churches the Glory of Christ.....................................	3–18
The Churches of Christ the Stewards of the Faith.	19–45
Church Characteristics as seen in the First Church at Jerusalem................................	46–64
Church Loyalty..................................	65–94
Dr. T. T. Eaton, on Matt. 16:18..................	69–72
Church Communion with Christ	97–131
Church Perpetuity is Scriptural	132–152
Petra—Petros.....................................	153–158
Church Perpetuity is Reasonable	159–191
Church Perpetuity is Credible...................	192–206
The Bogmils of Bulgaria and Bosnia	203–206
Church Perpetuity is Historical.................	207–306
Mosheim Epitomized on Baptist History.........	208–265
Traced Backwards to the 10th Century..........	208–233
Traced Forward to the 10th Century............	234–260
The Meeting Point...............................	261–265
Waddington Epitomized.........................	266–284
Another History Epitomized....................	285–296
Butler's History Epitomized....................	297–301
Dr. Thos. O. Summers..........................	300–301
Dr. John Dick and Theodore Beza	301
John Wesley.....................................	302–303
Oliver Cromwell and Dr. D'Anvers..............	303
President Gregg on the Waldenses..............	304–306
Dr. D. N. Lord, Hasse, Dr. Alexis, Masslin and Reinerius..	306
Church Perpetuity is Conclusive................	307–325
Dr. W. H. Whitsitt, and others	321–325
Perpetuity of Baptism as held by Baptists, 210, 211, 216, 217, 227, 229, 236, 237, 240, 243, 245, 246, 248, 250, 254, 255, 267, 268, 272. 277, 282, 289, 292, 293, 294, 295, 296, 298, 299, 309, 323.	

ADDRESS OF WELCOME

TO THE

SOUTHERN BAPTIST CONVENTION.

By J. B. MOODY, D.D.

Mr. President, Brethren of the Convention, and Visitors:

I have often visited the Southern Baptist Convention, but never had it to visit me before. I feel proud, elated, yea, I am almost beside myself.

I desire very briefly to introduce to you our city, and then to introduce you to our people. There are many kinds of cities in the world, most of them common, and but few uncommon. Ours is one of the few. The name does not express its only peculiarity. It is notably a city of hot springs, and it ought to be also for its cold springs, which abound in great variety, and are of the best quality. Out of the same mountain proceed both cold and hot water. This is a great mystery, which I trust some of you will solve. Truly, this is a place of "many waters," and I congratulate you in following the example of the first Baptists in resorting to such a place. If any should doubt there is much water because there are many waters, let me assure you that we have over five hundred places prepared for immersing the body in water. We all believe in immersion here. When we asked our bath-house men if the Convention might test our capacity to immerse a multitude, they cordially replied: "Certainly, send them on;" and one said, "Send them all to me." There was only one complaint, and that was, after tendering the baths they would not be accepted. If you don't accept you ought to be sent back and made to take a whole course. Get your tickets with instructions and your baths "as free as the water runs out of the ground," is the way one stated it. We welcome you to our many waters, cold and hot. Use them muchly and freely, both externally and internally. While this is not Washington City, yet it is a washing city. We take in washing—tons of it.

But not only the best of waters, but we have also the most precious stones. Passing by the baser metals, such as corruptible gold and silver, of which there are prospective mines more promising than the retrospective ones. Yea, we have mines in our minds more promising than those in our mountains. Passing by these, I introduce to you our crystal, the like of which is not found in all the world. No diamond can sparkle more brightly than ours; and the whole world is our market for whetstones. Bro. Moderator, as you are a lover of the beautiful, we present to you a Hot Springs crystal. That you may never feel poor, we present to you a Hot Springs diamond, and that you may never feel dull, we present to you a Hot Springs whetstone! These we have in great abundance. You may show this to your dull speakers.

But ours is also a Boarding city, and it is

needless to say we welcome our boarders. It is not customary to welcome customers, but to *thank* them. You have heard addresses of welcome belabored with eloquence, but eloquence is not needed now. You have heard it "spread on thick," which was necessary if the welcome was thin. But ours is thick enough, perhaps too thick, as some may covet not you, *but yours*. Not all of us, even in Hot Springs, are saints and angels. It is possible in a city like this for strangers to be entertained by angels unawares, but watch the angels, as there are two kinds. John says try the spirits, but he didn't refer to ardent spirits. Hot Springs has charge of that case. We keep them *for* trial, keep them *on* trial, and we keep *up* the trial. But let strangers beware lest these spirits try them. Indeed, if reports be true, we would not like to have them tried by every Baptist jury lest it happen unto them as it did to those evil spirits in the camp of Israel when "the earth opened her mouth and swallowed them up." Up is right, as they "fly to the head."

But I ask your attention to another peculiarity of our city. On a limited scale, here is perhaps the greatest combination of wealth and poverty, sickness and health, misery and pleasure, to be found in all the land. This is called the World's Sanitarium. The rich come here for pleasure, the poor for alms and the afflicted for healing. Of the latter classes you can hear stories, as true as holy writ, more horrifying than the ghost stories of your youth. Often are the poor shipped here on a charity ticket and dumped penniless at our depot. These are not our poor, but *yours*, and, as you are the representatives of the world's charity, I want you to know how we are imposed upon with the outside poor and afflicted. I hear that the Government bathes on an average of 600 to 1,000 daily of these indigent poor. But there is no charity fund here, and no charity home, and both these ought to be provided by those from whom the poor come, and to whom they rightly belong. We don't ask you to provide these, but to see that it is done. Acquaint yourselves with some of the facts, and your hearts will move with pity.

Next, I wish to interest you in our sore need as Baptists. Our church is out of place, and not in keeping with the place. A better church in a better place would give us access to hundreds that we do not now reach. If there is any place where the gospel can be preached to all the world, here is the place. Our people, sorely burdened with poverty and daily calls for charity, desire and deserve your sympathy and co-operation. Brethren, "if there be any virtue, any praise, think on these things, and those things which ye learn and see and hear, do; and the God of peace shall be with you."

But enough concerning ourselves. I wish now to introduce you to our people—to acquaint them with some of the peculiarities of our guests—I should say customers. Who are these that have come from the North, South, East and West, and have set down here to take council together?

Who are they? From whence came they? And for what came they? Whether any do enquire of this or that one, he is my partner, my fellow-helper concerning the truth; or if they all be enquired of, "*they are the messengers of the churches—the glory of Christ.*" In apostolic days the churches, with uplifted hands, chose messengers and sent them out on the Lord's business. But note well, they were the "*messengers of the churches.*" In the second and third centuries some of these messengers claimed to be delegates of their churches, which, of course, put church authority in their hands, and church authority is all the authority Christ left his people in the world. How the church could hold authority after delegating it I know not, or how they could delegate authority I know not, or how they could resist the delegated authority I know not; for they had been taught not to resist "the authorities." These delegates were generally the pastors of churches, and in two or three centuries they succeeded in wrenching authority from some of the churches, and thus arose an unscriptural congregational episcopacy. But not satisfied with authority over their church, they sought and fought to extend their authority over several churches contiguous to them. When they succeeded in this, they sought and fought to conquer more churches, and to conquer them the more. Thus grew the metropolitan episcopacy, and then the diocesian or provincial, and this grew into the national; and when the two greatest of these sought and fought for supremacy over the other, the bloody victory fell to the bishop at Rome, and he at length acquired the title of Universal Bishop, and from this he acquired the title of Pope, first of all christendom, and then of all the world. Not satisfied with the confines of this little planet, he extended his authority into heaven, and then into hades, and then into hell; and the final claim was, that all authority from the highest heaven to the lowest hell had been delegated to the pope of Rome. And this meant authority over men's bodies, minds, souls, property and destiny for time and for eternity. As all authority had been delegated by the Father to the Son; and as the Son had delegated it to his vicegerent, the pope, then the Father, Son and Holy Spirit must await, expecting till the pope, by fire and sword, should put all authority under his feet. Whether the pope, after subduing all things unto himself, proposes to deliver the kingdom back to the Father, and himself become subject, I know not, but I trow not, as he has "exalted himself above all that is called God or is worshiped." And, mark you, all this (and the half has not been told) was hatched out of that little egg that at first was innocently called "delegate." Are there any real delegates here claiming authority from their churches? We will save our welcome for you until the time of your departure, and if you are in a hurry for the welcome, then you must hasten your departure. Let me emphasize. I introduce to our people the "messengers of the churches." Not messengers or delegates of the

Convention. *Members* of the Convention and messengers of the churches. These are the glory of Christ. Delegates who rob churches of their authority dishonor Christ. These messengers claim no authority, not even over a hair on any man's head, nor will they allow any one to exercise authority over a hair on their head. These are the champions of civil and religious liberty, and their mission and commission is to make all men as free as themselves.

But note another peculiarity. These are not messengers of the church, but of the churches. Not one of them is a messenger from a State Baptist church, or Southern Baptist church, or national, or general, or universal church, for if so, he would be from a big church and the others from little low-down local churches, and there would be inequality and pre-eminence. A heavenly principle would be violated, and his place would not be in a Baptist Convention, but in the vatican at Rome, or some milder copy of it. *These be brethren.* They have no lords, no rulers, no masters. "Ye know that they which are accounted to rule over the Gentiles exercise lordship over them; and their great ones exercise authority upon them, and are called benefactors. But so shall it not be among you: but whosoever will be great among you, shall be your servant. And whosoever of you will be the chiefest, shall be servant of all."

Not even our President has the shadow of ecclesiastical authority. If there are sovereigns here they are on the floor. Our President, in allowing himself honored with election to this service, has really been abased. If we say go up he can go, and if we say come down he has to come. Don't you see how the earthly principle is reversed by the heavenly? No one-man authority here. The majority rules even the President. Even a delegate, claiming all the authority of the big church, would be cut off by the messengers of the churches. Christ built but one kind of a church, either a kingdom church to be increased, or a congregational church to be multiplied. These are messengers of the churches. Can you even imagine in that expression differing orders of rank either in the messengers or the churches? A telescope or microscope has never been invented that can bring such inequality even to the imagination. Christ is glorified in maintaining an equality of members, a parity of ministers and a comity of churches. To whatever extent preeminence goes to a messenger or a church, to that extent Christ is robbed of his glory, for he is head over all things to his churches—churches of same faith and order once for all delivered, else there might be scisms or divisions and heresies which cannot glorify Christ. There will be contentions about conventional matters, but that is to be expected from soldiers having on the whole armor and belonging to militant churches. But when the majority exercises its authority the fight will subside. They are sent here to fight for what they think is right, and then to abide by what the majority may decide. At one time you may say: Behold a fight in the camp of Israel, but when the vote is taken the war will end, and you can then say: "Behold how good and how pleasant it is for brethren to dwell together in unity."

The Baptists are a peculiar people. The churches sending messengers here are all modeled after the apostolic churches, and these after the church at Jerusalem, and that was the original first church which traveled about with the divine Carpenter and Master Builder. This first church, located for a while at Jerusalem, but getting too large and too lazy, the Lord permitted persecution to scatter it, and in their dispersion this church of Jerusalem became the church of Judea, Samaria and Galilee, going everywhere preaching the Word. But when they had rest they walked in the fear of the Lord and in the comfort of the Holy Spirit, *and was multiplied* by the members organizing themselves in their several places of abode into the churches of Judea, churches of Samaria and churches of Galilee, of which we afterward read: "Added to" in Jerusalem, but when persecuted it multiplied. Addition makes *more*, multiplication makes *many*. The Lord is glorified when his churches are multiplied. Indeed, addition, subtraction and division are all for a healthy multiplication. Multiplication is more important than location. Location is not always essential. The first church was not a local church. It located until it thought it necessary to be local, then it dislocated, by the will of God. We have all heard, and, I trust, read of the church that immigrated to this country from Europe. It was a church all the way. It is not right, because not Scriptural to call a church a local church. It was to an unlocal church that Christ said: "*Going*, disciple you all the nations, baptizing them in the name of the Father, Son and Holy Spirit, teaching them to guard safely all things whatsoever I have commanded you, and lo, I am with you in all the days, to the consummation of the age." What more authority has a local church? Christ may be more glorified in a going church than in a local one, however well located it may be. I don't object to a church locating as a means to multiplication; but I do object to using the word local as descriptive of our churches, unless we do it to distinguish from a migratory church. They don't have to be located to be churches of Christ. "Wheresoever two or three are gathered together in my name there am I in the midst of them." We don't have to locate in Mt. Gerizim or in Jerusalem. Our religion and churches and doctrines are *too much* localized. They ought to be going and discipling the nations. Seeds are for sowing—broadcast.

We are trying to change our location, but some are so wedded to the place that they had rather stay and starve than to move and thrive. Our literature abounds with these hurtful words, "delegate" and "local." I trust some one will move, and that the motion will receive a thousand, yea, two thousand seconds, to expunge these unscriptural terms from our nomenclature. They are misleading. Christ is more glorified in many little churches than one big one, and this discriminating adjective "local" is intended to disparage the congregational church. If the church Christ built is persecuted in one city, it can flee to another; but the church that occupies all space can't change its place. It can't even go to heaven, as that belongs to the universe. With this congregational construction it is proof against destruction. If all the mosquitoes were one, we could combine our forces against him and prevail; put as it is, it is a hopeless case. I never heard of a local mosquito, nor of local being used of any figure of the church. I never read of a local assembly, building, body, bride, city, congregation, candlestick, flock, fold, family, field, house, household, temple, vine, vineyard, woman, or wife. They may be local, but it is tautological tomfoolery to say so, except to distinguish them from some other kind. But there is no other. The kingdom is not local, but the church is necessarily so. When a church dies *in* a place, it dies only *to* the place, and scatters itself to others. Christ says, "I will *remove* the candlestick *out of its place.*" It is made of pure gold, the most enduring and indestructible of all metals. The more you melt it, the purer it becomes; the more you beat it, the more it spreads; the more you rub it, the brighter it shines. Christ does not destroy his candlesticks, but removes them out of their places. If Christ walks in the midst of the candlesticks and holds the stars in his right hand, how can you destroy them without destroying him? Christ is glorified in being the head of every man and of every church; and if being the head of every church makes him multicipital, being the head of every man makes him more so. If it is not necessary for every man to become one, that He may be the head, so of the churches. Behold these messengers of whom Christ is the head of every one, and they come from the churches of which the same may be said. Every man complete in himself, and every church complete in itself. Here is individual liberty and church independency. All with differing gifts and nationalities, yet in one Spirit have been baptized into one body, that is, one kind of body like the human body, with the head over the members, and the members having the same care one of another, "the whole body fitly joined together and compacted by that which every joint supplieth, according to the effectual working in the measure of every part, making increase of the body unto the edifying of itself in love." These have all drunk of one spirit, even the spirit of peace, truth and unity; having one Lord, one faith, one baptism, one God and Father of all, who is over all and through all and in all. The brother of low degree is exalted, and the brother of high degree is humbled, so there is equality, and they talk and walk and work together *as brethren*. While these messengers have been sent, and are servants, if the least one, in any particular, had preferred, he would have stayed away. His liberty was not lessened by being sent and being a servant. I speak in the language of Canaan. They were sent by the law of love and they serve in the law of liberty. What a peculiar people are Baptists!

A brother of another persuasion said to me the other day: "I am glad you have been sent back." "Sent," said I; "am I not free? Am I not free indeed?" After a long correspondence I despaired of getting clergymen's rates over the Union system of railroads, because I could not give the name of the moderator under whose appointment I was laboring at Hot Springs. Will Baptists never make themselves known? We are to blame for most of this. Who gave one man authority to order another in the service of Christ? If I should receive orders from any man, or body of men, to go anywhere or to do anything, it would not be my will at all to go to that place, or to do that thing. Who dare get between me and a throne of grace, or to supercede the Holy Spirit as my guide?

To be more explicit, and to make ourselves better known—and I am sure this whole Convention will endorse this confident spirit of boasting—if this, the greatest Convention that assembles on the earth, should *order* me to continue in my present field till further *orders*, I would resign next Sunday. This Convention, great in numbers and wisdom, is weak in authority, and why? Because He who has all authority never left it to a large annual gathering like this, but to a little weekly gathering like that on the other hill, called his church.

And again, in order to allay a little apprehension or suspicion among some of our own brethren, I make this further statement, and I am sure I will have the hearty, if not the audible, amen of even our Boards: If in your great wisdom you should suggest plans that my little church will approve, we will adopt, them, *but not otherwise*. You have the wisdom, and we the authority, and, trembling under a sense of that responsibility, we seek your wisdom to enable us the better to exercise our authority, and that is why we rejoice in your coming. Advise us in all things, command us in nothing. If it is right for the Spirit to contrary the flesh, and right to contrary wrong, it would be our duty to be contrary to any order that would be contrary to the liberty and authority, vested in us by the great Head of the church.

Let me repeat. These are messengers of the churches sent to serve, not as slaves, but as sons, free and willing, doing service from the heart, not unto men, *not unto men*, but unto Christ. A glorious service, in a glorious liberty, maintaining a glorious unity, and in this is the glory of Christ. And it is our mission in the world to make every man as free as ourselves. Those in bondage to men ought to pray for our success.

We welcome you, disciples, because you are the disciples of Christ. We welcome you, messengers, because you are the messengers of the churches. We welcome you, messengers of the churches, because you are messengers of the churches of Christ. We welcome you, messengers of the churches of Christ, because you are the glory of Christ. And as Christ is glorified in you, see that he is glorified by you and through you.

Glad you are here. Wish more had come. Hope you will stay a long time, and that your stay will be as profitable to you as to us. Especially are we glad to see our brethren from the East side of Jordan. I was a long time on that side myself, but hearing of the corn and wine and milk and honey that flow in Canaan, the promise land, I am here. And yet there is room. Come one, come all. Come to stay. Bring all the family and the folk, and their families and folk. Remember, you are just on the borders of this goodly land. We are the down-Easters. The Middle and Western States are all in the great beyond. It is further to the Pacific, than to the Atlantic. Out here you can raise most anything. But if you prefer to live on sand, stay where you are; if rice and sugar, come to our Louisiana; if corn and cotton and cattle, come to Texas; if you want to raise hogs not fattened on swill from the still, come to Missouri; if you want to raise a fuss, come to the Territory close down on the borders of Texas. Indeed, you can raise most anything in Texas, but I thought I would make a distribution of our Western products; if you want to raise the wind, come to Kansas; if you want to raise yourselves and a fine flock of children, come to Arkansas (and I suppose the difference between Kansas and Arkansas is the same as between angel and archangel.) How can you raise yourselves by coming to Arkansas? There are two ways open to you—the usual way and the unusual. The usual way you know, and if you should fail in that, you can try the other way, which is the Scriptural way, and that is to humble yourself, and you will be exalted in due time. This is one of the best States in the Union for that, as there is so much to help a man to humility, and when he gets there, then he can look to the Lord to lift him up.

I hope you all will take a ride or a walk over these mountains. A way is there prepared, yea, a high way. And as you go with exaltation of body and exultation of soul, don't forget that it all belongs to U. S.—us. Recognize it, yea, realize it; not only be at home, but feel at home. Seize the keys, do as you please and dwell at ease. If you desire next year to visit Asheville, N. C., the next year you must come back. Come out from there singing "Home Again," and "Home, Sweet Home." Hurry back to your fellow-disciples, who will be found fighting with devils below. And may the God of peace bruise Satan under our feet shortly.

(The following address was delivered at the B. Y. P. U. Encampment, at Estill Springs, Tenn., June 25, 1907. As many of the brethren expressed a desire to see it in print, I hereby comply, after having given it to my Bible Class.)

The Stewardship of the Faith.

On occasions like this, with limited time and a great subject, it is necessary to boil down to the last degree. Yet too much boiling boils dry or boils away. As I want to say something, and don't want that to be dry, I must not boil too much. I could not cry if I try, yet if my eyes are dry, I hope my mouth will not be, nor your ears. Often the dryness is charged to the speaker's mouth, when it is altogether in the hearer's ears. I don't believe in dry doctrines, not even in dry grace; for the grace that bringeth salvation is a bloody grace, while the body washed in pure water is the dedication that grace has ordained for service.

CHRIST TOOK TO WATER BEFORE HE TOOK TO SERVICE. And that was for our example. And then, by all authority in heaven and upon earth, he gave us his commanding precept as well as example. "Make disciples, baptizing them and teaching them all things whatsoever I have commanded." The baptizing and teaching are in the process of discipling. Disciple first to Christ for salvation, then disciple into His doctrine for service, and baptism stands between as the solemn profession of the first and the solemn dedication to the other.

So the gospel order for all men in all the age is. SALVATION, BAPTISM, SERVICE. As sure as faith comes before baptism, and as sure as salvation and its blessings are predicted of faith, and there is nothing surer, so sure is salvation before baptism. On this all Baptists are agreed. Now, just as sure as salvation is before baptism, that sure must baptism come after salvation. Who said so? The all authority in heaven and earth. And who is he that says that you may stop at salvation? Who is he? Where is he? What is he? Never will I excuse one from baptism. Now, another step. Listen, preachers! Just so sure as salvation and baptism come before service, just so sure must service come after baptism. And who is he that marks his Master's sheep and turns them loose, to starve and waste their wool? The unfaithful shepherd. And who is he that would turn the sheep loose without even a mark? Who? The traitor. The child should be clothed, and the soldier should be uniformed. Not clothed to become a child, nor uniformed to become a soldier, but because they are. As many as have been baptized unto Christ have put on Christ. The most shameful nakedness in this world is that found in the service of Christ. O, that they were clothed upon so as not to be found naked. Those not having this wedding garment will be found speechless. A patch on the forehead is neither uniform, nor clothing. Thomas Aquinas said: If there is not water enough for the body, let the head be dipped. If a man is going to serve Christ only with his head, let that be first baptized, or he will think wrong and wrongly. If only with his mouth, let that be baptized also, or it will talk wrongly. If his hands are also for service, let them be baptized, or they will work wrongly. And if his feet are also for service, let them, too, be baptized, or they will walk wrongly. A defect in the foundation makes the whole superstructure defective. This may be in bad taste, but it is not tasteless or dry, for "there is much water there." A bad taste is better than no taste, and often better than a sweet taste. I don't want you to sing, when I am through, "How tedious and tasteless the hour."

This is my prelude; now watch my interlude, and see how I conclude. I must first emphasize STEWARDSHIP—the STEWARDSHIP of the faith. Then faith—the steward of the FAITH. Then the two definite articles—THE stewardship of THE faith. The last may seem narrow, but definite articles are narrow, and the truth is narrow, and so is the way. Let us walk today in the narrow way.

A steward is a servant, hired to manage a fund or trust, according to instructions. Hence, it is required of stewards that they be found faithful. They must have an abiding consciousness, that what they have they received as a trust, to be guarded and used and distributed according to the will of the owner. The fund or trust was *his* before it was theirs; *his*, while it seems to be theirs; and *his*, by the same right when they give it out for him, or back to him. Stewardship requires careful deliberation, intelligent consideration and diligent administration of *what belongs to another*. In the case assigned me, and which we are to consider, the interest is so great as to require a co-stewardship, or brotherhood of stewards, and this requires a personal fellowship and active co-operation that recognizes that it and each and all belong to the owner. Whether goods, or faculties of mind or heart, or spiritual gifts—all were given and received that they might be wisely used and imparted.

Let several Scriptures settle the *Principle* involved. Then the Scriptures that contain the *terms;* then it will be easy to draw reasonable and right conclusions.

First then, the Scriptures containing the Principles involved; then those containing the terms. I have taken Jude, 3d verse, as a firm foundation on which to build my argument:

3 Beloved, when I gave all diligence to write unto you of the common salvation, it was needful for me to write unto you, and exhort *you* that ye should earnestly contend for the faith which was once for all delivered unto the saints.

The Stewardship is in the "earnestly contending;" the Trust is here called "The Faith;" and the Stewards are "The Saints." Jude begun with all diligence to write of the common salvation, but the Holy Spirit impressed him that it was more needful for him to write and exhort, that these Stewards should be earnest in their Stewardship of this great Trust, which was once for all delivered to the saints. And as the Trust was to be perpetuated "once for all," so there must be a perpetuity of faithful Stewards, with an earnestness of Stewardship adequate to all emergencies. It is of the utmost importance to know who the Stewards are, what Stewardship involves, and what the Trust is. What is this called here "The Faith?" And who are these called "The Saints?" I am sure we will all agree on the first answer to be given, but I fear we will not all agree on the second. I shall earnestly contend for a baptized and organized christianity, called "the church," and not the saints unorganized, though baptized. The gospel is to be preached not only to the lost for salvation, but also to the saved for service.

"SAVED TO SERVE."

Let us go first to the last part of the commission—Matt. 28:20. "Teaching them" (all the baptized disciples) "to keep safely" (the same as contend earnestly); and the "all things whatsoever commanded" is the same as "the faith once for all delivered." That this trust or commission was given to the church, a pattern of which he had built once for all, is evident from the acts of the Apostles, where the Lord added to the church those disciples, made and baptized, and that *every day.* Unorganized christianity has no trust or commission, as unorganized anything is incompetent to do anything. Persecution was made "*against the church;*" the gates of hades tried to "prevail against the church," for unorganized christianity never did offend anybody or defend anything. Material for a building is of no account until it is fitted into its place in the building. The loose, left-over pieces, go to the scrap pile for waste or for fuel. An unorganized saint that cares not to be baptized, or to join a church, would not care for the rest of the "like precious faith." He that is unfaithful in that which is least, would be unfaithful also in the much, and is unworthy and unfit to be a steward of anything for Christ.

My next Scripture is taken from John, 14th chapter, 15–17th verses.

15 If *ye* love me, *keep* my commandments.

16 And I will pray the Father, and he shall give *you* another Comforter, that he may *abide* with *you for ever*.

17 *Even* the Spirit of truth; whom the world cannot receive, because it seeth him not, neither knoweth him: but *ye* know him; for he dwelleth with *you*, and shall be in *you*.

As in the commission, the individuals, whether members, preachers, or apostles, were not to continue by reason of death, and as the divine presence was to continue through all the days to the end of the age with the "Ye," "You" and "Them," therefore Christ viewed them, not as individuals, or officers, but as an organization, which was to continue throughout the ages according to the hell-defying fiat of the all-authority in heaven and on earth. "The science of omission" here is the nescience of infidelity. So in the above. The "Keep" is the same word mistranslated "Observe" in the commission; and the "Ye" are the Stewards, with whom the Spirit was to abide forever; while the "Commandments" answer to "The Faith;" and by "earnestly contending for the faith once for all delivered," the Stewards are "to keep safely the all things whatsoever commanded." In 1st Cor. 3:16–17, we see this Spirit of Truth was to dwell or abide in the church. Hence, the "Ye" and "You" must be as abiding as the abiding Spirit.

See the same Principle in chapter 15:13, 14 and 19.

13 Greater love hath no man than this, that a man lay down his life for his friends.

14 *Ye* are my friends, if *ye* do *whatsoever* I command *you*.

(Not those who keep the essentials, but the all things whatsoever.)

19 If ye were of the world, the world would love his own; but because ye are not of the world, but I have *chosen you out of the world*, therefore the world hateth you.

He chose them out of the world and called them together, and these two make the *ecclesia* or church, a chosen-out and called-together body. He taught about his church in Matt. 16th and 18th chapters nearly a year before this. These personal pronouns must not hide the church. We will see about this further on. Here his "friends" are the Stewards, the "whatsoever I command" is the Trust, and the "Do" is a part of the stewardizing. The verb is used in Luke 16:2. The Principle of the Stewardship of the Faith is here clearly set forth, and the Stewards will be shown to be, not promiscuous persons, but saints, walking in the light and life and love and law of their Lord. The all things whatsoever include baptism and church membership. "To the church of God at Corinth, called saints." I say again, saints not in the church are unworthy of Stewardship, even in things that are least. See this Principle again set forth in Acts, 20th chapter, verses 17, 28-31.

17 And from Miletus he sent to Ephesus, and called the elders of the church, and said to them

28 Take heed therefore unto yourselves, and to all the *flock*, in the which the Holy Spirit hath made you overseers, to feed the church of God, which he hath purchased with his own blood.

(This flock or church of God was the one at Ephesus.)

29 For I know this, that after my departing shall grievous wolves enter in among you, not sparing the flock.

30 Also of your own selves shall men arise, speaking perverse things, to draw away disciples after them.

31 Therefore watch, and remember, that by the space of three years I ceased not to warn every one night and day with tears.

These elders or bishops were "in the church." He has no offices out of the church. The Lord has provided for the edification and perfecting of the church by giving them officers; but unbaptized and non-church saints he has made no deposit with as long as they are out of the church. The all-authority in heaven and on earth calls for their baptism in water and then addition to the church. Till then nothing is required at their hands and nothing committed to their trust. In a word, unbaptized and non-church christians are not the Stewards of The Faith. The Holy Spirit never wasted ink on nondescript christians. This church of God at Ephesus was a flock, to be flocked and fed, fattened and fleeced, to be watched over and warned of false apostles and elders, both outside and inside, who wanted to corrupt The Faith. These grievous wolves were trying to get in among them, that is, in the church at Ephesus, and their object was, by false doctrine, "to draw away disciples after them," "not sparing the flock." Christ commended this church for proving these false fellows liars. The elders or bishops were the leading Stewards, so that if the church should be destroyed by these wolves, their office would cease, as the offices *are in the church*. "The saints, bishops and deacons" constitute the church, so that the no-church saints can have no officers for their upbuilding in disobedience. That the churches are the Stewards of the Faith, see Rom. 16:17 :

17 Now I beseech you, brethren, mark them which cause divisions and offences contrary to the doctrine which ye have learned; and avoid them.

The "Ye" and "You" and "Brethren," who were to do the judging, marking and avoiding, were the Stewards of the Faith, and their Stewardship consisted in keeping and earnestly contending for it, as once for all delivered. This letter was addressed to "All that be in Rome, beloved of God, called saints;" yet the whole world is agreed that these saints constituted the church of God at Rome, and that they had been baptized. The word church does not occur in this Epistle till the last chapter, and there it occurs five times very instructively. Phebe was a servant of the church. If there were saints at Cenchrea out of the church, they sent no one, anywhere, to do anything, that the Lord requires. Such saints are often captured by the devil, and become exceeding zealous for error, and "transformed as the ministers of righteousness," ever preaching Christ of envy and strife," supposing they are adding afflictions to those who are set for the defense of the gospel. Such are the agents of the gates of Hades, and they are zealous to prevail against the church. All the Gentile churches thanked God for the faithful lives of Priscilla and Aquila, but if there were Gentile saints out of the churches, of course they cared for none of those things. We find also that house-hold saints constituted themselves into house-hold churches. The Lord wants all saints added to His church, without delay, though few in number as a household.

The saints must do nothing without the consultation, counsel and consent of the brethren of the church. The next two letters were addressed to "The Church of God at Corinth," sanctified in Christ Jesus, called saints. Both letters extended the addresses to others of like character, and some suppose to unorganized saints. But it is an unreasonable supposition. All the saints at Corinth were baptized. "Many of the Corinthians, hearing, believed and were baptized." That was the divine order, and no exception was allowed. Paul thanked God that he did not baptize all, but he never thought of thanking God that any or all were not baptized. Unspeakable evil has come from the recognition, and encouragement to the so-called, but miss-called "Stewards of God," who were and are unfaithful in the first and greatest commandment to the unbaptized saint. Saved they may be, thanks to divine grace, but not fit, ceremonially and mentally at least, to serve as Stewards of the faith once for all delivered. I repeat: the *only* duty of the unbaptized saint *is to be baptized;* TO BE BAPTIZED; and the next duty of the baptized saint is to be added to the church, to the church of which Christ is the author and builder and finisher and defender, and which has never been destroyed. So Jude's "Once for all delivery of the faith" is seen in the commission given by Matt., which was to the baptized disciples or saints. And so of all the rest, then, now and forever.

The next letter was addressed to the churches of Galatia, the Stewards of the manifold grace of God. They were instructed how to manage the trust committed to them. If there were saints in Galatia not in the churches, they were left out, as all such will be when Christ comes to gather his jewels. The Bride will be made up of the elect and select, who were the faithful collect. The Galatian churches were clearly recognized as the Stewards of the Faith. The letter to the Ephesians is supposed by some to justify the belief that Christ has a universal church, visible or invisible. I don't see how this can possibly be. Acts 20:17 and 28, just noticed, with Ephesians 2:17-19; and 3:15, as read in the Revision; with the whole of chapter four, make it impossible for me to interpret 5:23-33 in any different way. It is common to speak of a wife or husband, father or mother, horse or lion, jury or sunday-school, as the church is there spoken of; that is, generically, one of a species, comprehending all in the species. The church at Ephesus is so spoken of in Acts 20:28. A universal church, visible or invisible, must have organization and officers and doctrine and government, or it can do nothing. Such a church could not be a steward of anything. It never meets to consult about anything and has no officers to execute anything. This senseless error about a universal church has deceived more people and wasted more energy and begot more bigotry than perhaps any other deceitful device of the devil. I don't want everybody scattered over the whole creation, living, dead, and yet unborn, to administer on my estate. What is everybody's business is nobody's business. Everybody's responsibility destroys individual responsibility. Individual obligation to the church and church responsibility to Christ constitute the head and heart and hands and heels of my subject. The Stewardship of the Faith is in the church, each church, every church; and as Christ is the head of every man, so is he the head of every church. Not denominational, sectional, state or universal church, for Christ has none such, and I am sure he would not have. They are not worth having. All the good that can be done must be done by individual, or co-operative, *i. e.*, congregational effort. "The Church of God" is a congregation. The expression "Church of God" occurs twelve times, and any man, though blind in one eye and purblind in the other, can see it so in every case. The lion is a ferocious beast; every lion is a ferocious beast; but all lions are not a ferocious beast. That is an inconceivable conception; an unsupposable supposition and an unspeakable superstition. The executive ability is in the real beast and not in the unreal buster. So of the horse, man, jury, church, etc.

An *individual* father may rule well his own house and his own children, but a *universal* father, with universal wife and children, whether visible or invisible, would be as great a travesty as a universal bishop over a universal church. "The house of God, which is the church of the living God, is the pillar and ground of the truth." That means the church is the Stewardship of the Faith.

Eph. 2:19 Nov. therefore ye are no more strangers and foreigners, but fellow citizens with the saints, and of the household of God;

20 And are built upon the foundation of the apostles and prophets, Jesus Christ himself being the chief corner *stone;*

21 In whom every building fitly framed together groweth unto a holy temple in the Lord:

22 In whom ye also are builded together for a habitation of God through the Spirit.

All buildings can't be conceived of as one building, nor all churches as one church. This applies to the church at Ephesus and to every other church. Christ built just such a church, "to the intent that unto principalities and authorities in heavenly places might be made known through the church the manifold wisdom of God." This is again Church-Stewardship of the Faith. The church is offensive as well as defensive. The keeping or guarding or defending and earnestly contending implies danger and opposition and persecution, and the church is what has been persecuted, and what the gates of Hades have tried to prevail against." The dragon was wroth with the woman and went to make war with the remnant of her seed (left from previous persecutions) and which keep the commandments of God and have the testimony of Jesus Christ." Rev. 12:17. " Here is the patience of the saints; here are they that keep the commandments of God and the faith of Jesus." Rev. 14:12. Thus we see that where the Principle of Stewardship is taught, that the churches are the stewards, and the members and officers, each in his part, being dutiful to the church, enables the church to fulfill its responsibility to Christ. Now for some scriptures containing the terms.

Matt. 20: 1-16 is very instructive—the householder hiring laborers for his vineyard. The middle verse, the 8th, shows the work of the Steward and all the rest the work of the householder or owner of the vineyard. We see the Steward must do what he is told, no more, no less, and that the responsibility for results was with the master. The laborers did not murmur against the Steward who settled with them, but against "the good man of the house." That is a fine lesson. Study it.

In Luke 16: 1-12, we see where and how the responsibility of the Steward comes in. The first one, in Matt. 20, was faithful in doing what he was told to do; in this we see the "Unfaithful Steward" and the stewardship taken from him. And are not Christ's Stewards playing a like game today? Having all the commandments of Christ committed to them for safe keeping, are they not failing or refusing to contend earnestly for all the faith once for all delivered to them? Are they not saying to their Lord's debtors: "How much owest thou my Lord?" And in order to be popular, and to be received into their houses, are they not compromising by proposing to let them off with one-half or two-thirds? And think you that the churches of Christ, for failing or refusing to keep safely all things whatsoever Christ had commanded, that the Stewardship will not be taken from them, so that they will have to retreat and take shelter with those whom they excused from a full and faithful settlement with their Lord? When Christ said "all things whatsoever I *have* commanded," did he not use the perfect tense, and does not that mean that he would not give any other instructions to the end of the age? Had not the faith once for all been delivered when Jude wrote? Did not Jude use the past tense, which implied that the full deliverance had been made before he wrote? Are we not giving full credit to doctrines much later than these? Will something else do as well? Will other and later founded, formed and fashioned churches do as well? Are not many discounting the old and putting a premium on the new? Is not the church question a part of the trust? Are not modern bishops head and shoulders above the old Bible kind? Is all this and much more like it faithful Stewardship of the Faith once for all delivered. Can an unscriptural bishop be blameless as the Steward of God? Does not 1st Peter, 4:10-11 require *all members*, as well as the bishop, to be good Stewards of the manifold grace of God, and to speak as the oracles of God?

A bishop must be blameless AS THE STEWARD OF GOD, * * * "Holding fast the faithful word as he hath been taught, that he may be able, by sound doctrine, both to exhort and to convince the gainsayers. For there are many unruly and vain talkers and deceivers, whose mouths must be stopped; who subvert whole houses, teaching things they ought not for filthy lucre's sake. * * * Wherefore rebuke them sharply, that they may be sound in the faith; not giving heed to Jewish fables and commandments of men, that turn from the truth." That was the way to contend for the faith; to keep the all things and to fulfill the Stewardship; but, of course, Paul wrote and Christ lived in the olden time, before men begun to conceive of catching flies with molasses, as their high calling in Christ

Jesus. Vinegar catches many flies, but molasses is better. If flies were what we had to deal with, I should insist on molasses. But instead of flies, we, in our Stewardship, have to contend with "Foxes," "Hogs," "Dogs," "WOLVES," Serpents," "Vipers," "Ministers of Satan," yea, and Satan himself; so that is a poor steward who arms himself only with molasses. What may be fatal to flies might fatten the foxes, etc. Flies are more fatal to our molasses than the molasses to the flies. It draws and fattens and causes to multiply and drowns only a few. This Stewardship of the Faith requires the whole armour of God, even a sharp, two-edged sword; and if you have two swords better take both. That is, if you live out West where the church is yet militant. This holy war is not over with us, so we have to keep a regular standing army of real soldiers, armed and uniformed and in regular training and in constant fighting, or we could not keep the faith, as every article is constantly assailed.

The Bishop is the general, the deacons are the colonels, the teachers the captains, and the saints constitute the great army of God, so that "saints, bishops and deacons" must "stand fast in one spirit, with one mind, striving together for the faith of the gospel, and in nothing terrified by their adversaries;" and this spirit of unterrified faithfulness is a token of perdition to the adversaries, but of salvation to the Stewards. This conflict, begun by Paul, was to continue. If the war is over in the East, it is not in the West.

Or, the East may have gone into a truce or a trust; but in the West every victory yet requires a battle. Our God is a God of war, and he is still calling for stout and stalwart soldiers. We may cry peace, peace, but there is no peace. Stand, means to stand against, and contend, means to contend against. We are not beating the air out West. The gainsayers are there. We have not yet stopped their mouths. They won't quit, so we have "to quit ourselves," but like men, *i. e.*, after conquering a peace. They attack every part of the faith, and especially the Stewardship of the Faith. They sometimes propose to merge, but that means submerge. They want the wolf and the lamb to lie down together, but that means the lamb on the inside of the wolf, and that is too close. But I beg pardon for that and I beg permission for this. The universal church has been assumed, asserted and insisted on to the irrevocable damage of the faith for which we should contend. I don't believe in it. If there could be such a thing it could not do anything. It never has met, it has no doctrines, no officers, no government, no commission. You can't tell who is in it or how they got there. It is an invisible, impracticable, impeachable, impossible, impecunious imp, spread out into shallowness, enlarged into littleness and increased into nothingness. It makes a man feel too large for a contemptible little congregation that Christ organized for work. They think they are in the big church by reason of saving faith, and they don't see the need of being added to another church—a little, local, limited church, too small for their little finger. Let me magnify this minified and crucified church, which is the church of the living God. I have heard you magnify the other; now hear me magnify this, and be patient and sweet, that you may hear.

Paul made converts and then organized them into *churches* and afterwards visited these churches to establish *them* in the faith. He wrote nine letters to these churches. He wrote four personal letters to Timothy, Titus and Philemon, but they were all about the churches; how to officer them and to set them in order. But you say there are also catholic epistles. I don't believe it. Why should the Holy Spirit waste ink on unorganized christianity? What account is it? The letter to the Hebrews was to organized christians. See chap. 10: 21-25.

James wrote to the Twelve Tribes Scattered Abroad; but in chap. 5:14 he says: Is *any* among you sick? Let him call for the elders of the church. The universal church has no elders, and if it had, you could not call them.

Peter wrote to "the Strangers Scattered Abroad;" but in the 5th chap. he tells the elders about feeding the flock or church, etc. He says: the church at Babylon, elected together with them, greeted them. He also spoke of baptism saving them in a figure. Peter never wrote to unbaptized and non-church christians. Nor did John. How John did insist on keeping his commandments and walking in personal and doctrinal fellowship, and about some "going out from us to show they were not all of us." How could they go out of the universal church? Where could they go to? The Elect Lady had a church in her house, and he insisted that she nor we should give admittance or encourage any other doctrine than that received. His letter to Gaius was of the same sort. This son of Thunder hurled his lightning at the episcopal Diotrephes, who loved the pre-eminence and who exercised his assumed episcopacy by casting some out of the church.

And Jude speaks of certain men creeping in unawares. Creeping into what? Not the universal church. He calls them spots in their feasts of charity, feeding themselves without fear. They were those who separated themselves, yet would come to eat with them. Such were open communionists. Then Christ, in Revelation, addressed not a holy catholic church, nor the church of Asia, but the Seven Churches of Asia. There was no Church of Asia, for if so, it was beneath Christ's notice. These seven churches he urged to hold fast till he come. Ephesus was praised for exposing the false apostles and for hating the deeds of the Nicolaitans. Good stewards in doctrine and practice, yet bad in spiritual religion. Those of the synagogue of Satan were to try the church at Smyrna with tribulations and persecutions, and they were exhorted to be faithful unto death in their Stewardship of the Faith, and they would receive a crown of life. The church at Pergamos held fast His name and did not deny the faith, even in the days when Antipas, the faithful martyr, was slain among them. Yet they had those who held the doctrine of Balaam, and also those who held the doctrine of the Nicolaitans, which doctrine Christ hated. They were defensive, but not offensive. Thyatira *suffered* that woman Jezabel, who called herself a prophetess, to teach and to seduce the saints. Faulty again in aggressiveness. Sardis had only a few who had not defiled their garments with false doctrines or heresies. Philadelphia had the door of persecution closed on her and the door of missions opened, so she could preach the gospel to all the world. The Laodiceans, of which we are, were lukewarm—neither cold nor hot. We are saying, it makes no difference what a man believes, or what church he belongs to, or whether he belongs to any, or what he thinks of church or doctrine, just so he thinks very lightly. Lukewarmness hates straight-jacket orthodoxy and loves mother-hubbard liberality. This makes any church feel rich while it is miserable and poor and blind and naked. Laodicea was poor with its riches, while Smyrna was rich in her poverty. Now listen and hearken at this:

HE THAT HATH AN EAR, LET HIM HEAR WHAT THE SPIRIT *SAITH UNTO THE CHURCHES.*

HE THAT HATH AN EAR, LET HIM HEAR WHAT THE SPIRIT SAITH *UNTO THE CHURCHES.*

HE THAT HATH AN EAR, LET HIM

HEAR WHAT THE SPIRIT SAITH UNTO THE CHURCHES.

HE THAT HATH AN EAR, LET HIM HEAR WHAT THE SPIRIT SAITH UNTO THE CHURCHES.

HE THAT HATH AN EAR, LET HIM HEAR WHAT THE SPIRIT SAITH UNTO THE CHURCHES.

HE THAT HATH AN EAR, LET HIM HEAR WHAT THE SPIRIT SAITH UNTO THE CHURCHES.

HE THAT HATH AN EAR, LET HIM HEAR WHAT THE SPIRIT SAITH UNTO THE CHURCHES.

Christ spoke to his churches. The Spirit spoke to the churches. And if Christ or the Spirit were to speak again, it would be to the churches. Seven times repeated, yet men having ears will not hear. They think He has been speaking modernly to individuals, to men and even to women, telling them to change what He had spoken of old to His churches. Since Jude wrote, there have been many deliverances of doctrines to newly-invented churches of the denominational kind, which men are furiously contending for.

"I, Jesus, have sent mine angel to testify unto you these things in the CHURCHES." These churches are named only 111 times, but referred to more than a thousand and eleven times. The word does not occur in the 5th chap. of 1st Cor., for example, yet there are 27 places for it in those 13 verses. We hide it behind pronouns and signs and figures. Read 1 Cor. 1:iv-14, 10:14, and put church in the places of the pronouns and other substitutes. Try it on 8:16-17: "Know ye not that the church is the temple of God, and that the Spirit of God dwells in the church? If any man defile the church of God, him will God destroy. For the church of God is holy, which church ye are." We should not let these pronouns and other kinds of nouns destroy the church of God. In letters addressed to churches, pronouns mostly stand for the churches. In Matt. 16:19, Peter stands for the church, as these "angels" do in the churches of Asia.

Now a word about "The Faith." The King James Version *let* in the definite article 32 times before Faith, *forced* it in 11 times and *forced* it out 42 times—32 times right, according to the Greek, and 53 times wrong. Those saved by grace through faith are saints, and to these church saints a solemn trust is committed, called "The Faith Once For All Delivered To The Saints." Take a few examples. "A great company of priests were obedient to *The* Faith." First, faith in Christ, then obedience to Christ, called here "The Faith." This obedience begins with profession and baptism. "God be thanked, that having been the servants of sin, ye obeyed from the heart that form of doctrine delivered to you." Rom. 6:17. Paul preached *The* faith he once destroyed. He never destroyed faith in Christ. The devil tried that on Peter, but failed. He wrecked Peter's courage, but his faith and love abided. Hymeneus and Alexander made shipwreck of *The* faith of some. They erred concerning the truth, saying the resurrection is past already, and thus they overthrew *The* faith of some. Not the faith that had *saved* them, but the faith they were to save from such destruction. "Wherefore rebuke them sharply, that they may be sound in The Faith; not giving heed to Jewish fables, and commandments of men that turn from The Truth. See also 2 Thes. 2:16; 3:6 and 14; etc.

It is not the duty of any man to contend for any system of doctrine delivered since Jude wrote, or since Matt. 28:20 was spoken. Yet multiplied millions of professing Christians have furiously done this very thing. "Once for all" means for all time and for all saints. All the rest are doctrines of men which turn from the truth. They first say, the new will do as well; then the new is better; then they insist that the old will not do at all; then they make the stewards say: It makes no difference, just so you are sincere, as we are all going by different ways to the same place, although "The Faith" says there is but one way.

Now a word about the Stewardizing, or contending, or keeping. This must be with an agonizing earnestness and a faithfulness unto death. As the word used in Matt. 28:20, plucked up Episcopacy by the roots, by putting the responsibility and custodian care, or stewardship, with *all* the baptized disciples, therefore the translators translate it "observe." They did this about three times out of some 80 occurrences. This word does not apply to the unbaptized—never—but to the baptized. It is rightly translated "keep" in the following places, and every time addressed to the baptized, and means to guard or keep safely. If ye love me *keep* (guard) my commandments. Addressed to the baptized: He that hath my commandments and *k epeth* (guardeth) them, he it is that loveth me. If a man love me he *will keep* (guard) my words, and he that loveth me not *keepeth* (guardeth) not my sayings. If ye *keep* (guard) my commandments ye shall abide in my love.

Hereby we know that we know him if we *keep* (guard) his commandments. He that saith he knows him and *keepeth* (guardeth) not his commandments is a liar and the truth is not in him. Whoso *keepeth* (guardeth) his word, in him verily is the love of God perfected. He that *keepeth* (guardeth) his commandments, dwelleth in him, and he in him. By this we know we love the the children of God, when we love God, and *keep* (guard) his commandments. For this is the love of God, that we *keep* (guard) his commandments. Every time to stewards or baptized disciples.

This word does not mean to *obey*, or to *do*, but to *guard* from attacks, and perversion. "Whatsoever we ask, we receive of him, because we *keep* (guard) his commandments, and *do* those things that are pleasing in his sight—keeping, doing and obeying are different things. See also Rev. 2:26; 12:17 and 14:12. Here is the patience of the saints; here are they that *keep* the commandments of God and the faith of Jesus Christ." That is, guard and protect both the moral law and the doctrines of Christ. The *keeping* has to be done by earnestly contending. Contention for the right, in this wrong world, was the spirit of Christ, and is the spirit of the gospel. See Matt. 10:21-28; 34-39; and Luke 12:49-53; John 7:7; 15-18-20; and all of the Acts. 1 Thes. 2:2 says, that after shameful treatment at Philipi, Paul was bold in God to speak the gospel of God *in much contention.* "*Hold fast* the form of sound words, which thou hast heard of me, in faith and love which is in Christ Jesus." Paul's closing words were: "I have fought a good fight, I have finished my course, I have *kept* (or guarded) the faith." And it takes a good fight to keep the faith yet, and it will be so to the end. As the eyes, ears, nose, mouth, arms, feet, lungs, liver and heart perform their functions in and *for the body*, and as the body thus acts, so let the members of the body of Christ act *as members of the body*, each doing his best to extend, hold and preserve the faith; each responsible to the church, which is his body, and to which has been committed the Stewardship of the Faith. What is taken from the members is taken from the body, and what is given to the body is given to the members. Let us not become robbers of the churches by the isolation of its members, and by crediting the members with the honors and responsibilities that are due to the churches. "Despise ye the church," was addressed to those who were making the supper a social, or class meal instead of a church feast. Let all come together in one place, and tarry one for another, and eat it as a church. Members despise the church of God when they isolate themselves and divert their mission and other benevolent contributions from church channels. The Stewardship was given to the churches, and its members should help and honor the church with their services and contributions. Tell it to the church. Not to the preacher or presbytery. I close with Eph. 2:19-21:

19 Now therefore ye (Church at Ephesus) are no more strangers and foreigners, but fellow citizens with the saints, and of the household of God:

20 And are built upon the foundation of the apostles and prophets, Jesus Christ himself being the chief corner *stone:*

21 In whom every building fitly framed together groweth unto a holy temple in the Lord:

22 In whom ye are also builded together (into a church) for a habitation of God through the Spirit.

CHURCH CHARACTERISTICS.

Was the First Church a Baptist Church?

This great question calls for a careful consideration of CHURCH CHARACTERISTICS. Do Baptist churches of to-day possess the characteristics of the First Church at Jerusalem—the one Christ built? "On this rock I will build MY church." The pronouns are emphatic and prophetic. The Lord knew that many churches would be built on other foundations, and fashioned many ways, but he built his own church after the pattern of which all the other churches of the first century were patterned. Let us study the Characteristics of the First Church at Jerusalem, which was the church Christ built, and let us see how far Baptist churches agree with the mother church in Church Characteristics. Personal characteristics are to be considered only as they belong to the qualifications for membership and office. One may be a good man outside of church membership, and one may be bad with it. The church is the place for good men and not the place for bad men. This error with Baptists is accidental and not characteristic. A good man is no better for being outside of the church, and a bad man no better for being inside. The reverse would be better for both. Church membership can't make a man good, but it can make a good man better; and it also makes the bad man worse, as it makes him appear what he is not, and so far, and generally farther, he acts the hypocrite. So we enter now, not into a comparison of persons, but of churches. There are churches many that are of men, but there is but one church of Christ, and that must be like the one he fashioned in all essential church features. Let us study these in comparison with our own, and with others.

1. The First Church was Composed of Saved Persons.

If John the Baptist had baptized the multitude who applied for baptism (see Matt. iii. 7-10 and Luke iii. 7-9), it would perhaps have sealed their damnation. Why? Because they were destitute of the Spiritual prerequisites to baptism, and hence their baptism could only have been in "form" or, "according to the letter."

A man must first believe in Christ, and "whosoever believeth in the Son of God hath the witness in himself" (1 John v. 10); "hath everlasting life, and shall not come into condemnation" (John v. 24); "has been born of God" (1 John v. 1) and "overcometh the world" (1 John v. 4-5), "is justified" (Rom. v. 1). Yea, he must have the blessings predicated of Repentance, Faith, Love, Confession, or baptism will lead him away and astray, and that to his own destruction. How can a man obey in Spirit without Spiritual qualification? If Spiritual fitness is not inquired into, then soon it will not be required. You need not expect it if you don't exact it; if not taught it will not be sought; if not held it will not be had. If candidates go down into the water without having died to sin, and that means freedom from sin, and with no newness of life, then his baptism, so called, would be a solemn profession of falsehoods. Rom. vi. 1-11 has no reference to baptism of the Holy Spirit, or by the Holy Spirit, or in the Holy Spirit, yet it is Spiritual baptism. It is not the natural man conforming to the letter, but the Spiritual man conforming to both Letter and Spirit of baptism.

How inconceivably high does this lift us above the idea of a natural man submitting to a sacrament in order to be saved. How degrading the thought to a spiritual man. I would prefer idolatry in any of its forms to such a perversion of a holy ordinance and its implied holy doctrines. No likeness of any god can save any man from anything, not even any likeness of the true God or of his Christ. We were saved by the death and resurrection of Christ, and not by the likness of it. There is no more salvation in baptism than any other likeness of things or beings. If looking through the images to the gods is idolatry, so looking through this likeness to the reality is idolatry also. The reality comes first. We are not allowed to have any likeness of God or of Christ, but baptism, a likeness of salvation, is allowed and ordained as the profession of our previous hope before men. It is a "figure" of our salvation, not the putting away the filth of the flesh which is sin, but the answer of a good conscience by the resurrection of Christ. How was the answering conscience made good? "How much more shall the blood of Christ . . . purge your conscience from dead works to serve the living God." (Heb. ix. 14). "And the worshippers once purged should have no more conscience of sins." (Heb. x. 2). " Let us draw near with a true heart in full assurance of faith, having our hearts sprinkled from an evil conscience and our bodies washed with pure water. Let us hold fast the profession of our hope without wavering; for he is faithful that promised." (Heb. x. 22-24). Baptists are indeed distinguished for keeping the blood before water and Christ before the church. If baptism is the putting on of Christ and identifies us as Christians, ought we not to be Christians before we put on Christ? If the baptism of infants is infant baptism, and the baptism of believers is believers' baptism, then is not the baptism of Christians Christian baptism? And if so, where can you find Christian baptism except among the Baptists? Certainly no others hold it as the rule.

Neither John the Baptist nor Peter, on Pentecost, admitted any to baptism till they gave evidence of conversion, and as baptism is before church membership, the evidence of conversion was necessary to that also.

Read Acts, chapters 1 and 2, and it is clear that the whole church was composed of saved persons. Baptist churches today admit only such as profess to be saved. This is the rule only of Baptist churches. Others don't seek to have saved persons only. Armenians admit only those who are candidates for salvation. They think none are saved before death, and as death takes them out of their churches, none are saved while in their churches. They being witnesses, their churches have none in them that are saved— only in process and prospect of salvation; and this prospect exceeding poor, if they are to be saved by works, and that is their only hope and plea.

The question now to be considered is, what is this spiritual kind of material that in the beginning was put into the church—God's spiritual temple? There is an exception, but I think it helps to establish the rule. Christ knew from the beginning that Judas was a devil, yet he chose him, and put upon him all the honors that belong to a true disciple. He preached, wrought miracles, was treasurer, and had the best associations and influences that were ever provided for men. He was solemnly warned at the last supper, and was driven out on his devilish mission; and in the face of all this, he sold his Master and betrayed him with kisses. All this was necessary according to the divine purpose and plan, and as none but a devil could do a devil's work, a devil was chosen to do it. Now, if Judas, an unconverted man in the church, with all of his favorable advantages, was not deterred by detection and exposure "before the act" from its commission, on what ground can we found a hope that the church is the institution for a sinner to join? Yet the Catholic and Protestant world hold to this idea, and the writer entertains grave apprehension that we Baptists, in a large measure, have imbibed the damnable heresy. I fear many of our evangelists think that joining the church might do the sinner good, and with this salve on their doubting consciences they proceed to add fame to their name by large additions as a seal to their ministry.

But how was it in the beginning? With Judas out, the purged church was found tarrying in Jerusalem in protracted prayer-meeting, waiting for the promised enduement of power from on high. (Acts i). In the second chapter we find they all continued with one accord in one place. Not an unconverted person among them. They were all filled with the Holy Spirit, and spake as the Spirit gave them utterance. Their preaching was greatly blessed, and many were convicted of sin, and when they cried out, asking what they must do, they were not told to join the church for salvation. They were told to repent and be baptized, trusting upon the name of Jesus Christ for the remission of sins, and they (as well as the others) should receive the gift of the Holy Spirit. Peter preached the same gospel in Acts ii. 38 that he preached in Acts x. 43. The Greek idiom requires the above rendering.

The commission in Luke 24:47 has the same idiom: "Repentance unto the remission of sins, trusting upon his name, should be preached among all nations, beginning at Jerusalem." So Peter, beginning at Jerusalem, used the same idiom—epi before the dative, signifying trust, reliance upon, etc.

The change from the painful conviction of sin to the glad reception of the Word is evidence. To be publicly baptized in the name of Jesus Christ, whom they had crucified, and with wicked hands had slain, and that in the face of fiery persecution, is evidence again; and if further evidence is wanted, it is abundantly supplied in what follows:

"And they continued steadfastly in the apostles' doctrine and fellowship, and in breaking of bread, and in prayers. And all that believed were together, and had all things common; and sold their possessions and goods, and parted them to all, as every man had need. And they, continuing daily with one accord in the temple, and breaking bread from house to house, did eat their meat with gladness and singleness of heart; praising God, and having favor with all the people. And the Lord added to the church daily such as should be saved."

The last words, as translated, render this doctrine doubtful. Did the Lord add to the church the saved or such as should be saved? If such as should be saved, the Catholics and Protestants are right and the Baptists wrong. If they were saved before they were added, the Bapsists are right and the others wrong. The Catholic Bible reads: "And the Lord added daily to their society such as should be saved." King James follows with the such as should be saved." This makes the salvation prospective, and as all men should be saved, then all should join the church, even infants.

To keep one out of the church until he is saved, and saved forever, is peculiarly Baptist doctrine, and we claim that the text, rightly translated, will prove it. I will introduce a few translations here, just such as have come to hand; also a few commentaries. Were they saved before added or added before saved? That is the question of questions, and upon it rests the doctrine of **Regenerated Church Membership**.

In my Distinguishing Baptist Doctrines, chapters xiii and xiv, I quote from the following authors, to the effect that all are agreed on, say this one from Living Oracles, by Alexander Campbell, or by his disciple, H. T. Anderson, as the right translation, viz: "The Lord added daily the saved to the church." So say in substance Bible Union; Oxford Revision; Broadus, Hovey & Weston; Murdock's Syriac; Englishman's Concordance; Doddridge; Sawyer; Jamison, Fawcett & Brown; Sam'l Williams; Campbell—Rice Debate, pp. 436 and 459; McGarvey; Rotherham; Lyman Abbott; Homilitical Comt; Wesley; Adam Clark, who says, "should be saved is improper and insupportable. The original means simply and solely those then saved." That settles Acts 2:47.

Who but Baptists can boast so much of God's grace through faith before baptism and the church? Who is so free as we from baptimal regeneration and church salvation? Do not those who believe in these heresies acknowledge our doctrine of Regenerated Church Membership when they resort to the infantile rite for "regeneration and engrafting into the body of Christ?

But I must be brief on the other Characteristics.

2. They Were Discipled Before They Were Baptized. Matt. 28:19-20 and John 4:1. Others, as a rule, believe in discipling by baptizing. See A. Campbell, and Pedobaptist writers generally, and especially their practice.

3. They Repented Before They Were Baptized. Matt. 1:2, 7, 8; Luke 3:6, 8; Mark 1:4; Acts 13:24, etc. Baptist churches require evidence of Repentance before baptism. No others do.

4. They Were Convicted Before They Repented. John 16:8-9; Acts 2:37; 1 Cor. 14:26-27. Baptist churches only make enquiry about this work of the Holy Spirit. All Baptists do not, but they violate the old-time rule of Baptists.

5. They Repented Before They Believed. Mark 1:15; Matt. 21:22; Acts 2:38 and 19:4; Heb. 6:1. Baptists believe the order is of vital importance. The order reversed is fatal to both repentance and faith.

6. They Were Baptized When They Believed. Acts 2:41; 8:12; 18:8. Not when they repented, or when eight days old, etc., as the custom of some is, or when born of a believing parent or parents, as the rule of others is. When they believe, is the time. This is characteristic only of Baptist churches.

7. They Experienced Conversion Before They Were Baptized. Acts 2:37 and 41; 10:43-47; Matt. 3:8-10. "Works meet for repentance" are the voluntary fruits of a good tree.

8. They Were Baptized In Water, and Not With Water. Mark 1:5 and 9, etc. So say the Greek, and so translated by four English Versions out of six, viz: Tyndal, Wickliffe, Cramner, Rheims. Also Am. Stand. Revision and Twentieth Century. Also Geo. Campbell, Bengal, Lange, Myer, Abbott, Bennett, etc. Roman Catholics and Pedobaptists do not baptize in water, but "with" is their rule.

9. They Were Baptized by a Baptist Preacher. God had him thus named as the characteristic of his mission. Of course he looked after the necessary qualifications, or he could not have prepared a people for his Lord. Baptism was not his most important work, but his crowning work, which showed the vital work within. If one knows he was baptized by a Catholic, Lutheran, Episcopalian, Presbyterian, Methodist, Mormon, Campbellite, Christian, etc., then he knows he was not baptized by a Baptist, and weighed in this balance, he is found wanting in this very important particular, as seen in next characteristic.

(The class was asked to bring Scripture proof that the Apostles who were "first put into the church" were baptized by John. The following are some of the Scriptures used in proof: Matt. 3:11; Luke 3-5, 8; 7:20-30; Acts 1:4-5; 11:15-17 and 19:2-5, etc.)

10. They Were Baptized By One Who Had Authority From Heaven. Matt. 21:23-27; Mark 11:27-33; Luke 20:1-8; John 1:24-33; Eph. 4:4-5. All who were sprinkled or poured upon, or immersed as sinners, have a so-called baptism that is not of heaven, but of men. Those can't be churches of Christ that have the baptism of men.

11. The First Church Had Baptism Rightly Related to Repentance and Remission of Sins.

The following Scriptures, rightly interpreted, show this: Matt. 3:7-11; Mark 1:4; Luke 3:3; 24:47 (New Version); Acts 13:24; 19:4 and Acts 2:38. Baptist churches only hold these in right relation as a rule. It is our Characteristic.

12. Only the Saved and Baptized Were Added to the Church. Acts 2:41-47 (Revised Version) Dr. Jos. Smale, of Los Angeles, and some of our English churches, add the saved without baptism, but it is disorder, and they should forfeit their claim and recognition as churches of Christ. They are Baptist churches only in name. True church membership requires both salvation and baptism.

13. No Infants Were Baptized. Acts 2:41-42; 8:12, 18:8. Acts 2:39 with 5:25 and 13:32-33 were used in disproof. "Children," in these places does not mean infants, but descendents. Also the Greek words, teknon, teknion, paideion and brephos were also considered. No Pedobaptist, or rather brephorantist has a reasonable hope of membership in the church of Jesus Christ. That is, if churches in all time are to conform to the original pattern. And what are patterns for, but for copy? "See that ye make all things after the pattern shown in the mount."

14. The First Church at Jerusalem Was Complete in Itself With Christ as the Only Head. There was no Pope, or Bishop, or Presbytery, or Conference there or elsewhere, to which it gave the least heed, or to which or whom it owed the least allegiance. In Acts 1:14, we see they attended to their own business in their own way. Peter could only suggest the business, and others could only nominate the proper persons for the office. The whole church, directed by the Lord (verse 24), DECIDED the matter. That is just the way Baptist churches do today, and they only.

15. There Was No One Man in Authority. Matt. 20:20-26; Mark 10:35-45; Luke 22:24-27; Eph. 1:22.

16. There Were No Elect Few, Called Presbytery, Ruling Elders, etc., known in that day, and all who are thus ruled are not churches of Jesus Christ, for in them no one rules, but "all are brethren." Acts 20:28: Ro. 12:8; 1 Tim. 5:17; Heb. 13:7-17, etc., are Episcopal colorings. See elsewhere.

17. Church Officers. Christ put the first members into the church (1 Cor. 12:28) and made Peter the pastor or shepherd (John 21:15-16), and chose Judas as deacon and apostle. Acts 1:17 says Judas had the lot of this deaconship, and verse 20 says he had a bishoprick, and verse 25 says that Matthias was elected to take the deaconship and apostleship from which Judas, by transgression, fell. As the apostolic office was temporary, and no one could fill it but "an eye witness of his resurrection," this left only two offices to be afterward supplied by the whole church, under the guidance only of the Holy Spirit—Christ's vice-gerent on earth. Acts 6: 1-6. There is but one church with bishop and deacons elected by the church. Phil. 1:1 calls the whole church "saints, bishops and deacons."

18. It Had the Discipline of Its Own Members. Matt. 18:15; Rom. 16:17; 1 Cor. 5:12-13; 2 Thes. 3:6, etc. A church disciplined by an officer or officers is not the church of Christ. Baptists only possess this Characteristic.

19. It Stood for Religious Liberty. Acts 4: 17-20, 29; 5:27-29, 40-42. So did Paul and so have Baptist churches in all ages. See further on.

20. It Multiplied Like Baptist Churches. Acts 8:1-18; 9:31; 11:19-26. Whatever the circumstances or causes of their scatteration, if they chose, by the direction of the Holy Spirit, they congregated and organized on the voluntary principle, and elected their own officers. Any Baptist church can divide; or any part of it for a good reason can pull out and organize when and where it pleases, because individual liberty is not destroyed or impaired by church membership. The churches of Judea, Samaria, Galilee, etc., thus organized, were recognized by the mother church, and by the apostles, and Christ. **This is a golden mark.**

21. The First Church Was Persecuted. Acts 8:1-3. So it is characteristic of Baptist churches in all ages to be persecuted. This is a peculiar mark. Henry VIII, Luther, Calvin, etc., and the popes could fight each other, and fight viciously, but that is not suffering persecution. The world, and all that is of the world, hate a Baptist church for evident reasons, and that is why they have been persecuted. John 7:5-7 and 15:18-20. The world is afraid of the churches of Christ, but of no others. They are as terrible as an army with banners, yet they never carry the sword or carnal weapons, but weapons mightier than those to the pulling down of strongholds. A Baptist church testifies against the world that its deeds are evil. The world don't want anything better than a state church, for it can remain as corrupt as before. Indeed, the rule has been that such a church corrupts the world, that is, makes it worse, for the worse parts of the world are where state churches have ruled for centuries.

22. The First Church Kept the Ordinances as Delivered, both in their order and meaning. They were only memorial or emblematic, and Baptism was put before the Supper. Only Baptist churches follow in this. All the others pervert them into saving ordinances, and many put baptism first, even before heaven, and then change baptism in every essential feature. So having no baptism, they "can't eat the Lord's supper." 1 Cor. 11:20.

23. If Christ and the Apostles Should Return to Earth, They Could Not Join Any But a Baptist Church. All have decided that John's baptism was not a Christian baptism, and they could not, according to their rule, receive it. Baptist churches would gladly receive them on their baptism.

24. Such Churches Were to Continue, and Have Continued 'Till Now. Matt. 16:18; Eph. 3:21, etc. We claim to belong, not only to a church like the one at Jerusalem, but to one, the like of which has existed in all the centuries since. I would not belong to any other kind. And this is not left to blind credulity. Suppose you call for the proof. I would be glad to produce it. I have it in great abundance, and of the right kind—the proof that proves, and I can prove that the proof proves the proposition. See if I don't prove it. If Christ has not kept the gates of Hades from prevailing against his church, it was because he could not or would not. If he could not, his power failed; and if he would not, his promise failed; and in either case Christ is a failure, and there is no hope of the salvation of any man. All modern churches are built on the supposition that he failed to keep his church as he built it. He never built a denominational, sectional or national church, for no one ever saw reference to such a church in the word of the Lord. If denominational, which? If sectional, what section? If national, what nation? Some think he used it in a universal sense, including all the saved in all ages. Then he commenced it in the garden of Eden, and there never was a time when such a church was on earth, and will not be, for all the saved have not been here, and will not be before the end. If a part of the church is on earth and a part in heaven, then a very small part is here, as nine tenths of the host are infants and idiots, and that from the heathen. Was this church persecuted? Are the gates of Hades persecuting the church in heaven? What sort of a church did he build, and that has been persecuted, and driven from place to place, even into the mountains and dens and caves of the earth? Was the church of God at Jerusalem a universal church? Did the Lord add the saved to the universal church? Then the saved were not in it, and his church is not made up of all the saved.

25. The church at Jerusalem was called THE CHURCH OF GOD. So every Baptist church is THE CHURCH OF GOD. It is nothing less, nothing more. It is not a part of it, nor is a part of it somewhere else. It is composed of members each in his part, and all equal in authority. It can meet when and where it pleases, in or out of doors. It has Christ for its head, and the Holy Spirit for its heart. No man or men can exercise authority over it. No member in it has any authority. The authority is in the body when convened. What it binds or looses, is bound or loosed in heaven. There is no authority like this under the heavens. It is Christ's executive on the earth, and he has no other. All of this and more can only be said of a Baptist church. I heard a preacher say that he thanked God he did not belong to the church of Christ, but to a branch of the same. I thank God that I do belong to the church of God, and not to a branch of the same. Did members at Jerusalem, Rome, Corinth, Philipi, etc., belong to the church of God, or to a branch of the same? Every Baptist church is The Church of God, and not a branch of the same. Every branch has a trunk that bears it, and severed from the trunk, it is fit for nothing but to burn. Where is the trunk of these branch churches? Rome is the trunk of Protestant branches; but Rome has cut off all these branches and consigned them to the fires of hell. If Rome is the heaven-ordained trunk, then it had authority to bind and loose, to remit or retain sins, and that means to save or to damn. And that is what it claims. How can a man thank God that he belongs to a branch of such a trunk? Can a branch be better than the trunk that bore it? Shame on such church pride! A Baptist church is not a branch of that trunk, nor any other trunk. It is the thing itself, all to itself. Its members live in Christ, the vine. He is life to the members, but head to the church. The member gets life from the vine, while the church gets authority from its head. Others get life from sacraments and works, and authority from men. I glory in the church of God.

26. With others, church and denomination mean the same thing. The Methodist church is the Methodist denomination, whether taken as a whole or in its several parts. The Methodist Church South is the Methodist denomination South. And so, more or less, with all others. But not at all so with the Baptists. We cry aloud against a denominational church. With others the denominational church is all—with us it is nothing. It has no doctrines, no officers, no government, no meeting place, no mission and no commission. It never did anything, never will, never can. If all Baptists living could meet in one place, it would not be a church, because it could not be organized. As each person would be entitled to an equal voice in all matters, and equal authority in all things, the multitude would defeat every object for which a church meets. Such a church meeting would be as impracticable as the denomination is inconceivable. All the statistics that could be gathered of Baptists would leave many out. They are a host that can not be numbered. Many are numbered with other people. They are Baptists, but no one knows them. Of course, they are out of place, as Baptists often are, or God would not be calling on them to come out. And we doubtless have some numbered with us who are not Baptists. Wish we could exchange prisoners, as all such must be. Would be glad to give ten for one.

27. A Baptist church is composed of volunteers associated in congregational effort, each member in equal authority, and each church complete in itself and independent of all other churches and of all outside authorities. Thus it was in the beginning.

Hence, church fellowship is founded on a common experience of grace, and a common responsibility in worship, work, labor, sacrifice, doctrine and authority. Denominational fellowship is to be found in the comity of churches or individual concern for the welfare of all the churches instead of all Baptists. A member who is indifferent to the welfare of his own church must be indifferent to the general welfare of all the churches. If the hand or eye or foot respond not to the demands of the body of which it is a member, how can it respond to humanity in general? If any charity begins at home, this is the charity. If one has no self-respect, what cares he for other people? If we love not those whom we know and see, how can we love those we never saw? This loving all God's people alike is fanatical foolishness and ludicrous lunacy. A man that fellowships his own church will be a well-wisher of all other like churches, because all are engaged in the same cause. Individual association is for the church's good, and church association is for the general good. If all the members were loyal to the church's good, then the churches would be loyal to the denominational good, which with us can only mean the common good of all the churches. Hence, one must begin with individual loyalty to his church. No one is loyal to what he lightly esteems. Proper esteem compels loyalty. One who properly esteems his family or country would die for them—and so of the church. A Baptist should fellowship a Baptist not so much for his personal qualities as for his ecclesiastical qualities—he is a member of the body or church of Christ—both members of the same body or church or a similar body or church. So Baptists should have ecclesiastical rather than denominational pride. We can't promote the prosperity of the denomination except through the churches.

1 Cor. 11:22.—*Despise ye the Church of God?*
(Read Rom. 12:4-8 and 1 Cor. 12:12-28.)

CHURCH LOYALTY.

What think you of the cross of Christ? may be the greatest question for us; but perhaps a question of equal importance to Christ is: "What think you of the Church of God?"—which is his church, and for which he gave his heart's blood, and his life, and which he loves as he loves himself. So I ask you: "What think you of the Church of Christ?" After defining two terms, I will try to help you answer this great question. "Despise" means to think down on, to look down on, to subordinate, to lightly esteem. Hate is of the heart; despise is of the head. See the distinction in Matt. 6:24:

24 No man can serve two masters: for either he will hate the one, and love the other; or else he will hold to the one, and despise the other. Ye canot serve God and mammon.

This means that if you don't go so far as to love one and hate the other, you must subordinate one to the other; esteem one better than the other. In 1 Cor. 16:10-11, we read:

10 Now if Timotheus come, see that he may be with

you without fear: for he worketh the work of the Lord, as I also *do*.

11 Let no man therefore despise him: but conduct him forth in peace, that he may come unto me: for I look for him with the brethren.

The church could not keep the world from hating Timothy, for that was appointed to all faithful ministers; but they could keep the world from thinking lightly of him. That is to say, the reputation of the preacher is in the hands of the church. Not his character, but the how he shall be rated. They hated Christ, but they could not destroy his character. In Jer. 4:30 we read: "Their lovers shall despise them." A mother may despise her son whom she loves, because she knows he is good-for-nothing. So a wife her husband. None of you have a cause for hating the church of God; but do you despise it? How do you rate it as compared to other things claiming your Loyalty? This I will help you to answer.

Next I must define "The Church of God," for nothing under heaven needs so much to be defined. Nine-tenths of the so-called christian world think they do God's service when they use the term in a bewildering or perverted sense. There is but one God, one Christ, one church, one body, one faith, one baptism, though there be many that are called such. All the world, in all the ages, could not change the meaning of the word of God, not even by universal usage and legislation. Nay, let them seal their perverted meanings with the blood of millions of martyrs, yet the true meanings are written in heaven, and were written from heaven, and they will judge us at the last day. As Christ is yesterday, today and forever, so is his word. "The word of the Lord abideth forever." Woe to him who perverts it. May we know what The Church of God is? The expression occurs twelve times, and there is no excuse for mistake.

In the text it means "The Church of God at Corinth," and of which the Corinthians were members; all of whom "came together in one place to eat the Lord's Supper, and they should have "tarried one for another" before eating. This was the one body unto which, in one spirit of love and fellowship, they had been baptized with the one baptism; and they were censurable for not keeping the faith and ordinances as they were delivered to them, for safe keeping. Both of these Epistles were written to "THE CHURCH OF GOD AT CORINTH." Note that. "We have no such customs, neither the churches of God," means the churches of God in various places. In chapter 15:9, and Gal. 1:13, Paul says he "persecuted the church of God," which, in another place, he says, was "at Jerusalem." He persecuted no other. In 1 Thess. 2:14 he says: "The Churches of God which in Christ Jesus are in Judea." Not denominational churches, for there were none. In 2 Thess. 1:4 he says: "We glory in you in the Churches of God." In 1 Tim. 3:5 he speaks of a bishop, which always means the pastor of a single church, as "taking care of the Church of God."

In verse 15 he speaks of "behaving one's self" in the house of God, which is the Church of the Living God. That means that the congregation that meets in a house is the church of the Living God. In Acts 20:28, he tells of the flock, or church, at Ephesus, in which the Holy Spirit had made the Elders bishops, and that they "must feed the church of God which he had purchased with his own blood." But neither Paul, nor Christ, nor these elders, thought they were big enough to feed, or take care of a universal church of God. The Church of God, which Christ bought with his own blood, was, and is, a business-doing body—a called-out and called-together assembly; and these churches, singly and collectively, in co-operation, constitute the sole agency for advancing the interests of the kingdom of churches. The Church of God in a city, means the whole Church of God is there, and if the whole Church of God is there, then none of it is anywhere else. See the 86 places where the church is used in the plural number, and the 75 places where it is used in the singular, and if you don't then know what the Church of God means, then God can't teach you.

The following figures are also used for the Church, and confirms the one meaning. They are all local, but it is tautological nonsense to say so. Whoever was so foolish as to put the word local before these figures? Try it in your mind: "Assembly," "building," "body," "bride," "city," "congregation," "company," "family," "flock," "fold," "field," "house," "household," "lump," "temple," "vine," "vineyard," "wife," "woman," "Mt. Zion," "New Jerusalem." Introduce your wife as your local wife, and see what will happen. She would think that she was the contemptible, little wife, while the big one was somewhere else. And mind you, every time a man speaks of the "local church," he has in his mind a big church, compared with which the local is a contemptible, little thing. Hence, all such must despise The Church of God, because they subordinate it to another, which is not another. No error ever did more to destroy Church Loyalty.

I desire to disseminate and perpetuate the following editorials in *The Western Recorder*, by Dr. T. T. Eaton. The one followed the other in *The Recorder*.

ECCLESIA IN MATT. XVI, 18.

"*Editor of The Western Recorder*: Will you not give, briefly and clearly, your reason for believing that the word *ecclesia*, in Matt. xvi, 18, means the local assembly?
Fraternally,
A CONSTANT READER."

Most readily. We have seven reasons, but here we will take space for only three, either of which we believe to be decisive.

1st. It is conceded that, according to the *usage of classic Greek*, the word *ecclesia* means a local assembly. It is also conceded that it means the same thing according to the usage of *the Septuagint*, which is the Greek version of the Old Testament, in use in Palestine in the time of Christ. Can it be believed that our Lord, in using this word for the first time, would, without any explanation, give it a meaning entirely different from what it would be understood to mean by those to whom He spoke? It is not ingenuous for a teacher, without a word of explanation, to use words to his pupils with a meaning entirely different from what they understand the words to have. Christ knew that the Disciples would understand Him to mean a local assembly by His use of *ecclesia*. Knowing that, He used the word to them, without a word of explanation. To charge Him with using the word with an entirely different meaning is to charge Him with disingenuousness, and this is not to be considered for a moment

2nd. The usage of our Lord Himself compels us to believe that He meant local assembly when He said: "On this rock I will build my church, and the gates of hell shall not prevail against it." Christ used the word *ecclesia*, so far as the record tells us, just 22 times. We will set aside, for the sake of the argument, this passage, Matt. xvi, 18, as doubtful, and look at the 21 passages, to determine our Lord's usage of the word. Whatever that usage is, must be applied to this passage. In Matt. xviii, 17, Jesus says: "Tell it to the church, but if he neglect to hear the church." This is the local assembly. In Rev. I, II and III Christ uses the word *ecclesia* 18 times, e. g., "the seven churches," "to the angel of the church at Ephesus," etc., and in every one of these cases there can be no sort of question that He means the local assembly. It is Christ that says this, because the one who told John to write what is here recorded, says of Himself: "I am he that liveth and was dead, and behold I am alive for evermore, and have the keys of hell and of death." Again, in Rev. xxii, 16, we read: "I Jesus, have sent mine angel to testify unto you these things in the churches."

Certainly here *ecclesia* means the local assembly.

Thus in every one of the 21 instances in which Christ uses the word *ecclesia*, there can be no question that He meant the local assembly. The probabilities, therefore, are twenty-one to nothing that He meant local assembly in Matt. xvi, 18—the passage which, for the sake of the argument, we set aside as doubtful. A probability of twenty-one to nothing is a certainty. Hence, it is certain that Christ meant the local assembly when He said: "On this rock I will build my church."

3rd. Christ, in Matt. xvi, 18, promised to build His church, which certainly was very dear to His heart. He did not promise to build but the one. If He meant anything else than the local assembly, then we have this result, viz: He promised to build His church and then never made the slightest reference to it afterwards; but in speaking on the subject of church twenty-one times, He, *in every case*, referred to something entirely different from what He promised to build. That He should speak twenty-one times about the church *He did not* promise to build, and never make the slightest allusion to the church He *did* promise to build, is simply incredible. Can there be a reasonable doubt that the church Christ spoke of twenty-one times, and the only one He did speak of, is the church He promised to build?

These are three of our reasons, each one of which, by itself, we think is decisive. We have four others we will not now give. "A three-fold cord is not easily broken."

After this comes the following:

Our neighbor arranges its "deadly parallel" on us, and claims to see a contradiction in the following quotations from the editor's tract, "Faith of the Baptists."

"Turning to the New Testament we find the word church used in two special senses, first as a local body of baptized believers, and second as including all the redeemed of all ages and lands."

"These local churches, the only kind known to the New Testament, were independent bodies and were subject to no central authority."

It would have been amusing had our neighbor attempted to point out the alleged contradiction. The "two senses" are simply the literal and the figurative. "All the redeemed of all ages and lands" are conceived figuratively as a church, when they become a local assembly in Heaven. We reaffirm both those sentences. We will give a chromo to the man that will point out the contradiction.

This editorial was endorsed by the following:

Dr. Jesse B. Thomas writes:
"I go farther than you in questioning whether the 'church' is *ever* used in the New Testament as 'universal'—for exegetic reasons assigned."

President B. L. Whitman:
"I am bound to say that I see no flaw in your position."

President Henry G. Weston:
"From your point of view you make out your case on the question you are discussing."

Dr. Wm. C. Wilkinson writes:
"Your editorial is a good specimen of steel-chain logic."

President G. M. Savage writes:
"All that you say on the church, I believe with all my heart. I accept what you there accept, and repudiate what you there repudiate. * * There is but one thing in your article that I wish you had plainly said, additional; that is, that the rock (*petra*) foundation is Christ."

No doubt but nine-tenths of Southern Baptists would be glad to add their endorsement. The other definitions of " church " are full of deadly poison.

If a woman is to keep silence in the church, and the church is universal, then she must keep silent in the kitchen and the parlor, for she is everywhere in the universal church. Indeed, she must be silent in heaven, if she gets there, for it is claimed that the universal church will meet in heaven, to part no more.

So the first charge is made out: Those Despise the Church of God Who Subordinate the Real to the Unreal; the Congregational to the Universal; the Practical to the Theoretical. At the first, the Lord added the saved, who, it is claimed, were in the universal church by virtue of saving faith; these he added to the church which was at Jerusalem, and which he himself had built. If they were in the big church by faith, why add them to the little church? Were there two churches at Jerusalem?

(2) Those Despise the Church of God who subordinate it in matters of Judgment. "Judgment begins at the house of God," "Which is the church of the living God." In 1 Cor. 5th chapter, we see that "The Church of God at Corinth" had judgment of those that were within; and in chapter 6, we read that they shall "judge the world," and even "angels." In Rom. 16:17, the church is called on to judge doctrine, and to withdraw from those who cause offenses contrary to sound doctrine. In 2 Thess. 3:6, the church is charged to judge those who walk disorderly, and to withdraw from such. The same in verse 14: "Have no company with those who obey not the word." Read also Phil. 1:9-10:

9 And this I pray that your love may abound yet more and more in knowledge and *in* all judgment.

10 That ye may approve things that are excellent: that ye may be sincere and without offence till the day of Christ.

Only those who have exercised themselves in righteous judgment here, will be qualified to sit on Christ's throne to judge the world and angels. Those who go to the courts of unbelievers for judgment, esteem them superior in judgment to the Church of God.

(3) Those despise the Church of God who appeal from her Authority. There is no higher court. Every appellant says by his actions, which speak louder than words, there is a higher court of Authority than the church of God. Christ says in Matt. 18:17: "Tell it to the church, and if he neglects to hear the church, let him be unto thee as a heathen man and a publican." That settles the case. There is no higher tribunal and no other tribunal. The Church of God is the Supreme Court of heaven on the earth; so that whatsoever it binds on earth has been bound in heaven; and whatsoever it looses on earth has been loosed in heaven. No king, or czar, or potentate ever had such authority as this. Christ left authorities on the earth to try earthly things; but the heavenly things belong to his church. I knew a man turned out of a church for selling whiskey, just before the meeting of the association, and he laughed at the church, saying he would appeal to the association. He tried it and found out for

the first time that there was no authority in such matters in an association—none of any kind outside of the church.

(4) Those Despise the Church of God who subordinate her peace and prosperity to their personal whims and family interests. Often this is a theological whim, or notion, or opinion, or hobby. How many pastors and churches have been sacrificed by one member because their doxy was not his doxy. If the pastor should be too loose or too strict on some moral or doctrinal question, as he holds it, then destruction sets in. He may be a very strong or very weak Baptist, and may believe that the majority should rule, but he considers himself the majority. The church is small compared with him. It is not quantity that he counts, but quality. If he is a drunkard or adulterer, or some such mishap has fallen on one of the family, then the church must not put her honor, or the honor of Christ, or his cause above his and his family. Such would be willing, yea, would insist on discipline of such cases on others, but not on him and his. Who has not seen churches wrecked and ruined because the church was put above the individual and his family. One such said to the visiting committee: "If I must choose between the church and the horse race, the church can go to hell." Others have put it in milder form about card playing, flinch, dancing, etc. Their whims are put above church honor and authority. They despise the church of God.

(5) Those Despise the Church of God who

esteem Lodge Membership and Fellowship above that of the Church of God. Of course this is limited to those who profess to belong to Christ. I have seen them regularly at the lodge, and seldom at the church. In front in the lodge, and in the rear of the church. Early at the lodge, and late at the church. Forward at the lodge, and backward at the church. At home in the lodge, and a stranger at the church. Brothers those in the lodge, and misters those in the church. Proud of the lodge, and ashamed of the church. Gives to the lodge, and withholds from the church. By putting the lodge above the church, do they not Despise the Church of God?

Zelucas, king of the ancient Locri, made a law, and the penalty for first violation was the forfeiture of one eye, and for the second violation the penalty was the forfeiture of two eyes. His son was the first to deserve the double penalty. Will the king ignore his law? Then he is not worthy to be king. Will he ignore his son? Then he is not worthy to be a father. What will the king do? He will both vindicate his law, and have mercy on his son. So he required his son to forfeit one eye, and he forfeited the other. Thus justice and mercy met together and kissed each other. Thus it should be in the church. Principle before personal pleasure or profit; the church above self.

(6) Those Despise the Church of God who put Association with the world above that of the Church. They have professed to be saved, and

they know their Lord wants the saved added the same day to his Church, but they prefer to be identified with the world. Everyone is identified in association either with the world or church. He takes his choice. He claims to belong to Christ, but he don't want to belong to his church. He is invited, urged, exhorted, and may be pulled and pushed and persuaded by a host of anxious friends, as well as church, pastor and the Holy Spirit, and impelled by an inwrought sense of duty, yet despite all this, he prefers so stay out and continue to be identified with the world. Of course, he will soon go back and walk with the world, and forget he was ever purged from his old sins. He is told he will walk in darkness, and soon in doubt. He cuts himself off from the means of spiritual life, and the result will be worse than cutting off from the means of physical life; but he persists, and WHY? Because he had rather be associated with the world than the Church of God. The archangel, with the most powerful telescope, or microscope, or any other kind of scope, can't detect a flaw in that verdict. If he is converted, it is far better for him, and the church, and the cause, and the world, to associate with the people of God, but he prefers to be numbered with the world. Did Christ say, come out from the world, and be separated from the world? Yes; but he prefers not to do it. Christ's honor and authority, with individual and church pleasure and profit, are not enough to induce him to break fellowship and membership with the world. He prefers to be in the devil's big church; in the kingdom of the world, which is soon to go down and come to an everlasting and ignominious end, than to be in the everlasting kingdom and dominion which is soon to fill the whole earth. Such will not be cast out, because they are already out. And when he comes and shuts the door, it will be too late to knock for admittance. Saved they may be, but so as by fire, and they suffer loss, and what a loss! Eternal loss! There will be no rewards for well-doing after the judgment. Great are the rewards of those who go in and labor in the vineyard. The same with Trunk, Lapsed or Excluded members. They ought to bleat, and bleat, and bleat until they get back into the fold. I was never lettered out of a church, and if I should be excluded, I will bleat to get back, and when I shall die out, I expect to join the general assembly as soon as I can. I beat my letter every time the letter gets behind. I join first opportunity if I can, letter or no letter. I belong to the company called saints, and that means the church of God..

If the devil can thus blind saints, and lead them contrary to their eternal interest, then what can he not do with sinners? I try to magnify God's Saving Grace to sinners; but is not that amazing grace, indeed, that "keeps" those who have tasted the good word of God, and the powers of the world to come, and who, it seems, *try* to fall away, or don't care if they do. It takes more grace, it seems to me, to preserve an enlightened, quickened, forgiven, justified, sanctified, saved saint, than it does to save a poor, blind, depraved sinner, led captive by the devil at his will. Think of a sinner saved by grace, and, in return, prefers to serve the devil. The Lord wants the service of no man until he is baptized and joins his church. I repeat: The Lord took to water before he took to service, and walked 65 miles to do it; and in the beginning the Lord added daily the saved to the church. Don't want to be associated with the saints? Rather be associated with sinners? Then see how they play with so-called, but miss-called letters of dismission. Right here the churches are reaping the fruits of their own folly. A church can't dismiss a member by letter. It can only recommend him. Paul calls them, in 2 Cor. 3:1, "Letters of commendation from you, or to you." He is dismissed from your membership, and you are no longer responsible for his conduct *when he joins another church*. But he thinks he is dismissed by the letter, and is out of the church, and back again in the good old fold of the devil, and he feels good, and perfectly at home, and perfectly at peace with the world, the flesh, the devil, and may think he is at peace with God, but he has only to wait till the good shepherd comes feeling around with his rod. Yes, there are thousands who take their supposed letters of dismission, and put them down deep in the trunk, or far back in the drawer, to keep safely, that is, keep safely from the church. Others will put the letters or themselves in the church, and then hide themselves out. Thus they run from the service of the Lord into the service of the devil.

They go about the streets begging the world to employ them, and the Lord to excuse them. What an easy prey for the devil! And if the devil don't use them, it will be because he doesn't want them. This scandalous conduct of christians has called forth such designations and classifications as Regulars and Irregulars, Oncers and Noncers, Workers, Jerkers, Shirkers, Dirkers, Hired, Tired, Retired, Attired, Billy, Silly, Nilly, Lilly, Trunk, Spunk, Defunct, Skunk, Annual, Quarterly, Monthly, Weekly (spelled both ways). "And such are some of you."

(7) Those Despise the Church of God Who Subordinate her Worship and Decline Attendance on her Meetings. They are bound by covenant to do so if God permit. They are all bound alike, and it is as much the duty of one as another. But see how they put the church on trial, perhaps before they arise in the morning. The devil suggests something for their attention and attendance instead of the church meeting. If it is business, the devil wants them to decide that their business is of more importance than the church. He may do this even on the Lord's day. Or, he may tempt with a diversion, such as a visit, an excursion, lounging at home, loafing with another of the same stripe, or sponging on a church-going member, to keep him away. One of these, or such like things they put up against the church early in the morning. Reason is the attorney, comparing this with that; judgment is the court that decides the case; and the will is the sheriff that executes the decree of the court.

Thus the church is put on trial perhaps early every Sabbath morning. Which will win? One must go up and the other down. WHICH? Why of course the one you think is of the most importance will win. You can't put any of these things above the worship or service of the church without subordinating or despising the Church of God. You attend to the most important things, of course. Better read Zech. 14:16-19; Heb. 10:25; John 20:19 and 26; Acts 2:1; 1 Cor. 16:1-2, and many such like.

If the Church of God is the most important institution in the world, then its meetings are the most important in the world.

> " I love thy church, O God,
>   Her walls before thee stand,
> Dear as the apple of thine eye,
>   And graven on thy hand;
> For her my tears shall fall,
>   For her my prayers ascend,
> To her my toils and cares be given,
>   Till cares and toils shall end.
>
> Beyond my highest joy
>   I prize her heavenly ways,
> Her sweet communion solemn vows,
>   Her hymns of love and praise.
> Sure as thy truth shall stand,
>   To Zion shall be given
> The greatest glories earth can give,
>   And brighter bliss of heaven."

Where the church is, there Christ is in the midst. Some had rather be where Christ is not, and where the devil is. All who despise the church meeting despise the church.

(8) Those Despise the Church of God Who Subordinate her Service. We profess to be servants of the church, as that is the way we serve Christ. But God and angels and men know that we are the servants of those whom we serve, and of that which we serve. We are all servants. The Church must be served. The world also demands our service. When these seem to conflict, then which? Why the one we esteem the highest and most important. Even a fool knows that much. These need not conflict, but when they do, the best comes first.

Let a pastor work his garden at the Saturday hour of meeting, and let the passing member ask him if he is not going to church, and he replies that his garden needs his attention more than the church; and it would be no plainer from the conversation than from the silent action. Of course, it would be too ugly in the pastor, but how does it look to the pastor when the member does the same thing. But you say the pastor is paid to serve. But the members promised to serve without pay. This was the way Christ ordained it. Then is not the obligation of both equally binding. You obligate yourself to render your little service without financial compensation, because it requires but little of your time. The pastor gives his whole time to service, and, of course, his temporal wants must be provided for. But the obligation to serve the church in these respective ways is equally binding on both. "Go in my vineyard and work today," is spoken to every saved man and woman. "To every one his own work." They are all rewarded according to their works, and all chastened for unfaithfulness. Read here Rom. 12 and 1 Cor. 12. Read the whole chapters. Also Eph. 6:10-18. Also Matt. 6:24; John 8:23; Rom. 6:16, etc. Nothing must be put above the Worship or the Service of the Church.

(9) Those Despise the Church of God Who Withhold Their Support. There are many things needing and deserving our support, and there should be no conflict; but when there is conflict, which is neglected most? The least esteemed, of course. The devil would hardly deny it, liar as he is. It is a principle of universal application. We support those things most we like best and deem the most important. Which gets the most of your support—the lodge or the church? The theater or the church? The circus or the church? I have seen a whole wagonload of church members come in 10 to 20 miles, in bad weather, and stand and freeze and starve waiting for the show; and they pay more to the show than they pay to the church in a whole year. They go to the races, now called Fairs, to catch the silly saints, and they will stand around all day for days, and thus give more sacrifice to that than the church of the living God. Some give more for whiskey and tobacco than they give to the church. Christ paid his way through the world, and he wants his people and his church to do the same. He never wrought but one

miracle for himself, and that was to pay a doubtful debt for him and Peter. The Church must live, and the world is not expected to support it. We support a thing as we esteem it. How does the church stand this test?

(10) Those Despise the Church of God Who Fail in its ASSISTANCE. The Church must not only be supported, but Assisted. It must not only live, but it must work. It has the greatest mission of any institution on earth. More good and everlasting results will come from its mission than all others. The Church must not only support itself, and the cause at home, but it must assist other churches in evangelizing the whole world. Those who sit in darkness and in the shadow of death must have the light. Those under the dominion of satan must be delivered. The Church is the divine human instrumentality in saving men. Every man engaged lawfully in this work must be a member or an officer of the Church, and all things must be done by her direction, or sanction, or authority. None others have any authority in these things. Not only the first part of the commission, but the middle and the last were committed to the church, so that all engaged in this important and responsible work must be under subjection to the wisdom and counsel of the brethren, and even then corruption of doctrine and practice creep in. To turn every fanatic loose with his ambitious, ambiguous, ambidextrous, amaurosious, amorous, amphibious, amble, amiable amenities to deceive the very elect, would

have wrecked the object and purposes of the gospel. Christ had too much common sense to have inaugurated such a perilous policy. In the multitude of counselors there is wisdom. Let all things be done decently and in order, and let nothing be done without the consent of the brethren. Not only must individuals combine in churches for the nearer and smaller matters, but the churches must combine in the greater and more distant matters. Educational institutions, publication societies, orphan asylums, and many such like things are essential to the progress of these great interests. These are the greatest works in the world. The Church of God needs the assistance of all its members. Other interests also need our assistance, and when there is to be discrimination, *which will get the advantage?* Of course, that which we most highly esteem. There can be no other answer. Did you ever know a church member to pay the merchants, doctors, lawyers, teachers, laborers, etc., and put the Church of God last? I have, for I was a deacon for many years. Religious papers are a great help to the cause of truth, yea, a necessity in these times. The truth must be printed and read. Paul wrote letters to the churches, and asked that they be read. Col. 4: 16. That was the best that could be done in those days. The devil has his printing presses; so has the world; so have errorists; so must the Church of God make occasions to cut off these other damaging and damning occasions to injure the cause of truth. The greatest work in the world is in the church. It needs assistance. "Help, Lord!" "Ye men of Israel, help!" "Curse Meroz, because they come not up to the help of the Lord against the mighty." Which will you help most? That, that you think is the most deserving. If you think down on the church; if you subordinate its interests and work, then you Despise the Church of God. A great secretary said, that if the Baptists would send him all the bones that rot on their lands, that he would have more missionary money than was ever put in his hands for the work. A wise man, Dr. Solomon, said, that if he had all the money that go to buy feathers for the women's hats, that he could burn and rebuild all the churches in Kentucky, and give all of them pastors for every Sunday, and at a good salary. O, God's "people will not consider." "They are perishing for lack of knowledge." A woman who gives more for a hat than for the Church of God, puts her hat above the Church of God. I don't ask you to give more than you give, *but to give more wisely.* Give less to the little things, and more to the great things, and it will be better for you, for others, and for the cause of Christ. Prophecies, tongues, and the getting of knowledge will come to an end; but there are eternal interests, and those who spend their all on things that are temporal, and that perish with the using, to the neglect of the things that are eternal, are doing themselves and the cause irreparable and eternal wrong. If you would see the great mission of the church, read the Epistle to the Ephesians. What is to be compared to that? "To the intent, that now unto principalities and authorities in the heavenlies, might be made known by the church the manifold wisdom of God, according to the eternal purpose, which he purpose in Christ Jesus, our Lord." O, that we knew how to "behave ourselves in the house of God, which is the Church of the Living God." Perhaps we all work enough and give enough to other things, but we don't Assist the Church of God enough. Each one is honor bound, yea, with double honor, to do and to give according to his ability. If all were thus honorable, the Church of God would not be so poor as to beg bread and live on the cold charities of the world. "Let there be equality, and not the few burdened, and the many eased." Here is where the trouble comes. Our financial system, if we have any, is contrary to the word of God, and, of course, we suffer.

God directed the building of one house for his glory, and that was the costliest house ever built. Neither David nor Solomon would live in a finer house than God's. I don't believe any blood-bought man or woman should spend more on themselves than they spend for the Church of God. I believe we would all have more to spend on ourselves, and enjoy it more, and get more out of it, if we did not rob God by withholding what is his due. Duty means debt, and we are all indebted to God more than we can pay. So he asks only a small proportion of our income. If Judaism owed God one-tenth, what does

Christianity owe him? Certainly not less. But being now no longer under the law, but having the liberty to purpose in our own heart what we shall give, let us not abuse this liberty, for God loves a liberal and cheerful giver. If we sow sparingly, we shall reap sparingly; and if we sow bountifully, we shall also reap bountifully. Give, and it shall be given to you, good measure, heaped up, pressed down, shaken together, and running over. Now, fathers and mothers, will you continue to spend your money for that which is not bread? Will you continue to give your children stones for bread, and scorpions for eggs? Yea, poison for food? This you do when you feed them on the secular, fictitious and filthy trash of the day.

(11) Those Despise the Church of God Who Usurp her Functions. The Church is the Steward—the custodian of the Faith. The doctrines and ordinances were committed to her. All authority was left with her. She judges of the qualifications of those seeking her membership, or the unworthy would rush in to destroy her peace and prosperity. The devil would want no wider door than to allow any one to judge of his own fitness. The unworthy often think they are too fit for the really worthy. The Church judges those that are within, so as to put away such as she deems unfit. The Church imposes and deposes official obligations. The Church judges of the qualifications of deacons and preachers and pastors. The Church must call its own pastor. Now, when some Diotrephes presumes to take

these functions from the church, and to officiate on his own responsibility; that is, decide who should become members, or who excluded; or to appoint deacons, and to depose them; or to appoint or disappoint pastors, or to impose, oppose or depose them; or authoritatively decide doctrine; or to ordain preachers, or to locate them; or to administer ordinances, either baptism or the Supper; and all these have been done by usurpers of authority, and I charge all such with despising the Church of God by thus putting themselves above the church in such functions.

They may think they are big-hearted by thus relieving the church of such responsibilities, but such usurpation never came out of a big heart, but always out of a big head, and the *definite* article might be the one to use in all such cases. The eleven inspired apostles would not dare to fill the vacancy caused by the death of Judas without submitting the matter, both the nomination, and the election, to the whole 120 disciples. Nor would these twelve appoint deacons without submitting the matter to the whole multitude of disciples. Acts 6:5 : "And the saying pleased the whole multitude; and THEY chose the seven." One of our greatest men was baptized without church authority, and another ordained without church authority, and another said before a minister's state meeting that the commission was not given to the church, but to disciples as such, and he meant unbaptized disciples. If that is not anarchy, then I don't know what that means. Who begun the execution of the commission on the day of Pentecost? Were they left unbaptized, and out of the church? Were the 120 an unorganized mass? If "God put in the church first the apostles, then prophets, teachers, miracles, gifts of healing, helps, governments, diversities of tongues, then where was the church, for all of these were there, before, and on that day? Did they work as a mass and not as a church? Then why a church?

If the mess of a mass in a muss would be more effectual than organization, why did Christ do so foolish a thing as to build a church? If the whole divided christian world is the Church of God, then how could the church at Corinth be the Church of God? And if there were "churches of God" in those early days, even in a province, were they the same as we have now in the denominations? Are the denominations as such churches of God? If so, are they the same as we read of in the Sriptures? Is the sum total of the churches of God the Church of God? Why this dogged effort to break down all the scripture characteristics of a church, if not to destroy church functions, and turn them over to any fanatic and free booter, who, Diotrephes like, would love the pre-eminence, and take in and cast out of the church whom he would. It is those who love to have the pre-eminence that usurp church functions. They first try to get everybody in the church; then the church, of course, can't operate by reason of the multitude, and multitudinous disagreements; so Mr. Diotrephes can have the pre-eminence. The same authority that administers one ordinance administers the other. They begin to usurp baptism and ordination, and the rest will come in time. All these roads lead to Rome. When messengers are made delegates, and anybody can be delegate, then the gates of Hades have prevailed against the church. God forbid!

(12) Those Despise the Church of God Who prefer the churches (?) of men. As there have been gods many, and lords many, and christs many, and bibles many, so are there churches many. Any one who has sense enough to choose, and a few have been allowed that privilege, or rather have that privilege because they escaped conscription; and millions have been conscripted with the sword; and millions by the sword of the mouth; and millions have been kidnapped in infancy; yet millions escaped all these, and deliberately chose a church which they knew was started in modern times, and by uninspired men, and some of these church founders were the wickedest men the world ever saw, and the rest the most presumptuous the world ever saw; and yet they prefer that to an institution of God, set up by Christ himself, who called it: MY CHURCH, and said the gates of hades should not prevail against it. These gates will surely prevail against all other institutions, including these churches of men. These all say, no salvation out of the Church of God, and they are certainly out, and if judged out of their own mouths, as Christ says he will do, and also out of his word, which we know he will do, then what will they say in

the Judgment? Every member of such organizations either went in by choice, or they stay in by choice, and in either case they prefer that to the Church of God.

The Church of God is over 1800 years old, and has come down through persecutions, even baptisms of fire and blood, all of which did not and can not prevail. It is in the world to-day, doing business for its Lord as in the beginning, having the same government, officers, constitution, ordinances and doctrines, differing however as at first, because each has the right to think and decide for himself. But freedom to differ, and even to fight for the supposed right, is a thousand times better than enslavement of mind and soul to usurpation of popes and bishops, such as the Bible knows only to condemn. But those made free to differ, are as united as the others, and they have the only agreement that counts for anything in the kingdom of Christ and of God. The agreement is intelligent and voluntary, and not slavish, for that kind is an abomination to God, and ought to be to all men. If one can be in the Church of God and will not; if he can be free with that freedom that comes from a knowledge of the truth, and will not; then the consequences are of his own choosing, and that without excuse, unless God requires us to know things we can't know, and perish such a thought! Everyone can know where his church (?) started, and when, and who started it, and he takes his choice between that and the one that has come down through 1260 years of opposition and persecution, acccording to prophecy. Was your church persecuted 1260 years? The true church was. But you may ask, can we tell which of all the so-called churches of to-day was this persecuted church? If you can't know, then you are under no obligation to know. But if you can know, then you must know, or suffer the consequences. Can it be both identified and traced. Read what follows in this book, and decide for yourself. The Lord has no denominational churches, nor can such be forced on him, for he decided in the beginning not to build such, and he is the same yesterday, to-day and forever. What account would such a thing be, if indeed such a thing could be? It never met, never did anything, and never will, and never can. Everything that was ever done was done by individuals and organizations of individuals, called bodies, and a congregation is not a body unless it is organized for business. We read of an unofficial assembly in Acts, 19th chap.; but it was a mob, a mass, a mess, and all it could do was to get up a muss. It was unlawful—not the congregation, but its presumption in undertaking the business of an ecclesia, which is always a lawful assembly. They were told that the lawful assembly, or ecclesia, would prosecute them for trying to do business; and so all lawful churches ought to prosecute the unlawful ones for trying to take business out of their hands, or into their hands, which is the same. So all unlawful assemblies, to-day, which have taken the Lord's business in their hands, have and aim to take it out of the hands of lawful assemblies. If infant rantism prevail, and this is their aim, then believers' baptism is at an end. If Episcopacy, or Presbytery, or Papacy prevail, then that church government, given from heaven, and which has done more for this world than all the gold in its banks and bowels, will be overthrown. All liberty, and freedom, and individual responsibility, etc., that have come to natural and spiritual men, are the fruits of this heavenly democracy, united into congregationalism. There was no democracy in this old, tyrannical world till Christ brought it from heaven; for he came to lift up the lowly, to pull down those exalted, and "to make men free and equal." "There shall be no one in authority among you, for ye are all brethren." Now, why choose to belong to an unscriptural church, and that means unlawful, so far as Christ's rule goes, and it will ultimately go all the way, as he is to uproot all the Father did not plant; why, I say, choose to belong to a so-called church, that Christ never organized or authorized, rather than the one that has Bible characteristics? If you put these above The Church of God, then you Despise the Church of God. But maybe you have not thought of these things. Then think of them now.

The body that exalts itself above the head is a "beast," and the "Beast" did this when it thought to "change times and ordinances." Then this beastly body must have seven heads and ten horns. So there is no end to this unholy ambition.

A human body is the likeness of Christ's church. In this body we see unity in diversity among its members. Services differing, like those of the hands, feet, eyes and ears, yet all working together, "fitly joined together and compacted, by that of which every joint supplieth, according to the effectual working in the measure of every part, making increase of the body unto the building up of itself." This is inexplicable and inapplicable except to a congregation. These members of the human body are not only "joined together," and working together, but in full sympathy, "having the same care one for another," so no one can say to another, "I have no need of you." "Not one member, but many." "If all were one member [as bishops in the general conference], where were the body?" "But now are there many members but one body." The feeble and uncomely members are necessary, and ought to have more abundant honor, for God tempered the body together so there should be no schism. "Now ye [church of God at Corinth] are the body of Christ and members each in his part." 1 Cor. xii. Look a little at the likeness. "Joined together"—congregation; one head—Christ; complete in itself—*a* body, or *the* body. The eyes "oversee," but do not lord it over the others; the tongue speaks, but never against the members; the hands strike, but in defense of the members; the feet, the servant of all, and lowest of all—these all working together to execute, not the law of the hands or eyes, for these can make no laws, but in all their co-operative labor, they do the will of the head. When a body gets to making laws, it puts itself on an equality with the head, or exalts itself above the head, and thus shows itself the body of a beast. I would not belong to such a body. The figure of a human body is an argument in favor of congregationalism, so potent that flesh and blood, and principalities and powers, and rulers of the darkness of this world and spiritual wickedness in high places, can't answer. If all the human bodies were made into one body, and became a great image, like the one Nebuchadnezzar saw, some little stone might strike its toes and grind it to powder, or it might fall of its own weight; but organized as it is, on a small scale, each complete in itself, the human body becomes an institution which the gates of hades can not prevail against. These gates may close on one every second, yet the multiplication is so rapid and widespread that the body, as an organization, is destined to ride the surging billows and land at last on the uttermost shores of time. "I speak concerning Christ and his Church."

Why belong to a church of man's devising? "Come out of her, my people!"

CHURCH COMMUNION.

1 Cor. 10:16, 17. The cup of blessing which we bless, is it not the communion of the blood of Christ? The loaf which we break, is it not the communion of the body of Christ? For we the many are one loaf, one body, for we all partake of the one loaf.

Acts 4:23 contains one of the most philosophical statements to be found. "And being let go, they went to their own company." These two suffering apostles did this from both principle and choice. Many do so to-day from choice, and not principle. I am glad all have the civil privilege to choose their own company. This is the result of Religious Liberty, "the trophy of the Baptists." No one has the *moral* or *scriptural* right to associate himself with a company of errorists in either morals or doctrine; but all have civil liberty, and with this they have associated themselves with the company of their own liking, and often without regard to the truth as it is in Jesus. Hence, we have the Methodist communion, Presbyterian communion, Baptist communion, etc. This means the place we have chosen to commune. The word translated "Communion" twice in the text, is also thus translated only in 2 Cor. 6:14 and 13:14.

The same word is translated "Fellowship" 18 times, and "Partner" and "Partaker" 14 times. I prefer the last two to the first.

When one chooses his community to live in, he becomes a partner or partaker of the common interests of the neighborhood, and having so many things in common, there is a communion in the common interests. There is fellowship, partnership, communion. This is the right sense of the word, and the mystical or spiritual communion is the result of the partnership. Partners in business have not only a financial fellowship and partnership, but this should beget a sympathy in other matters—a sort of personal fellowship extending to the family in matters of health, hope and happiness.

Communion, partnership, fellowship are based on agreement. "How can two walk together except they be agreed?" Partners in business must be agreed, or they will not have sweet fellowship and communion. We choose, or should do so, the church company or communion we most agree with, for without agreement there will be no fellowship. Differences of a serious character require divisions. "Mark those who cause divisions contrary to the doctrine ye have learned, and avoid them." Rom. 16:17. This is the cause of so many denominations. They are divided on what they esteem important doctrines, and for the want of agreement they are compelled to separate themselves.

THINGS THAT DIFFER MUST DIVIDE. On this principle cosmos was brought out of chaos. Chaos was mixed communion, which was not pleasing to God. So he made things that differed to divide. He told the waters to separate themselves from the land, the light from the darkness, etc. "And God saw that it was good." Anyone can see that. Then he made the seeds, animals, birds, fishes, etc., each after its kind, and told them to preserve their species by non-intercommunion. Mixed communion would have frustrated the divine plan in creation. The Lord don't want half-breeds, but full-bloods. A hybrid and mongrel are abominations to God. Pure gold and silver, etc., means that all unlike substances called "alloy" are separated from the metals. There is such a want of agreement in the mixed substances as to injure their beauty and value. Let things that differ divide, is the universal law of God. Let corn, oats, wheat, etc., be sown in separate fields, lest they mix and become corrupted. Let "birds of a feather flock together," and animals of a kind herd together. Flocks of quail, geese, duck, sheep, bees, ants, etc., may appear selfish to ignorant people, but it is a selfishness that is well-pleasing to God. The peace and prosperity of all depends upon keeping separate. "Thou shalt not plow an ox and ass together." Deu. 22:10. Why? There is too much difference. They are not agreed. There is no fellowship, and there should be no partnership. They can't commune together. The greatest travesty I ever saw was a two-horse show called "The Happy Family." There was as great a variety as the owners could get together. There were fowls, beasts and serpents. It was the most miserable set I ever saw. The monkey was the only happy one, and his happiness consisted solely in tormenting the others. If they had been let go, how they would have gone to their own company. They were sick of mixed communion. There was no agreement, hence there could be no fellowship and no partnership. Do you ask if there was NO fellowship? Yes. How much? As much as there was agreement. I can commune with a hog in hunger, thirst and suffering, because we hold those in common. But I could not go any further in communion than we are agreed. When he eats filth and wallows in the mud, I must be excused. On those points we must separate. Should the hog insist and accuse me of selfishness, I know such selfishness is well pleasing to God and man. Where we differ we must divide.

Let us now apply this rule to the race of man. There are differences that necessitate divisions, or destruction would follow.

God made of one blood all the nations that dwell on the face of the earth; but because of differences he divided them into nations, and gave each its bounds of habifation. If God had left all together they would have worked their own destruction with greediness. There is such a thing as race fellowship and also national fellowship. If one should boast of his liberality, and transgress the race line, and marry an orang-outang, and his so-called partner didn't kill him, then God or man should attend to it at once, for such a man is not fit to live on the earth. Race fellowship is destroyed when carried beyond the bounds. So National fellowship must be confined to one's own nation, or he will be accused of having no national fellowship. There is a difference in color that makes social fellowship impossible. No sensible white or black man would want to give his son or daughter in marriage to the other color. The black companion may be the equal or superior in many respects, yet differences exist that forbid such a union. Dr. Eaton told of a visit to a South Sea Island king, and in his company was a black man and a mulatto. The king cordially received all but the mulatto. God made the white and black man, and he wants them to continue as he made them.

A politician destroys his Political fellowship when he tries to hold communion with both or all parties alike. A man is required to take sides on political questions, and show his colors or hold his peace. No one can fellowship both sides of any question. Such fool pretenders are found only in religion. Those who pretend to have so much religion that they can fellowship all, are generally found to have none at all. Mark all such, and avoid them.

There is also such a thing as Social fellowship, and woe to those who do not restrict it. We have a golden custom of introducing strangers. A mutual friend, knowing both parties, thinks there would be pleasant association because of agreeing qualities. Thus the unfit and unworthy are not admitted. To throw open the doors of social fellowship would be disastrous in many cases, and especially so with females, as a great multitude of male dogs would spend their lives seeking whom they might devour. These rascals are generally the best dressed and best polished in manners. The only safety is in close social communion.

So of Craft fellowship. Farmers, merchants, doctors, lawyers, teachers, preachers, etc., confine their craft fellowship to those of their craft. When Paul was in need he introduced himself to a tent-maker, and being of the same craft, he found fellowship.

Let farmers, doctors, bankers, teachers, lawyers, etc., hold their conventions and consult or commune together. So of firms. What is everybody's business is nobody's business; and the man who tries to attend to everybody's business has none of his own. Christ said, when you make a feast, don't call the well-to-do, but the poor, maimed, lame and blind. Let the unfortunate get together and have fellowship in their sufferings.

But society takes on more serious forms of organization, which requires still more restrictions. When a man and woman seek a partnership for life, the utmost care should be taken to secure Matrimonial fellowship, or communion. "Let every man have his own wife, and every woman her own husband." Monogomy is close communion; polygamy is open communion. The parties must seek points of agreement and congeniality. No old fool should marry a young one. The cultivated and the uncultivated would make a mismatch. The rich may marry the poor with the understanding that one has enough for both. Some differences may be adjusted, but the greatest care should be taken lest, for want of agreement, matrimonial fellowship or communion be broken.

After this comes the family, and family fellowship must be restricted to the family. If a man come to your house boasting that he is too liberal and too large for one woman and one set of children, kick him out of your house, and out of your yard, and out of your front lot into the public high-way; then let the public take up the kicking, and let the kicking continue as long as there is anything to kick. Such a man (?), too big for one woman and one set of children, is too big for God or man, and is not fit to live with us little fellows. Some men are too large for one church, yea, too large for one denomination. Some are too large for all Protestant denominations, and they try to take the Catholics into their communion; yea, some, after studying "Comparative Religions," become too large for any one of them, or all of them, so they take in Atheists. There may be some that take devils into their fellowship. When a man grows beyond the proper size, there is no telling where he will stop.

After the family comes Consanguine fellowship, and this, like all the others, must be restricted to the bounds appointed, or it will be destroyed.

The man who claims kin with everybody knows nothing of consanguine fellowship. Paul and Barnabas had ministerial fellowship, and fellowship in labor and suffering, but it all went to pieces when it came in contact with consanguine fellowship. Barnabas wanted to take his nephew, John Mark with them on their second missionary tour, but Paul objected, and they both being strong-minded men, they had a sharp contention, and separated, each taking his chosen companion, and they went their own ways. A beautiful illustration of this is recorded in Gen. 29:10-14:

10 And it came to pass, when Jacob saw Rachel the daughter of Laban his mother's brother, and the sheep of Laban his mother's brother, that Jacob went near, and rolled the stone from the well's mouth, and watered the flock of Laban his mother's brother.

11 And Jacob kissed Rachel, and lifted up his voice, and wept.

12 And Jacob told Rachel that he *was* her father's brother, and that he *was* Rebekah's son: and she ran and told her father.

13 And it came to pass, when Laban heard the tidings of Jacob his sister's son, that he ran to meet him, and embraced him, and kissed him, and brought him to his house. And he told Laban all these things.

14 And Laban said to him, Surely thou *art* my bone and my flesh. And he abode with him the space of a month.

The kissing was an expression of consanguine fellowship. But this should be restricted to the kin, and very close kin at that. The man who would kiss all because kin to all, is a little lower than the beasts, for, as a general thing, they have their own families and friends they prefer to the rest.

Let us now pass from the natural to the religious relations and fellowships. The world is full of religion, and religions. They are too numerous to mention. Budhhism, Confucianism, Mohammedanism, Judaism and Christianity are enough for us. How much Religious fellowship is there among these religions. As much as there is agreement, and can't be more. Read the 8th chapter of 1st Cor. and the last half of the 10th chapter. I quote some of the latter. The word translated in 18th verse: "Partakers," and "Fellowship" in the 20th verse, is the same translated "Communion" in the 16th, which is our text. Read and digest.

18 Behold Israel after the flesh: are not they which eat of the sacrifices partakers of the altar?

19 What say I then? that the idol is any thing, or that which is offered in sacrifice to idols is any thing?

20 But I *say*, that the things which the Gentiles sacrifice, they sacrifice to devils, and not to God: and I would not that ye should have fellowship with devils.

21 Ye cannot drink the cup of the Lord, and the cup of devils: ye cannot be partakers of the Lord's table, and of the table of devils.

22 Do we provoke the Lord to jealousy? are we stronger than he?

27 If any one of them that believe not bid you *to a feast*, and ye be disposed to go; whatsoever is set before you, eat, asking no question for conscience sake.

28 But if any man say unto you, This is offered in sacrifice unto idols, eat not for his sake that shewed it, and for conscience sake.

We will have use for this principle further on.

In Acts 14:15-17 and 17:22-29, Paul struck on to some points of agreement, and thus religious fellowship begun. This increased as he turned them to his doctrine of the true God, and our relations to Him. When he saw so many altars of sacrifice, and one to "The Unknown God," he met them at that altar, because there they were agreed in some way. When he saw them making sacrifice for sins, he had fellowship in that, because Paul knew that sin requires sacrifice. They differed about the kind of sacrifice; but both had the same experience of a troubled conscience. They both were partakers of a like experience of a coming condemnation and death. But this was as far as Paul could go at first. Before they could have more fellowship they must have more agreement. So Paul led some on into Christian fellowship: "Howbeit certain men clave unto him, and believed, * * and a woman named Demaris, and others with them." They could not fellowship Paul's religion until they agreed with him in it. Then they became partners, and changed their company and communion.

CHRISTIAN FELLOWSHIP.

We will now dismiss the other religions, and study those called Christian. There are many of these in name. Here fellowship, partnership and communion increase as agreement increases, and it can't possibly go any further, and we need not deceive ourselves and others about it. I have a great deal of religious fellowship for the Jews, because I agree with them on the Old

Bible, its prophets, and many of its teachings and prophecies. We have the same God, the same law, the same Abraham for our father, the same Moses; but we divide on Christ and christianity; hence I can not have Christian Fellowship for them. As far as we agree we can walk together, and any further is hypocrisy.

I can fellowship Catholics only so far as we can agree. We agree on the dead, risen and ascended Christ, but their living Christ lives in Rome, while mine lives in heaven.

But dropping them out, let us study communion with the Protestant Divisions of christendom. Here Fellowship greatly increases, but the rule holds good-fellowship only as far as there is agreement. Any more is pretense, if not worse. Why are we divided? Because we differ on christian doctrine. Who set up the divisions? They did. The Baptists had been protesting for a thousand years. They are yet doing business at the same old stand and in the same old way in all essential things. When they came out of Rome, we did not disfellowship them, but they us. They set up their own communions, and disdained and persecuted us. God called them out of Rome, but he did not call them to create divisions and offenses contrary to the doctrine we had received. I rejoice that we are now increasing in agreement, but we yet differ as to the church and ordinances, to say nothing of many vital doctrines. For these differences they would exclude any of us, and we any of them, and at the same time recognize the excluded as genuine christians. If I wanted to unite with any of them and preach what I now preach, they could not receive me without suicidal results. If any of our preachers announce that he believe what is peculiar to any of these denominations, we would depose if not exclude him. This is necessary for us and them. No one will deny this, and no one will condemn it. The Lord's Supper being in the Lord's Church, and to this we are all agreed, they having another sort of a church, and having different ways of getting in the church where the supper is, then the difference must keep us from the same table. We invite all to it the way we got there, and the only way left us, and "keeping it as delivered," we must be faithful to the trust.

Christian Fellowship may and should abound as far as there is agreement, but divide we must when differences require it. And don't forget that we are not responsible for a single one of these differences. If they had not first differed from us, we would not have been compelled to differ from them.

But let us magnify some points of agreement, and be very thankful to God for them, and pray earnestly for a continuous growth in nearness to a real union. Let us joyously walk together as far as we can agree. As many as believe in public prayer, come and pray with us. Can you join us in our songs of Zion? Come and welcome. Our songs and prayers are very much alike. Is any in our neighborhood poor and in distress? Pass the hat to all for a collection.

Each may take care of its own poor, but some are of the world; yet they are citizens and the poor of all christian people of the neighborhood. Let all partake, and thus become partners in such cases. Do you believe in public worship? So do we; come and worship with us. But do we not also agree in mission? Yes; but not in mission work. Pedobaptists believe the nations should be discipled by sprinkling the babies. So their name and creed say. We can't join them. But you say, we all believe in preaching the gospel to adult sinners who have not been "engrafted into the body of Christ" by a sacrament. Suppose, in a union effort, such are led to Christ— then what? Let the convert take his choice of "modes" without instruction? But our orders read: "Teach them all things whatsoever I have commanded you." You say, we must not do that. Christ says, we must. Whom shall we obey? If we attempt to walk together where we do not agree, we will lose what little fellowship we have. The way to get along peaceably is to divide wherever the differences require it. There is only one rule for us all, and those who depart from it are responsible for themselves; and those who fellowship them by association, patronage, or any other way, become partakers with them in the transgression. A union with Pedobaptists in mission work is union in pedobaptism. They not only carry that doctrine with them, but they carry it out. Let us walk together in social, civil, moral, political, and also in religious matters, as far as agreed. We adhere strictly to this rule in all the other matters; why not in religion? We withdraw social, civil, political and moral fellowship from those of the contrary part. This is right. But how much more so in religion? If we can't compromise the lesser matters, how can we compromise the greater? Like animals, birds, plants, political parties, etc., we differ, and the world knows it, and the world also knows these differences have caused divisions. Then why lie about it? Unity is a thousand times better than union. Let us work on our differences and getting them healed, we will not have to touch the union question with one of our fingers. That will take care of itself. Any magnetic needle will point to the pole if there is no hinderance. Remove the hinderance, and you don't have to show the needle where the pole is. If you force it to point to the pole despite the hindering cause, the force must continue as long as the hindering cause remains. Such force would be against nature, as regards the needle, and against religion in the other case. We ought to have some religious common sense. Those who meet in Christ by repentance and faith have christian fellowship. Two christians met in a foreign land, and they knew not each other's tongue. Each wanted congenial companionship, and this required signs. One made a cross with his two forefingers, then laying one hand on his bosom, with the other he pointed to heaven. They embraced, and became loving companions with no further knowledge of each other's doctrinal views. They could pray and sing together in different tongues, and love and help each other in many ways, but they could not baptize each other or commune at the Lord's table, because Christ did not leave those solemn ceremonies to be thus used and abused. We agree on this. If one should say, those two men could set the Lord's table, I have no controversy with him. I have no ammunition small enough for such. They have Christian communion, but not church communion, unless they belong to the same church.

DENOMINATIONAL COMMUNION.

The Lord put the supper in the church, but not in the Denomination, because there was no such thing. Some want Denominational Communion, and some inter-denominational communion, but both these must be unscriptural, because the Scriptures knew no denomination. Yet circumstances have brought about the denominations, and as everyone ought to be in the one of his own choice, he must have Denominational fellowship, partnership, communion. This, like all the others, must be restricted to his own denomination. The man who has as much for one as another has none at all. There are such vain talkers, but they are deceivers. Every honest christian works for his own denomination. When you find one carrying around for distribution the books setting forth the peculiar doctrines of other denominations, with the boast that he was as ready to work for one as the other, you know that like Judas, he is after "the thirty pieces of silver." The man who would willingly sell false doctrine would also sell his Lord. What denomination would want or have him? If Denominational Fellowship is selfish, then it is a holy selfishness. God is pleased with the principle, and so are all right-minded men. The world knows these devisive denominations exist, and the man is to be pitied or despised who would in any way try to lie out of it. If he has chosen one of them to walk and work with, I can respect him, but not otherwise.

CHURCH COMMUNION.

So far we have spoken of the Communion twice spoken of in the 16th verse. That is a communion with Christ in his broken body, and shed blood. That is, the communicants thus express their fellowship, partnership, or common interest with Christ in the sacrifice of Himself, as He was sacrificed in our stead. "Died for us" means died in our stead; that is, died the death we owed to God's just law, which says, "the soul that sins shall die." If he died in our place, then we died with him; and if he arose for our justification, then we arose with him. If he is our substitute for both sin and righteousness, then we stand in him. We are to be made like him in mind, soul and body. This he secured for us in his suffering and sacrifice for us. Hence, we are partners with him in that great transaction, in all that was or will be accomplished by it. But WHO ARE THE WE of the two texts? Not everybody. Then WHO? The 17th verse tells us who the "We" are that sit at the Table. We have been considering in verse 16 church communion and union with Christ. Now it is community and unity between the members. Communities are not always in unison; fellowships are not always fraternal; partners are not always peaceable. In the Lord's Supper it is required that there shall be both community and unity, as well as communion and union. Not union in everything, for then we could not eat the Lord's Supper; but union in some essential things to be now considered.

We mentioned some of the variety of fellowships and partnerships, and the word translated communion twice in the text, and in only two other places (2 Cor. 6:14 and 13:14) is also translated "fellowship" thirteen times and "partner" and "partaker" fourteen times.

There are the fellowships growing out of race, color, nationality, society, both simple and organized, whether for business in its various professions, or marriage, family and consanguinity, etc. Here are fellowships and partnerships requiring some sort of unity and community.

Then we spoke of Religious fellowship, Christian fellowship, Doctrinal and Denominational fellowships, and have now the next and most important of all—Church Fellowship, Church Partnership, or Church Communion. In most of these matters, especially the political, professional, social, religious, christian, denominational and church fellowships, everyone has, or should have, CHOSEN his own company. So that each belongs to the communion of his choice, and that means his choice of a place to commune, and since all should have a place, he should be restricted to his place, or it would not be necessary for all to have a place. If any place is right then one place is wrong. Such a view leaves no place for fellowship or partnership, and converts union and communion into a flimsy farce that would be sacrilegious at the Lord's table.

If the Lord's table was intended for the whole race, then none are restrained but beasts and birds. Yet that would restrict it to the race. If for the whole religious world, then it must be restricted to them, and the irreligious restrained. And all of these "must meet in one place," and " tarry one for the other," and that after exercising discipline, lest some professing the qualifications should not possess them.

If it was intended for the whole Christian world, then Jews and heathen must be restrained and the table restricted to Christians. And these must "all come together in one place," as the table is local, and "tarry one for another," and the unworthy of these must be restrained, as "with such we should not eat."

As this would be impractical and impossible, the table of the Lord was not intended for all Christians. All Christians should have access to the table, but there are other requirements, such as baptism, church membership, and orderly walk, both in doctrines and morals. If the table was intended for all Christian denominations, or to one such, then the same "impossible" practicability confronts us as in the above. It could never be observed by our denomination for the same reason. But a community of some kind must observe it. "The many" must be "one body" of some kind. The Christian world is not a body, but a mass, and as for unity, it is a mess. So of each denomination. When the number gets too large and too much scattered, you can't get them into one place and one body; nor can you wait for them to come together, or know whom to discipline.

Christ did not put his table into a large portion of a denomination, such as "Conference," Convention," "Assembly," or "Association," for there were none of these in apostolic days as a permanent organization. The one that met at Jerusalem, after attending to its special business, adjourned *sine die*, and did not eat the Lord's Supper.

So we are driven by logic, facts and scripture to locate the table in the church. Paul was writing to the church at Corinth. The four "we's" in the text and the thirty-three pronouns in the latter half of the next chapter, all refer to the church, or to members of the church, and they are about the Supper. It is Christ's will that every saved man shall be baptized, added to some church, and to continue steadfastly in the Apostle's doctrine, as qualifications to his table; and those who approach it unworthily, that is, in an unworthy manner, and that includes the proper qualifications, established by thorough self-examination, and church discipline, eats and drinks condemnation to themselves.

The table is in the church, and for orderly church members. Here is the Community and Unity we desire now to ascertain. I will give you several translations of the text, such as are before me.

Anderson.—Because the loaf is one, we, the many, are one body, for we are all partakers of the one loaf.

Ox. Rev.—Seeing that we, who are many, are one loaf, one body, for we all partake of the one loaf.

Emp. Diaglott.—Because there is one loaf, we, the many, are one body; for we all partake of the one loaf.

Living Oracles.—Because there is one loaf, we, the many, are one body; for we all participate in the one loaf.

Rotherham.—Because one loaf, one body, we, the many are; for we all of the one loaf partake.

Gould.—Because we, the many, are one loaf, that is, one body, for we all partake of the one loaf.

Mine.—Because of the one loaf, one body the many are; for these all from the one loaf take a part.

Bible Union.—Because we, the many, are one loaf, one body, for we all share in the one loaf.

Syriac.—As therefore that bread (loaf) is one, so we are all one body: for we all take to ourselves from that one bread (loaf).

American Edition.—Seeing that we, who are

many, are one bread, one body; for we all partake of the one bread. (Loaf in the margin).

Conybeare and Houson.—For as the bread is one, so we, the many, are one body; for of that one bread we all partake.

Twentieth Century.—Just as there is one loaf, so we, many though we are, form one body; for we all partake of the one loaf.

Wesley.—For we, being many, are one bread, and one body; for we are all partakers of the one bread.

Broadus, Hovey and Weston.—Because we, the many, are one loaf, one body, for we all share in the one loaf.

Worrell, Sawyer, etc., translate like many above.

So it is clear to any mind not beclouded with prejudice, that those who partake of the one loaf must be one of the body that partakes. That the body means the church, see 1 Cor. 12:27; Eph. 1:22-23; 4:3-6 and 16; 5:23-24; Col. 1:18, 24, etc. That the body spoken of in the text means the church at Corinth, is plain enough for anyone who can intelligently read the eleventh, twelfth, fourteenth and sixteenth chapters of this epistle. Any other conclusion is inexcusable and censurable. Membership in a supposed universal church by reason of faith and salvation, is not counted as sufficient by our Lord, since it is his will that all "the saved be added to the church" which he built—the business-doing congregation or body to which his interests and ordinances are committed. The one who partakes of that one loaf says, by that most solemn of all acts, that he is a member of that body or church observing the ordinance. But some "sport themselves with their own deceivings," "feeding themselves without fear." If it is right for one who is not a unit in the body to partake of that one loaf, then Christ was wrong in setting the example, and the Holy Spirit was wrong in writing our text, and also in all the restrictions and qualifications prescribed. No proposition is clearer to my mind than this—that the unity of the text requires every participant to be a unit in the body partaking. The one cup and the one loaf are forty times mentioned, and many times made emphatically emphatic by repeating the article and pronoun. So the first item of unity is Church Membership—Church Fellowship—Church Partnership.

But this unity also requires Moral Fellowship. "With such do not eat" refers to moral characters. They refer to church members; but not all church members are to commune. The man referred to in 1 Cor. 5th chap. was wrong in his moral conduct, but he was no worse than those in the church who had been leavened by his example and influence, which they favored by consenting to such a marriage. A man who lives in adulterous marriage has no right to partake, nor have those who favor, or apologize for, or try to excuse such a marriage, for they are all alike guilty. Nor has a church who retains such characters in her membership and fellowship any right to set the Lord's table. Do they not provoke the Lord to jealousy. All such should judge themselves, and condemn themselves, and be chastened of the Lord, lest they should be weak and sickly and die, and be condemned with the world. This unity requires moral integrity, both in sentiment and practice. But another requisite of this unity is Personal Fellowship. That these should first be adjusted, see Matt. 5:23-24; 18:15, with their connections.

The fellowship expressed by membership must be real. "If you love not your brother whom you have seen, how can you love God, whom you have not seen?" "If you forgive not your brother, neither will your heavenly Father forgive you." The celebration of Christ's sufferings and death is no time and place for a farce. It is no place for hypocrites. But you don't have to agree with a brother in politics, nor in ethical codes of man's devising, but in God's ethical code.

Again, the unity of the text requires fellowship in Doctrine. Ro. 16:17. "Now we beseech you, brethren, mark them which cause divisions and offenses contrary to the doctrine which ye have learned; and avoid them."

Difference on some doctrines should be tolerated, but there are vital doctrines that to err on is fatal. Such as the Divinity of Christ, the Inspiration of the Scriptures, the Personality of the Holy Spirit, the Necessity of Repentance and Faith, Salvation by Grace, and the Resurrection. Doctrines contrary to these should cause immediate separation. Lest this should look like an apology, let me say that we should aim at the Unity Christ prayed for in John 17:6, 11, 22; and for which Paul prayed in 1 Cor. 1:10; see also 12:25; 11:19-20; Eph. 4:3, 13; Ps. 133.

"Purging out the leaven" means first out of ourselves after self-examination; and then out of the church after church examination or discipline. The members and the church need at least an annual spring cleaning. The seven days of unleavened bread should teach us the importance of giving ample time to the casting out of malice and wickedness; first out of our own hearts and lives, and lest we fail to detect it in ourselves, let us subject ourselves to the brethren who are united with us in this responsible matter. For the New Scriptural use of leaven, see Matt. 13:33; 16:6, 12; Mk. 8:15; Luke 12:1; 13:21; 1 Cor. 5:6, 7, 8; Gal. 5:9. It symbolizes both bad morals and bad doctrines.

There is an insane clamor for Union in these days, whether we are One or not. Let such remember that unite occurs but two times in the Word of God: Gen. 4:6 and Ps. 86:11; Unity but three times: Ps. 133:1; Eph. 4:3, 13; while One occurs a thousand times; such as one body, one fold, one shepherd, one faith, one baptism, etc. Now, we have many bodies, many folds, many shepherds, many faiths and many baptisms; and unity and union is impossible while that state of things exists.

Christ did not pray that his disciples might be united, but that they might be one. He made Jew and Gentile one—of the twain one new man—reconciling both to God in one body by the cross, and by one Spirit, they both have access to the one God, through the one Lord Jesus Christ. It is not said of the Trinity that the three are united, but that they are one.

A man and wife may be united and yet not be one. So of church members. The church should not only be united, but one—like the loaf. The grains in their natural state could not be united into one loaf. They must go through the powerful process of the upper and nether millstones, and the winnowing and sifting, so that the leaven of disunity might be removed; then the pure flour can be made into one loaf. The many natural non-cohesive men and women, by the powerful operations of the nether millstone of the convicting spirit, and the upper millstone of saving and sanctifying and cleansing grace, are united into one body, Jews and Gentiles bond and free, male and female, and have become one body.

This one body is symbolized by the one loaf, and those who partake of the one loaf say, by that most solemn act, that they are members of the one body, and that means church; and church or body never means denomination. Never; no, never.

Inter-Church communion means Denominational communion. The restriction is to the denomination. That would make it a denominational ordinance, and that would make the denomination a church, and the observance of it impossible. Who are in the denomination? All of those whose baptism we receive. The two must go together. This also requires a church to sit in judgment on the denomination, while it has only "judgment of those within." Interchurch communion also requires one church to sit in judgment on members of another church, or do away with discipline. Christ made no provisions for church members to run around, and lie out, and loaf about, and "eat the sacrament," and then do as they please, or do nothing if they please, and then force themselves on those who have no confidence in them, but whom they are bound to invite, because the commandment of God is made void by our tradition. "With such no not to eat," but "withdraw from them." This confines to discipline, and hence to the church. The other is evil only, and that continually, as it makes void scripture example and precept by an unscriptural sentiment.

But, say some, does not Acts 20:5-11 show that Paul and his companions communed with the church at Troas? King James' Version may justify such an inference, but any new translation that I have seen settles that clearly. It reads thus:

Luke, the author of the Acts, after naming seven brethren who had gone before, says:

Verse 5. "But these had gone before, and were waiting for us at Troas." Waiting for whom? Of course, for Paul and Luke, who were to come after. Who were waiting? Those, of course, who had gone before.

Verse 6. "And we sailed away from Phillipi,

after the days of unleavened bread, and came unto them to Troas in five days, where we tarried seven days." Who were the *we* who sailed from Phillipi? Of course, Paul and Luke. Who were the *them* to whom they came? Evidently those who had gone before and were waiting for Paul and Luke.

Verse 7. "And upon the first day of the week when we were gathered together to break bread, Paul discoursed with them, intending to depart on the morrow, and prolonged his speech until midnight." Who does *we* here refer to? Evidently, of course, to those who had come to Troas. Who does *them* refer to? Of course, to those to whom *them* refers in the 6th verse. (Here a break occurs in Paul's discourse by the fall of Eutychus.)

Verse 11. "And when he was gone up again and had broken the bread, and eaten, and had talked with them a long while, even till break of day, so he departed." To whom does *them* here refer? Evidently to the same brethren previously mentioned. Let it be observed that no one is here mentioned as eating except Paul, which was evidently a common meal, as it was natural for him to have taken some refreshments before departing on his journey. So say Sherwood, Albert Barnes, Jameson, Fausset and Brown, Alex. Campbell, and others.

Verse 13. "But we going before to the ship, set sail for Assos, there intending to take in Paul; for so he had appointed, intending himself to go by land." Who does *we* refer to here?

Evidently to those who went to Troas, and who, while there, came together to break bread, and the same with whom Paul talked a long while, and the same who came away from Troas and sailed for Assos.

Now, if there was a church there, it is strange, indeed, no mention is made of it, or that its members greeted Paul or his companions on their arrival, or that those members took leave of them when they departed. Such mention is made in other places where resident disciples were met with. Upon what legitimate hypothesis can you account for the omission here? Now I do not *know* there was not a church at Troas; neither do you *know* there was. But if there was, I must say that, which you will admit, it is one of the strangest things that Luke could give all the incidents he did in connection with the visit of Paul and his companions and yet avoid making the slightest allusion to it. Therefore, I think the most natural and reasonable conclusion is, that there was no church at Troas at that time, unless it was composed of Paul and his fellow-travelers.

But if this were true, then it was a church without a local habitation.

The truth is, from the simple expression, "when we came together on the first day of the week to break bread," is drawn the inference that the Lord's Supper was celebrated, and that by a regularly organized church, and that that church was located at Troas. The absurdity is plainly on the face of any such inference.

Long after this, Christ sent seven messages to "THE SEVEN CHURCHES OF ASIA," and left out Troas. No where is there an allusion to a church there. All admit that Church Communion was practiced at its institution, and at Jerusalem, and at Corinth, and in all other places where referred to. Then why press a known error in Acts 20:5-7, for an exception, and for confusion and contradiction? Errors of translation beget errors of practice, which errorists are loath to give up. Thousands of Baptists loaf around another church all their life, doing nothing for the cause, and, as a poultice for their evil conscience, they insist on " eating the sac-rament," to get what magical or mystical virtue it might possess. They support the church they left behind with their absence, which, in most cases, is a great blessing. "Spots they (often) are, sporting themselves with their own deceivings while they feast with you," "feeding themselves without fear." A man who was publicly drunk on Saturday, came with a good member, both of another church, and both presented themselves for "communion." "With such no not to eat." What should be done? Invite both? They are both in good standing in their own church, as their church, like thousands of others, has no discipline. Some have not life enough to exclude a member for anything. Both must be invited, or the church must judge the members of another church. In either case the Scriptures are ignored. If the Supper must be protected by discipline, as all admit, then the question is settled, and the limit is fixed to members of the church. If the Supper is in the church, and is to be eaten by the church, and as a church, then the question is settled from that standpoint. It is like voting, whether to receive members, exclude them; or the call of a pastor, or what not; if it is to be done by a church, in church capacity, then the voting must be limited to the church. And all agree that the Supper is a church ordinance; but some think that, by "courtesy," the invitation may be extended to visiting Baptists, while the same "courtesy" should not be extended in voting. Do you ask, what harm can come of it? I answer, a world of harm. When all authority in heaven and earth says: "With such an one no not to eat," but "purge out the leaven," and "put away from yourselves that wicked person," you set up a custom of "courtesy" without warrant or precedent that makes void this great commandment. It is impossible to obey this great commandment, to protect this solemn ordinance, by discipline, while bound by that senseless, useless "courteous" custom. It tramples under foot all the all-authority in heaven and earth.

Let the world see that we are sincere when we call it a church ordinance, and that we practice what we preach, and practice on our own people, and this bug-bear of a bugaboo will vanish to the realm of shades and spooks and hobgoblins, where it was born, and where it belongs, and where it should die, and be buried to rise no more, forever more. Amen.

When Baptists say, it is close baptism, they may be sincere, but are inconsistent; for when one leaves the Baptists and goes to the world, as thousands do, or to other denominations, they are still baptized, but debarred; so that can't give satisfaction. As long as we practice such an inconsistency they will browbeat us and bully us, so that thousands are kept away from us, or enticed away. The scripture, precept and practice on this would hush the fuss and stop fight on this subject. And what do we gain by the modernly-invented custom? We simply quiet the croakings of a few roustabout Baptists who want to eat the sac-rament to compensate for their lay-outs from duty. If we can make it an expression of fellowship of members of other churches, then it can be made an expression of fellowship, and Pedobaptists have the argument on us. Christ "put in the church first the apostles," and after "purging out that Judas of the leaven of malice and wickedness," as he tells us to do, then he instituted the ordinance with only the elect Eleven, leaving out his mother, and thosands of Baptists who were in Jerusalem at that very hour. If this is not an argument for church communion, then I don't know what an argument is. It ought to settle and satisfy all who want to know the truth.

But indulge a few more remarks. I write this at such moments as I can snatch from other pressing duties. Attribute the repetitions to this, as I can not re-read every time I write. Moreover, the repetitions are the things that are prominent in my mind, and such as I esteem important. Some logs are so hard to split, and some rocks are so hard to break, that many blows are necessary to do the work. But the hardest resistence, and the toughest obduracy, and the most stubborn prejudices in all the world confronts religious truth. When Baptists tell other christians that they should be baptized like Christ was baptized, and like Christ taught, it hits hard, and ought to be irresistible; but when a Baptist tells a Baptist that he ought to observe the Supper as the Lord did in instituting it, and like he commanded it through those who spoke and wrote, as the Holy Spirit brought to their minds His teaching on this subject, for no one will say that Christ practiced one thing and taught another; then what shall we say when they treat it just like the prejudiced ones on baptism? It needs explanation, and here it is as near as I can give it. One has been made to believe that John baptized "with water," and the other has been made to believe that "Disciples," in Acts 20:5, was the church, and that Paul and his compannions communed with them when they (the church) came together on the first day of the week. But both are misled by false translations. And the Baptist is most to blame, because all new translations leave out "The Disciples," while all do not correct the "with water." While no argument can be made for error, yet some arguments for truth are more plausible than others. The last three requirements in entering a Baptist church are, a satisfactory profession of saving faith, baptism and reception into membership. Some Baptist churches put the first and last together—the last to be valid after baptism. But there is the vote to receive them into membership. The table is in the church (not the house), but the "BODY" wherever it may meet. You can't partake unless you are one of the body. "For we, the many, are one body, one loaf, for we all partake of the one loaf." There is but one way to get to the table. On this we are all agreed. The "visiting brother" has the first two requirements, but not the last; he has not been received into membership. Shall this be required of some and not of others? Some say, invite the visiting Baptist as a member of another church, and some say, by a like "courtesy" we can regard him for the time being as a member of our church. Then he is, or is not, a member. If not, it is a farce and a falsehood.

If he is really for the time a member, and should be one of those that we should not eat with, then try him, and purge him out, and with him "no not to eat." Especially do this, as is often the case he is a member of a church that is too dead to do that much-needed thing for him. He is a member or not a member, and why falsify at that the most solemn place and time in our lives? Not commune with a Baptist? Have you no fellowship for Baptists outside of your own little company? That is the slogan borrowed from Pedobaptists. It is as respectable when one uses it as when the other uses it. Yes, a thousand times yes, commune with all Baptists and all christians; but that is not the way or when or where to show it. We all tell Pedobaptists that it is a perversion of the holy ordinance, to detract it from church fellowship with Christ in his "broken body and shed blood," to an expression of our feelings for christian people. And I tell the "visiting brother" the same thing. We have plenty of ways of expressing our feeling for one another, but this is not one of the ways. The fellowship one for another was expressed when they were received into membership in the body, and by continuance of the same; but at the table we express the fellowship between the church and Christ, or the "body and the head." Language can not make this clearer. In one ordinance-baptism, "each one" expressed his individual fellowship for his buried and risen Lord, and his individual partnership with him in his great sacrifice of himself for us individually. But he also "gave himself for his church;" he "bought it with his own blood," and it is proper that this ordinance—the Supper—should be kept sacred for the expression of that one thing. Anything else is a perversion. One is heaven high above the other. I saw my wife partake once when she seemed to realize that it was her last time; she seemed to use all her powers to lift herself to a "discernment" of its true import. Her agonizing countenance melted my heart, and I prayed as perhaps I never did for the Lord to help her to a spiritual feast of that sacrifice. As the feast of the Passover was necessary to sustain Christ's body on the way to the cross, so might that spiritual feast give her strength for the awful ordeal awaiting her. I communed with her, though I did not partake of the Supper, not being a member with her there. Christ gives us a thousand times and places and ways to commune with one another, and sets one time and place and way to commune with him, and shall we rob him of that? Then let Baptists quit communing with one another at the Lord's table, and let the church, as such, hold communion with her Lord. I have never, thank God, violated his expressed will in this holy ordinance in that way. I officiate in ordinances for churches, but they are the church in all church actions.

Perhaps baptizing is rightly classed with ministerial function, but not so with the Lord's Table. That is not a preacher's *ex-officio*. A church should observe that ordinance—preacher or no preacher—as it is a church ordinance, and the ministry is an office in the church; so the church is before and above and independent of all of its officers. But baptism, while in the care of the church, is administered to those that are without. One is outside and the other inside; not inside the denomination, but inside the church, and there is no lawful way to it but through the door of the church. And baptism is not the door, but the uplifted hand lets them in or puts them out. Guard well that door, lest the unbidden of the Lord enter.

CHURCH PERPETUITY

PREFACE

In May, 1900, I delivered twelve lectures, by request, on "Distinctive Baptist Doctrines," at the Soutwestern University. Ten of these, by request of the class, were published in book form, by Folk & Browder, Nashville, Tenn. The book closes with these words: "My two lectures on Church Perpetuity, which, with the others, were requested for publication, are withheld for the present; but I trust soon to give them with good measure. To all who heard or may read, fare ye well."

In the following pages I try to fulfill that promise. I have added much to the matter of these two lectures. There is a strange and strong effort to discourage and suppress investigation along this line. My conviction that the subject is of immense importance and profit, compels the venture of "what I have written." Let those who object, inspect.

Church Perpetuity is Scriptural.

INTRODUCTION

There are three words used almost indiscriminately in the discussion of Church History, viz: "Succession," "Continuity" and "Perpetuity." Not one of these words expresses the whole idea, but each one is nearly right, and sufficient for honest inquiry. In the sense of popes and kings succeeding each other, the word is not to be used of church history, because one church does not take the place of another. Sometimes one church dies as an organization, and some of the members may constitute in the same, or another place, and thus one may succeed the other. But this is hardly involved in this discussion, except where churches may have been driven from place to place, or from one country to another. The church at Jerusalem was multiplied into the churches of Judea, Samaria, etc., but these did not succeed the church at Jerusalem, because that church had not died, as when popes and kings succeed each other by death. That particular idea of supplanting, or taking the place of another, must be eliminated.

"Continuity" is not far from the true idea, as

these churches were a continuation and extension of the first church. So out of continuity there came perpetuity, as in human history. These other churches did not spring out of the ground, but came from the first church. There was continuity, but this is not what we are to prove in this discussion by history. If that was the principle of propagation, clearly established in the beginning, and is the principle yet, and has been as far as we know, then, as in Beehives, we can reach a satisfactory conclusion, unless the opposite is clearly proved. Perpetuity fits the kingdom better than the church, unless we use the church in the kingdom sense, a sense I wholly and heartily and holily discard. The kingdom "endureth forever," is "everlasting," but these terms don't fit the church, which is an organized body within the kingdom. The exact relation of the church, or churches in the aggregate and kingdom, I may not clearly discern, nor can I clearly discern the exact relation of Father, Son and Holy Spirit; nor that of soul and spirit; nor the natural and spiritual, or day and night, or winter and summer. There is a blending, a place of meeting, but who can tell where? We don't have to, thanks to goodness and mercy. We know the kingdom was first mentioned, and that the church did not supplant the kingdom. They both must be entered. It is not enough to be in the kingdom. Matthew mentions kingdom nearly as often after the church was mentioned as before; Mark, Luke and John never mentioned church, but kingdom often. The kingdom was before the church, as the church was composed of citizens of the kingdom, organized for work and worship. The Lord added those in the kingdom to the church.

There are many things predicated of the kingdom that can not be of the church, and *vice versa*. We know that when the church became the most frequent term in use, that the kingdom was not done away, but is often referred to even to the end of Revelation. We know the church and the kingdom are not the same, nor is the aggregation of churches commensurate with the kingdom, as many are in the kingdom who are not in a church, and many in the church, who are not in the kingdom; that discipline can put out of the church, but not out of the kingdom; that one can die out of the church, but not out of the kindom; that many lose membership in the church by lapses, disintegration of the church; but none of these forfeits citizenship in the kingdom. There is room and need for both church and kingdom; they are not hostile, nor in competition, nor is either in the way of the other, but both helpers together. We can discern both, but we can not discern the exact difference, nor the exact relation of the two. Thus it is in many things closely related.

The exact relation of husband and wife is often perplexing, even to the parties themselves. The continuousness of the kingdom is not disputed—I mean the kingdom set up by Christ. But as to the continuousness of that institution that Christ called his church, which the gates of hades should not prevail against, that shall be the aim of the following pages to establish. The race, family and church have existed from their beginnings. As the kingdom and the church are so closely related, we will go over the ground covered by both. The same power that could perpetuate the kingdom, could preserve the church. Perpetuity of the kingdom, and continuity of the churches in the kingdom are both plainly and abundantly taught in the Scriptures. This ought to be enough for the faith of the saints, in the absence of all history. But history shall also testify. Let us go on to see:

1st. IF PERPETUITY IS SCRIPTURAL.
2d. IF IT IS REASONABLE.
3d. IF IT IS CREDIBLE.
4th. IF IT IS HISTORICAL.

CHURCH PERPETUITY IS SCRIPTURAL.

First let us notice a few scriptures concerning the Kingdom. Kingdom is a correlative term, like husband and wife, parent and child, master and servant; that is, it depends upon its correlative parts. No husband, no wife, no parent, no child, etc. So a kingdom must have a king, subjects, laws, territory. So of the kingdom of heaven. The kingdom set up by Christ in the days of the Caesars was to endure for the age. See the following scriptures on the kingdom.

Ps. 145—13 Thy kingdom is an everlasting kingdom,
And thy dominion *endureth* throughout all generations.

Ps. 146—10 Jehovah will reign forever,

Thy God, O Zion, unto all generations.
Praise ye Jehovah.

Dan. 2—44 And in the days of those kings shall the God of heaven set up a kingdom which shall never be destroyed, nor shall the sovereignty thereof be left to another people; but it shall break in pieces and consume all these kingdoms, and it shall stand for ever. 45 Forasmuch as thou sawest that a stone was cut out of the mountain without hands, and that it brake in pieces the iron, the brass, the clay, the silver, and the gold; the great God hath made known to the king what shall come to pass hereafter: and the dream is certain, and the interpretation thereof sure.

Dan. 4—3 How great are his signs! and how mighty are his wonders! his kingdom is an everlasting kingdom, and his dominion is from generation to generation.

Dan. 4—34 And at the end of the days I, Nebuchadnezzar, lifted up mine eyes unto heaven, and mine understanding returned unto me, and I blessed the Most High, and I praised and honored him that liveth forever; for his dominion is an everlasting dominion, and his kingdom from generation to generation; 35 and all the inhabitants of the earth are reputed as nothing; and he doeth according to his will in the army of heaven, and among the inhabitants of the earth; and none can stay his hand, or say unto him, What doest thou?

Dan. 7—14 And there was given him dominion, and glory, and a kingdom, that all the peoples, nations, and languages should serve him; his dominion is an everlasting dominion, which shall not pass away, and his kingdom that which shall not be destroyed.

Dan. 7—18 But the saints of the Most High shall receive the kingdom, and possess the kingdom forever, even forever and ever.

Dan. 7—21 I beheld, and the same horn made war with the saints, and prevailed against them; 22 until the ancient of days came, and judgment was given to the saints of the Most High, and the time came that the saints possessed the kingdom.

Dan. 7—25 And he shall speak *great* words against the most High, and shall wear out the saints of the most High, and think to change time and laws: and they shall be given into his hand until a time and times and the dividing of time. 26 But the judgment shall sit, and they shall take away his dominion, to consume and to destroy *it* unto the end. 27 And the kingdom and the dominion, and the greatness of the kingdoms under the whole heaven, shall be given to the people of the saints of the Most High: his kingdom is an everlasting kingdom, and all dominions shall serve and obey him.

Luke 1—31 And behold, thou shalt conceive in thy womb, and bring forth a son, and shalt call his name JESUS. 32 He shall be great, and shall be called the Son of the Most High: and the Lord God shall give unto him the throne of his father David: 33 and he shall reign over the house of Jacob forever; and of his kingdom there shall be no end.

Heb. 12—26 Whose voice then shook the earth: but now he hath promised, saying, Yet once more will I make to tremble not the earth only, but also the heaven. 27 And this *word*, Yet once more, signifieth the removing of those things that are shaken, as of things that have been made, that those things which are not shaken may remain. 28 Wherefore, receiving a kingdom that cannot be shaken, let us have grace, whereby we may offer service well-pleasing to God with reverence and awe: 29 for our God is a consuming fire.

Rev. 11—15 And the seventh angel sounded; and there followed great voices in heaven, and they said, The kingdom of the world is become *the kingdom* of our Lord, and of his Christ: and he shall reign for ever and ever.

There was great effort to overthrow the kingdom, which, of course, was visible, and the same power that could preserve the kingdom could preserve the church, although the powers and authorities, visible and invisible, did their utmost against both, and all, as we will see.

THE THRONE ALSO EVERLASTING.

I quote these scriptures, not for the teachers of theology, but the learners, who might not turn to them.

Ps. 89—27 I will also make him *my* first-born, The highest of the kings of the earth.

28 My loving kindness will I keep for him evermore; and my covenant shall stand fast with him. 29 His seed also will I make to endure forever, and his throne as the days of heaven. 34 My covenant will I not break, nor alter the thing that is gone out of my lips. 35 Once have I sworn by my holiness: I will not lie unto David: 36 His seed shall endure forever, and his throne as the sun before me. 37 It shall be established forever as the moon, And *as* the faithful witness in the sky.

Isa, 9—6 For unto us a child is born, unto us a son is given; and the government shall be upon his shoulder; and his name shall be called Wonderful, Counsellor, Mighty God, Everlasting Father, Prince of Peace. 7 Of the increase of his government and of peace there shall be no end, upon the throne of David, and upon his kingdom, to establish it, and to uphold it with justice and with righteousness from henceforth even forever. The zeal of Jehovah of hosts will perform this.

Heb. 1—But unto the Son *he saith*, Thy throne, O God, *is* forever and ever: a sceptre of righteousness *is* the sceptre of thy kingdom.

Rev. 3—21 To him that overcometh will I grant to sit with me in my throne, even as I also overcame, and am set down with my Father in his throne. 22 He that hath an ear, let him hear what the Spirit saith unto the churches.

So we see the Throne was not to be overthrown.

THE KING IS ALSO EVERLASTING.

Ex. 15—17 Thou wilt bring them in, and plant them in the mountain of thine inheritance, The place, O Jehovah, which thou hast made for me to dwell in, The sanctuary, O Lord which thy hands have established. 18 Jehovah shall reign forever and ever.

Ps. 5—15 Break thou the arm of the wicked; And as for the evil man, seek out his wickedness till thou find none. 16 Jehovah is King forever and ever.

Jer. 9—10 Jehovah sat *as King* at the Flood; Yea, Jehovah sitteth as King forever. But Jehovah is the true God; he is the living God, and an everlasting King: at his wrath the earth trembleth, and the nations are not able to abide his indignation.

Mic. 4—6 In that day, saith Jehovah, will I assemble that which is lame, and I will gather that which is driven away, and that which I have afflicted; 7 and I will make that which was lame a remnant, and that which was cast far off a strong nation; and Jehovah will reign over them in Mount Zion from henceforth even forever.

John 12—32 And I, if I be lifted up from the earth, will draw all men unto myself. 33 But this he said, signifying by what manner of death he should die. 34 The multitude therefore answered him, We have heard out of the law that the Christ abideth forever: and how sayest thou, The Son of man must be lifted up? who is this Son of man?

1 Tim. 1—17 Now unto the King eternal, immortal, invisible, the only wise God, *be* honour and glory forever and ever. Amen.

THE TERRITORY IS ALSO EVERLASTING.

"The earth is the Lords, and the fullness thereof. He made it and redeemed it for an eternal possession." The meek shall inherit the earth, and dwell therein forever. Read Gen. 13: 15; 17:8; 48:4; Ps. 2:8-9; 37:9-11, 18, 22, 29, 34; 72:7, 8; Prov. 2:21, 22; Isa. 2:2-4; 60:21, 22; Ez. 37:21-28; Amos 9:11-15; Mic. 4:1-7; Matt. 5:5; Ro. 4:13; Gal. 3:18, 29; Rev. 11:15; 21:1-3, etc. The Hebrew *erets* occurs six times in Ps. 37, three times translated "land," and three times "earth." The late revisors say, in margin, they all should be earth. Christ says, in Matt. 5:5, "Blessed are the meek, for they shall inherit the earth;" and Paul, in Ro. 4:13, says the promise to Abraham was the "WORLD." So read:

Ps. 37—9 For evil-doers shall be cut off; But those that wait for Jehovah, they shall inherit the (earth) 10 For yet a little while, and the wicked shall not be: Yea, thou shalt diligently consider his place, and he shall not be. 11 But the meek shall inherit the (earth) and shall delight themselves in the abundance of peace. 18 Jehovah knoweth the days of the perfect; and their inheritance shall be forever. 22 For *such* *as be* blessed of him shall inherit the earth; and *they that be* cursed of him shall be cut off. 28 For Jehovah loveth Justice, and forsaketh not his saints; They are preserved forever; but the seed of the wicked shall be cut off. 29 The righteous shall inherit the land (earth), and dwell therein forever. 34 Wait for Jehovah, and keep his way, and he will exalt thee to inherit the land (earth): when the wicked are cut off, thou shalt see it.

Eph. 1—13 In whom, having also believed, ye were sealed with the Holy Spirit of promise, 14 which is an earnest of our inheritance, unto the redemption of *God's* own possession, unto the praise of his glory.

Rev. 5—9 For thou wast slain, and hast redeemed men to God by thy blood out of every kindred, and tongue, and people, and nation. 10 And hast made them unto our God kings and priests: and they shall reign on the earth.

So the earth is to be redeemed from the curse of sin, and will become a "new earth," wherein the righteous are to dwell forever with the Lord. At last the Father will come down also out of heaven to tabernacle with men, and the kingdom will be given back to him. See Rev. 21st chap. and 1 Cor. 15:23-28.

"THE STATUTES," "BOOK OF THE LAW" OR "WORD OF GOD" WAS ALSO TO CONTINUE, OR "ENDURE FOREVER."

"The Word of the Lord liveth and abideth forever." It was thought to be lost in the Babylonian captivity, but see Nehemiah, chap. 8, what interest is taken in the reading of the blessed book. Since the days of Christ what diabolical efforts have been made by Pagan emperors and

Papal popes to utterly destroy the Word of the Lord; but He who preserves all things was watching The Laws of His Kingdom. It was hidden in the dens and caves of the earth and buried in the graves of Papal archives with the rubbish of relics, but God brought it out of both. It has been counterfeited, and interpolated, and misinterpreted, and wrested, and reviled, and spit upon, but it still lives and abides, shining the brighter by the rubbing off of the rust and rubbish. Now He who could preserve the Law of the Kingdom could also preserve his SUBJECTS. It was prophesied of them that they should be persecuted as He was, by men and devils, but they should not prevail. Remember, the church is not a house, but a household, composed of "Living Stones." Read:

Matt. 5—11 Blessed are ye when *men* shall reproach you, and persecute you, and say all manner of evil against you falsely, for my sake. 12 Rejoice, and be exceeding glad: for great is your reward in heaven: for so persecuted they the prophets that were before you.

Matt. 10—21 And brother shall deliver up brother to death, and the father his child: and children shall rise up against parents, and cause them to be put to death. 22 And ye shall be hated of all men for my name's sake: but he that endureth to the end, the same shall be saved. 23 But when they persecute you in this city, flee into the next: for verily I say unto you, Ye shall not have gone through the cities of Israel, till the Son of man be come.

Mark 10—29 There is no man that hath left house, or brethren, or sisters, or mother, or father, or children, or lands, for my sake, and for the gospel's sake, 30 but he shall receive a hundredfold now in this time, houses, and brethren, and sisters, and mothers, and children, and lands, with persecutions: and in the world to come eternal life.

Luke 6—22 Blessed are ye, when men shall hate you, and when they shall separate you *from their company*, and reproach you, and cast out your name as evil, for the Son of man's sake. 23 Rejoice in that day, and leap *for joy:* for behold your reward is great in heaven; for in the same manner did their fathers unto the prophets.

Luke 21—12 But before all these things, they shall lay their hands on you, and shall persecute you, delivering you up to the synagogues and prisons, bringing you before kings and governors for my name's sake. 13 It shall turn out unto you for a testimony. 16 But ye shall be delivered up even by parents, and brethren, and kinsfolk, and friends: and *some* of you shall they cause to be put to death. 17 And ye shall be hated of all men for my name's sake. 18 And not a hair of your head shall perish. 19 In your patience ye shall win your souls.

John 15—18 If the world hateth you, ye know that it hath hated me before *it hated you.* 19 If ye were of the world, the world would love its own: but because ye are not of the world, but I chose you out of the world, therefore the world hateth you. 20 Remember the word that I said unto you, A servant is not greater than his lord. If they persecuted me, they will also persecute you; if they kept my word, they will keep yours also. 21 But all these things will they do unto you for my name's sake, because they know not him that sent me.

John 16—2 They shall put you out of the synagogues: yea, the hour cometh, that whosoever killeth you shall think that he offereth service unto God.

2 Tim. 3—12 Yea, and all that would live godly in Christ Jesus shall suffer persecution. 13 But evil men and impostors shall wax worse and worse, deceiving and being deceived.

Rev. 12—17 And the dragon waxed wroth with the woman, and went away to make war with the rest of her seed, that keep the commandments of God, and hold the testimony of Jesus.

Rev. 17—4 And the woman was arrayed in purple and scarlet, and decked with gold and precious stones and pearls, having in her hand a golden cup full of abominations, even the unclean things of her fornication, 5 and upon her forehead a name written, MYSTERY, BABYLON THE GREAT, THE MOTHER OF THE HARLOTS AND OF THE ABOMINATIONS OF THE EARTH. 6 And I saw the woman drunken with the blood of the saints, and with the blood of the martyrs of Jesus.

Also Matt. 13:21; 23:34; Acts 8:1; 22:4-8; 26:11-15; 2 Thess. 1:4; Rev. 6:9-11; 7:13, 14; also Dan. 8:12, 24-25, etc.

This part of the prophecy has been verified by history. The true witnesses have been thus persecuted. Have the Promises been fulfilled? Then the true church is in the world to-day. Notice some of the Promises of Preservation and Perpetuity:

Matt. 16—18 And I say also unto thee, That thou art Peter, and upon this rock I will build my church; and the gates of hell shall not prevail against it.

Matt. 28—18 All authority hath been given unto me in heaven and on earth. 19 Go ye therefore, and make disciples of all the nations, baptizing them into the name of the Father and of the Son and of the Holy Spirit: 20 teaching them to observe all things whatsoever I commanded you: and lo, I am with you always, even unto the end of the world.

Ro. 8—35 Who shall separate us from the love of Christ? shall tribulation, or anguish, or persecution, or famine, or nakedness, or peril, or sword? 36 Even as it is written, For thy sake we are killed all the day long; we were accounted as sheep for the slaughter. 37 Nay, in all these things we are more than conquerors through him that loved us. 38 For I am persuaded, that neither death, nor life, nor angels, nor principalities, nor things present, nor things to come, nor powers, 39 nor height, nor depth, nor any other creature, shall be able to separate us from the love of God, which is in Christ Jesus our Lord.

1 Cor. 15—24 Then *cometh* the end, when he shall deliver up the kingdom to God, even the Father; when he shall have abolished all rule and all authority and power. 25 For he must reign, till he hath put all his enemies under his feet. 26 The last enemy that shall be abolished is death.

Eph. 1—19 That ye may know what the exceeding greatness of his power to us-ward who believe, according to that working of the strength of his might 20 which he wrought in Christ, when he raised him from the dead, and made him to sit at his right hand in the heavenly *places*, 21 far above all rule, and authority, and power, and dominion, and every name that is named, not only in this world, but also in that which is to come: 22 and he put all things in subjection under his feet, and gave him to be head over all things to the church, 23 which is his body, the fulness of him that filleth all in all.

Eph. 3—20 Now unto him that is able to do exceeding abundantly above all that we ask or think, according to the power that worketh in us, 21 unto him *be* the glory in the church and in Christ Jesus unto all generations forever and ever. Amen.

Eph. 5—23 For the husband is the head of the wife, as Christ also is the head of the church, *being* himself the saviour of the body. 24 But as the church is subject to Christ, so *let* the wives also *be* to their husbands in everything. 25 Husbands, love your wives, even as Christ also loved the church, and gave himself up for it; 26 that he might sanctify it, having cleansed it by the washing of water with the word, 27 that he might present the church to himself a glorious *church*, not having spot or wrinkle or any such thing; but that it should be holy and without blemish. 28 Even so ought husbands also to love their own wives as their own bodies. He that loveth his own wife loveth himself: 29 For no man ever hated his own flesh; but nourisheth and cherisheth it, even as Christ also the church; 30 because we are members of his body. 31 For this cause shall a man leave his father and mother, and shall cleave to his wife; and the two shall become one flesh. 32 This mystery is great: but I speak in regard of Christ and of the church. 33 Nevertheless do ye also severally love each one his own wife even as himself: and *let* the wife *see* that she fear her husband.

Be sure to read Dan. 7:21-26 and Rev. 11:15-18; 19:1-21. I would like to comment on these scriptures, but any comment, I think, would weaken the scriptures. If in the face of these Words of God, one should doubt the perpetuity of the church, then reason would be useless. And don't forget that this discussion is made necessary by such doubts, yea denials, and that of late by some of our own people, who have apostasized from the faith of our fathers. They laugh and mock at this, as the higher critics do at Inspiration, etc. How could an invisible church provoke opposition and persecution? How could they persecute what they could not see, or touch, or handle? "Has reason fled to brutish beasts?" The church that started has continued through persecutions. Is that true of your "church," dear reader? Why was yours started? Did Christ start it, and has it come down through floods and flames? If not, you don't belong to the church of Christ. It is the church of him who started it, whether Henry, Luther, Calvin, Wesley, Campbell, J. Smith, Mrs. Eddy, etc.

PERPETUITY IN PARABLES.

There are seven of these in the 13th of Matt. The first, the seed of the kingdom, represents the word, falling on four classes of hearers, three of which it seems was wasted, but the fourth brought forth 30, 60, 100 fold. So the sowing was not a failure. In the next the seed represents good and bad men. Christ and the devil are the sowers. The tares came up with the wheat, but did not choke out the wheat, nor root it up, but itself was routed out in the time of harvest, at the end of the age. The tares greatly damaged, but did not destroy. The tares did not turn to wheat, nor did the wheat turn to tares. The field endured both to the end. So the gates did not prevail. Again, the kingdom of heaven was likened to a grain of mustard, the least of all seeds, yet it grew to be the greatest of all herbs. That means success. In the next it is like to leaven, which operated till the whole was leavened. In the next it is like a treasure hid in a field which a man bought. The field is the world; the man, the son of man; the treasure, the hidden people of God. Christ sold all he had and bought the field containing the hidden treasure, and the treasure was "sealed until the redemption of this purchased possession, unto the praise of his glory." The devil would take this field if he could, but if Christ's word is true, then the devil and his forces are to be cast out at the last day, and he will reign with his saints on the earth forever. So that will not be a failure. So of the pearl of great price. A man who would sell all he has, and give it for one pearl, will very likely look after the pearl, and keep and defend it if he can. Christ would die for that pearl. Yea, it is hid with Christ in God. So the devil must first take God and Christ before he can get the pearl. "Kept by the power of God."

In the next we see that the gospel net that was cast into the sea, did not break, though it gathered of every kind, but was drawn to the shore, which is the end of the age, when the separation will take place. The bad fish did not turn to good fish, nor did the good turn to bad.

So in all of these trials through which the kingdom and church were to pass, defeat was threatened, but the success was final. All the organizations of so-called churches, is on the theory that there was a failure; that the kingdom or church did come to an end, and that it is the pretense for the starting of others. The King had a hard time of it in this wicked world. They got him on the cross, and in the grave, with a stone sealed, and a guard, "but he was not holden of it," or them, but triumphed gloriously. The Word of the kingdom also has had a hard time of it. It has been imprisoned, tortured, and burned, but here it is, "living and abiding forever." The Subjects of the kingdom have also received the same treatment. 2 Cor. 5:8-11: Troubled on every side, perplexed, persecuted, but not forsaken, cast down but not destroyed. 10 Always bearing about in the body the dying of the Lord Jesus, that the life also of Jesus might be made manifest in our body. 11 For we which live are alway delivered unto death for Jesus' sake, that the life also of Jesus might be made manifest in our mortal flesh.

Some one said "that Baptist succession has not yet been proven, and we very humbly add that nothing vital depends on proving it."

Perhaps not. Yet the honor, power, majesty, glory and dominion of Jesus Christ depends on the *fact*. If succession is not a fact, then those who have fallen asleep in Jesus have perished. He promised to keep his church, and if he has not, either his power or veracity has failed, and, in either case, we are without hope in the world. If he did not keep his bride in exile, when all the world persecuted her, and when she counted not even life itself dear unto her, but left all and clung to him, and trusted him, if he did not keep her then, it was either because he would not, or could not—either of which would be fatal to our hopes. Yet nothing may depend on *proving* it.

Why this catering and pandering to infidels about ability to prove an acknowledged fact, I know not. It stuns reason, defies judgment, imagination refuses to conjecture. Let us leave it to the barred and bolted vault of God's hidden mysteries, hoping that in eternity it will be explained, and we will be advanced enough in knowledge to understand it.

Comparing my faith with that of Abraham, the father of the faithful, I find his faith characterized as follows: Rom. 4:20-22. "He staggered not at the PROMISE of God through unbelief; but was strong in faith, giving glory to God; and being FULLY PERSUADED that what HE HAD PROMISED, HE WAS ABLE ALSO TO PERFORM, AND THEREFORE it was counted to him for righteousness." Now this is a parallel case. Did HE promise to keep his church? "*That's the question.*" Then I stagger not at the *promise* of God through *unbelief;* but am *strong* in *faith*, giving glory to God, and being fully persuaded that what HE had promised HE is also able to perform, and therefore walk in the steps of that faith of our father Abraham.

That Christ made the promise, and spoke the fiat concerning the perpetuity of his church, no one is reckless enough to deny.

If the church of Christ died in the wilderness, or anywhere else, during the persecution, or any other time, show us the place and time in history.

Who or what was it that prevailed against it? Show us "where they laid it, and we will take it away." In what mortuary report can we find a record of its death? Where is the historian that has chanted its obsequies? The body of Christ dead!!! Where is the place of its inhumation? Tell us, that we may go and weep there.

Who saw the dismal glare of the funeral pyres,
And sung the requiem by the sullen fires?
Had it funeral rite or curfew's tolling dirge?

Produce the supposed dead body of Christ, and grant us an autopsy, and we are ready to lift up our hand toward heaven and swear by him that liveth forever and ever, that it is neither dead nor sleepeth. For he himself, willing more abundantly to show unto the heirs of promise the immutability of his counsel, confirmed it by an oath; that by two immutable things in which it is impossible for God to lie, we might have strong consolation, who have fled for refuge to lay hold on the hope set before us: which hope we have an anchor to the soul both sure and steadfast and which interreth into that within the veil; whether the forerunner is for us entered, even Jesus, made a high priest FOREVER after the order of Melchisedec.

Could Christ take care of his church? If he could and did not, it was because he would not. Then he forsook it, and broke his promises and oath. Yea, the Father also, and also the Spirit.

Then where are we? What are we? What hope have we? But you say it can't be proved. That means, it has not been proved to you. Like doubting Thomas, do you demand the utmost demand of your natural senses? Thomas got it and surrendered. Christ's word and others should have satisfied him, and it ought to satisfy you. Don't fail to read on, for who knows but you, even you, may not yet say: "My Lord and my God." If His word is not true, then let us all go a-fishing. But we are not through with the subject yet. See this whole subject foreshadowed in the following illustration:

Matt. 7—21 Not everyone that saith unto me, Lord, Lord, shall enter into the kingdom of heaven; but he that doeth the will of my Father who is in heaven. 22 Many will say to me in that day, Lord, Lord, did we not prophesy by thy name, and by thy name cast out demons, and by thy name do many mighty works? 23 And then will I profess unto them, I never knew you: depart from me, ye that work iniquity. 24 Everyone therefore that heareth these words of mine, and doeth them, shall be likened unto a wise man, who built his house upon the rock (petra): 25 and the rain descended, and the floods came, and the winds blew, and beat upon that house: and it fell not; for it was founded upon the rock (petra). 26 And everyone that heareth these words of mine, and doeth them not, shall be likened unto a foolish man, who built his house upon the sand: 27 and the rain descended, and the floods came, and the winds blew, and smote upon that house: and it fell: and great was the fall thereof.

Would Christ be so foolish as to build his house on sand? No; He built it on the petra or firm foundation. Let us study this Church foundation.

PETRA—PETROS.

"On this Rock I will build my church." Is this Rock Peter, or Christ, or Peter's Confession, or God's Revelation of the Divinity of Christ to Peter? Or the inner Revelation and Confession? Some things plausible may be said of any one of these positions. The Catholics and some modern Baptists hold the first; Protestants and most Baptists hold the second. I have almost been convinced that the third is the true interpretation; then I shifted to the fourth, and then fell back to the second. Plausible arguments can be made on most any position, even the first. But this is the way I now view it, and the reasons therefor. God is called a Rock in the following places: Deut. 32:4, 15, 30, I. Sam. 2:2; II. Sam. 22:2, 3, 32, 47; Ps. 18:2, 31, 46; 28:1; 31:2, 3; 42:9; 61:2; 62:2, 7; 71:3; 78:35; 89:15; 94:22; 95:1; Isa. 8:14; 17:10, etc.

Petra is found in the new Scriptures sixteen times: Matt. 7:24, 25; 16:18; 27:51, 60; Mark 15:46; Luke 6:48; 8:6, 13; Romans 9:33; I. Cor. 10:4; I. Peter 2:8, etc.

Thayer says the distinction between *Petra*, the massive living rock, and *Petros*, a detached fragment, is generally observed in classic Greek. *Petra* is never used of a man, and God is never called a *petros*. Christ is called *petra* more than once, and Peter is called *petros* over 160 times. I. Cor. 10:4: "They drank of that spiritual Rock (*petra*) that followed them, and that rock (*petra*) was Christ. Again I am confirmed in this by by what was said of the foundation, and that was what Christ was talking about—building his church upon a firm foundation, so that because of the foundation, the winds, rains, floods, etc., of persecution, beating upon it, and furiously assailing it, should not overthrow it. The stability is not predicated of the building, but of the foundation. So the church can not be overthrown, not because Christ built it, but because he built it on Peter (?). Its stability is in the foundation—Peter, a bowlder (?). In Matt. 7:24 it is *petra*, not *petros*. Peter was the personification of unstableness, as we will see. I believe Christ was the *petra*, because Isa. 28:16 says: "Therefore thus saith the Lord God—I will lay in Zion for a foundation, a stone, a tried stone, a precious corner-stone, a sure foundation, and he that believeth shall not make haste." See also Gen. 49:24; Ps. 118:22; Matt. 21:42; Acts 4:11, 12; Romans 9:33; 10:11; I. Cor. 3:10, 12; Eph. 2:20; I. Peter 2:48. In all these we know that Christ, and not Peter, is the foundation stone. 1 Cor. 3:11: "For other foundation can no man lay than that is laid, *which is Christ Jesus*." If this does not prove it, then what need have we of proof.

This is further confirmed by a change of gender. Thou art *Peter*, and on this *petra*. He did not say, thou art Peter, and on that rock, but on this rock, a very different kind. Nor did he say, thou art Peter, and on *Thee* I will build. That would have been so plain. *Petros* is explained in John 1:42 as signifying a stone, not *petra*, but *Kephas*. He is thus called in I. Cor. 1:12; 3:22;

9:5; 15:5; Gal. 2:9. Christ is the foundation, the chief corner-stone, the head of the corner, the cap-stone, etc. *Petros* and *lithos* go into the building, but *petra* never, for the building, with its foundation, is on the *petra*. The idea of building Christ, the apostles, prophets and saints to the end of time on Peter! That road certainly leads to Rome. Christ is the foundation, and *petra* supports the foundation, therefore Peter supports Christ (?). Was Christ and his church built on Peter? Did he say on that *petros* or on this *petra?* If Peter could support Christ and his church, then he could have built the church on himself. Christ, and not Peter, is the *petra*, the foundation, the chief corner-stone, the capstone, "the all and in all."

See this movable, changeable, contemptible Petros in several places. In Matt. 14:28-31 he starts to walk on the water, but soon turns coward, and cries like a baby for help. In Matt. 15:15 Christ rebukes his want of understanding. In Matt. 16:22 Peter opposes his Master (pope like), and in reply Christ rebukes him, saying: "Get thou behind me, satan, for thou art an offense to me." (Infallible pope?) In Matt. 17:4, we find him talking foolishness, on the mount of transfiguration. See him in Matt. 26:33, "following afar off." Hear him lying to a little maid; cursing and swearing. What a stable foundation (?) In verse 40, Christ begs Peter to stay awake and watch with him just one hour. Begged him three times, while in that awful agony, but the sleepy head slept on. Hear him in John 13:8, saying: "Thou shalt never wash my feet," and then, with the fallibility of a pope, changes to: "Not my feet only, but my hands and my head." See this rash pope (?) cutting off the ear of Malchus, the High Priest's servant, and the Lord had to undo his work. He raced with John to the sepulchre and got beat. John had sense enough to stop on the outside, but Peter ran into the tomb, where there was no Lord. Hear him, disheartened, saying: "I go a-fishing"—back to his old trade. When the Lord asked him: "Lovest thou me?" he cowardly dodged the question three times. In Acts 10:13-14, the voice from heaven said: "Rise, Peter, slay and eat." But he said he would not do it. In Acts 15, James beats him making a speech in solution of the vexing question. In Gal. 2:11-14, Paul rebukes him for acting the hypocrite. In his first epistle, 5:1, he calls himself not pope; not the foundation of the church, nor the *petra* supporting the foundation, but simply elder; and in his second epistle, chapter 1, he calls himself a slave. Peter was in the foundation, but so were the other apostles and prophets, and Christ only in a special sense—"the chief corner-stone."

Peter knew that the twelve were addressed through him as their representative, just as the "angels" were in the second and third chapters of Revelation; that the binding and loosing power was not in him, but in the church, as is infallibly taught in Matt. 18:17-18. We know that the great power conferred in John 20:22, 23 was on all the apostles alike. Peter knew that in the council at Jerusalem, when a great question was to be decided for all time, that he had no authority to decide it, for when James made the speech that "pleased the apostles, elders and the whole church," that the settlement came in the appointed way. He knew that he had no power to appoint a successor to Judas, or to appoint deacons in the sixth chapter of Acts. That was also done by the whole church. In Acts 8:14, the other apostles sent Peter and John into Samaria. Did Christ build the Kingdom on Peter? Is Christ the foundation of the kingdom, and Peter the foundation of the church? Now, those who try to put the church on Peter must have a kingdom-church in their minds. Catholics say the Visible, the others say the Invisible church. I wonder if the devil can see the invisible church, and what he wants to destroy it for. It never did anything.

Our sunday-school literature of 1907 has the church built on Peter. I quote as follows: "There can be no reasonable doubt that Jesus' words, fairly interpreted, mean that the "rock" on which the church is to be built is not Peter's faith, nor the Messiahship and divinity to which his confession referred, but Peter himself."

From another: "Peter" means rock, and it was as if Jesus said, "Thou art stone, and upon this stone I will build my church." The "church" includes those who believe in Jesus Christ and make the confession that Peter had just made, being taught, as he was, by the Holy Spirit."

From Western Recorder: "*Thou art Peter, and upon this rock*"—evidently referring to Peter as spokesman for the apostles. The apostles and the prophets are the foundation. (Eph. 2:20).

The new Jerusalem has the twelve apostles for its twelve foundation-stones. (Rev. 21:14).

But Christ said, Luke 6:46 And why call ye me, Lord, Lord, and do not the things which I say? 47 Whosoever cometh to me, and heareth my sayings, and doeth them, I will shew you to whom he is like: 48 He is like a man which built an house, and digged deep, and laid the foundation on a rock: and when the flood arose, the stream beat vehemently upon that house, and could not shake it: for it was founded upon a rock.

In both places the rock is *petra*. Better put your foundation on sand than a *petros*—bowlder.

But read further from the Recorder: "*My church*"—his elect people, and no "visible" organization. When such are spoken of, it is the church in Rome, the churches of Galatia, etc. "*The gates of hell*"—the gates of death. There shall never be a time when some of that elect people shall not be living upon the earth."

Then Christ did not build a church. He has always had an "elect people." Did he build them into a disorganization, or an invisible organization? Then it is a sin to have a visible organization. Where is his building? Were these 12 foundation-stones, with Christ the chief corner-stone, laid on Peter? Forgive the thought.

Here is another scripture that fits this subject: Luke 14:28 For which of you, desiring to build a tower, doth not first sit down and count the cost, whether he have *wherewith* to complete it? 29 Lest haply, when he hath laid a foundation, and is not able to finish, all that behold begin to mock him, 30 saying, This man began to build, and was not able to finish. 31 Or what king, as he goeth to encounter another king in war, will not sit down first and take counsel whether he is able with ten thousand to meet him that cometh against him with twenty thousand? 32 Or else, while the other is yet a great way off, he sendeth an ambassage, and asketh conditions of peace.

Did Christ begin to build and was not able to finish? Did he fail to reckon the strength of the opposition to his church? Did he make peace with the adversaries, or did he surrender? Will you "mock" him with a failure to do what he started out to do?

IT IS REASONABLE.

Reason and Revelation Confirmed by Analogy and History.

Some things are of the earth earthy, and some are of heaven. The heavenly things all bear the marks of their divine origin. "Every house is built by some man," and since it is man's work, man may build at any place and time that necessities may require. This, like all human works, bears the marks of human origin. The mordant tooth of time will devour it, will bring it to an everlasting end, because it has no reproducing power in itself, and it has not this power because man, the builder, could not impart it. No house, or watch, or work of man's hand, ever contained life or seed in itself. Nor need they, since men are always, and everywhere, and when their work is needed they are generally glad to perform it. And this is the very best man can do. But God is one, and creation's day having passed, his works have come down through the journey of ages, through the self-perpetuating power which he put within them; otherwise he could not have "rested from his labors." When he made the grass, and herbs, and trees after their kind; fishes, fowls, beasts after their kind, he only made one or one pair of each, and then put in them the self-propagating principle; and if you can bear it, each one of all these species on earth today is the legitimate product of its predecessor, and thus has come down by succession from the original. Mules and mongrels and hybrids don't propagate their species. The line may be long, and impossible to trace, but this we know—God finished his works of creation in the beginning, and stamped them with perpetuity, and put the law within. We see this law in operation today, and so far as history testifies, this law of self-propagation has ever operated; hence the conclusion in favor of succession is irresistible.

So of the church, if it is of God's building, and designed for perpetuity. Let us study the principle from Reason and Analogy.

THE RACE.

This is true of our own species. I know I am in the succession, not because I can trace it, but because God originated the race with this law of self-propagation—a law we see in operation now, and so far as history testifies, it has thus ever operated; hence the proof and conclusion are irresistible. You may tell me I can't trace it. You may urge variety of complexion and countenance, and customs, as unfavorable to one origin; I may concede these differences from each other, and from the original, and then point out sufficient marks of unity to establish the identity. We may possess many marks in common with other species—such as two eyes, two ears, one nose, etc., and many marks dissimilar to our original, yet who is troubled in establishing the fact, that "of one blood he has made all nations that dwell upon the face of the whole earth?"

None but God could originate a race like ours. He made the first pair, gave them self-propagating power, and commanded them to multiply and fill the earth, and we are right sure the race was not overthrown in the long wilderness journey. It was often wasted, but never exterminated. The gates of hades did not prevail. I claim to be in the succession. Men may challenge the historical proof, and it may never be furnished, yet the proof, the right kind of proof, is abundant, and the succession is sure.

HARVESTS.

God, who made man, and who undertook to provide for him, promised that seed-time and harvests should not fail to the end of time. God gave the first harvest to begin with, and put in it this law of progeniture, and promised perpetuity. We know that our last harvest came out of its predecessor, and that may be as far as we can trace it, yet, from principles previously laid down, we assert the succession with dogmatic assurance.

Wasting and decay have continually operated, but have not prevailed, and the law of propagation has never changed. There have been many and sore famines, but harvests have continued by the only law of propagation. One harvest must furnish seed for the next. Man can't make seed. Degenerate seed may be improved, but can't be made better than the original, and man can't originate seed with life, though he is an expert at counterfeiting.

THE FAMILY.

This is a divine institution.. So is the church. It has constitution and government. So has the church. The father is the head, and the mother the heart. So Christ is the head of the church, and the Holy Spirit the heart. Natural children have an instinctive disposition to love and obey the parents, and the parents are naturally disposed to love and care for the children. So of the church. God ordained the family for a perpetual institution. So of the church. God intended for every natural man to be a member of a natural family. So of the spiritual church. God intended that all natural increase should be by the family. So of the church. All have not been, as there have been many unlawful marriages and births. Yet the general rule has prevailed, and families have in the main absorbed by adoption, and other social methods, the many who, without culpability of their own, have been born bastards, or of unholy wedlock. But the family has not been overthrown. So many spiritual children have been born out of spiritual wedlock, but as they have a spiritual disposition, they have generally turned into the fellowship of supposed "lawful assemblies." Neither the family nor the church has been overturned by these lawless proceedings. In the beginning of families there was one family in Eden. In the beginning of churches there was one church in Jerusalem. The first family increased in numbers and multiplied in families. So of the first church. The devil caused the first family to be cast out of Eden. So he did with the first church out of Jerusalem. The scattered members from Eden increased, and multiplied the families. So of the first church. Every family was called after its head, as the family of Abraham. So all the churches are called after their head — "the churches of Christ." All the families that came out of the family of Abraham, are never called the family of Abraham. So all the churches of Christ are never called the Church of Christ. The word family occurs nearly 300 times. The word ecclesia occurs over 200 times. Both are often used in the singular and plural numbers. Each is distinct and complete in itself. The singular is never extended beyond its bounds. ("The whole family in heaven and earth" is a mistranslation; it should be every family or fatherhood.) The families have succession, though it can't be traced. So of the churches. Proof is sufficient, but not historical proof. Then why doubt the continuity of churches, since they have tenfold more and better proof than the other, and that in the face of the hell-defying fiat of all authority in heaven and in earth; yea, the keys of hades and hell were in his possession. Ah, the multitude of irregulars say it must not be. So we have this cowardly, conciliating, compromising, conforming conservation of error with truth. What is needed is more courage to testify to what truth we have.

THE JEWS.

Here is another illustration of our principle. Matthew begun with Abraham, and traced the succession up to Jesus. Is that to be laughed at? Does it make no difference whether he descended from Abraham and David? Luke begins at the other end, and traces the genealogy or succession backward. He takes a different route, but they both get there. If this succession fails then Christ fails. If he is not the seed of Abraham, and the offspring of David, and of the tribe of Judah, he is not the Christ. So an inspired man now could give more than one route in the genealogy of Christ's churches. It might take an inspired man after the wholesale destruction of historic evidence, as it did with the other. Luke was bold enough to trace the succession on up to Adam, who he said was the son of God. Let those who laugh at succession, laugh here. Read the first chapter of Matthew, and the third of Luke, and the second of Ezra, and the seventh of Nehemiah, and especially the 78th and 105th Psalm, and Acts 7th and 13th, and if you are disposed to laugh at succession, you can exercise your risibles to satiety.

In Abraham's day, God separated the Jews for a peculiar people, and promised perpetuity, and though the nations tried to exterminate them, and often carried them into wasting bondage, the first over 400 years and the last over 2,000 years, yet they are preserved a peculiar people, and they will, in due time, receive all the promises to the letter, with good measure, heaped up, pressed down and running over. Yea, they often tried to exterminate themselves. They intermarried with Gentiles and conformed to their religions. Nevertheless God forgot not his promises nor his oath to their fathers. God did not promise to perpetuate their kingdom, but them. Not for their sakes, nor the father's sake, but that he purposed, promised, and predestinated, therefore he had mercy on them, and "led them according to the integrity of his own heart and guided them by the skillfulness of his hand." Ps. 78: 72. "When he slew them, they sought him; and they returned and enquired after God. They remembered that God was their rock, and the high God their redeemer." Ps. 78:34, 35. While wars without and within, and intermarriages, and conformity to other religions, did not help God to fulfill his promises, yet all of these and all else did not frustrate the promise of God. He made them put away their wives, and in due time brought them to repentance. If God could feed those millions for forty years with bread from heaven, and give them water out of the rock, and give them all the countries before them; if all this and more for national Israel, what could he not do for the spiritual bride of his son? As the Samaritans were not counted for Jews, neither are halfbreeds counted today. The Jew who is not in the succession today is not a Jew, either outwardly or inwardly. Satan got into Eden through the serpent, and into the apostolic church through that serpent, Judas Iscariot, and he has gotten into all churches, and sometimes set them on each other, and the world on them also, yet the gates of hell shall not prevail against God's churches. Here is a lesson from Analogy that greatly confirms my faith. I know he is able to perform what he promised.

THE BEES.

All we know about the propagation of bees is that hives swarm out of hives. Until some one can prove that at some time, and for some time, this law was violated, then we must believe that there has been continuity, as all the knowledge we have is that way. The want of proof has nothing to do with it. There must be certain infallible disproof of the right kind. The want of historical proof cuts no figure in it. As we see the law in operation today, and all history testifies to the same, the conclusion is safe, viz., Bee-hives have continued to swarm out of bee-hives. Or, if you could prove that for a long time there was no honey, or honey but no bees, or honey and bees but no bee-hives, then I would be under no obligation to believe that cinch-bugs, or house-flies, or other insects, or several at or about the same time, and some at distant times, resolved themselves into bees, and hived themselves, and went to making honey, in order to keep up the honey business. That would be a great strain on my credulity, and I know that I would not invest very much in the honey. Great swelling words of flattery might be spoken concerning the new bees, so-called, that they had no stings, were more sociable, etc., yet I would be compelled to question their right or ability to make the genuine article. I would greatly prefer the original, yea, would avoid the substitute. "This is a great mystery, but I speak concerning Christ and the church."

HUMAN SOCIETIES.

Lodges and societies have adopted the divine method of propagation, but their origin is not of divine authority. Prayer-meetings, Sunday-schools, social and benevolent gatherings are of divine permission, but not of divine organization. They are not the appointed guardians of laws, doctrines and ordinances, and they have nothing to do with them, having no authority in the kingdom of Christ. Privilege, permission and authority are very different things. When men mete out authority, they must meet with authority, and that means by authority. Authority does not spring out of the ground, but comes down from heaven. "The baptism of John, was it from heaven or of men?" This answers the question of authority. Any unauthorized gathering, even of good men, to execute judgment and justice, even with the best of motives, would be a mob. Such a gathering we find in the 19th of Acts, but it was unlawful, and they were told that they were amenable for their assumed authority. There was a lawful assembly to which they were referred for the execution of the law. Good men might organize to release an innocent prisoner, or to punish the guilty, and in either case the ends of justice might be subserved, but it would be lawlessness, and if it involved killing it would be murder, though the person might deserve to die. And why? Because God has authorized only "the authorities that be" to take the life of the guilty. God ordained these authorities for the punishment of transgressors. Private citizens have no authority in such cases. They may meet and take counsel, but not council, as they can't execute. Any other view runs into lawlessness and anarchy. "By what authority doest thou these things?" "This is a great mystery, but I speak concerning Christ and the church." That is where the authority resides, and to this all agree, though they differ as to what the church is.

THE HIGH PRIEST.

There was a period of about 1370 years, with about 80 High Priests mentioned in the genealogy. It may be impossible for us to trace the succession of those named, even with so much inspired history. But who will say that there was no succession because we can't trace it?

Does the existence of things depend on our knowledge? Many things have been long in existence of which men know nothing. But this we know, God planned the succession of the High Priests; therefore succession is pleasing to God, and men should not laugh at God. Melchisedec was out of the succession, and in this he typified our Great High Priest, "who sprang out of Judah, of which tribe Moses spake nothing concerning the priesthood." This made it necessary to change the law of induction. God ordained Aaron to begin the succession, as he did John the Baptist to begin another, and Christ honored this last appointment by walking 65 miles to John, to be baptized of him. Korah, Dathan and Abiram, with 250 others, thought this succession unnecessary, "as all the people were holy and God was with them." If the people had gone to some other than John to be baptized, they would have deserved the same fate of these intruders. "This was written for our admonition, upon whom the end of the age has come." We may ridicule the idea of a "successional juice," but God is pleased with all the succession he requireth, and we know he was pleased with this priestly succession, and also with church succession. Otherwise let every church be a bastard, and not a legitimate child of any mother church. Churches legitimately multiplied, as far as we know, in the beginning. There was continuity of churches; so when this is ridiculed now, the same ridicule belongs to the other end of the line. If God had said: On this rock I will build my High Priesthood, and it shall continue, then we know he is pleased with continuity; and if it failed, the fault was his, and the obligation to continue as at first is unaltered. If I knew that millions have been wrongly baptized during the centuries, thus obscuring the way, that would not relieve me in the least from being baptized according to the law of baptism, one item of which is, that the administrator must have authority to baptize. As sure as there were qualifications and ceremonies required in the one case, so in the other. Suppose there were no restrictions to the priesthood, or church, or ordinances, what would have become of them? I plead for order, the others for anarchy. "This is a great mystery, but I speak concerning Christ and the church."

THE BIBLE.

Now let us bring our illustrations nearer the subject. I have before me a Bible. I now refer to all the books as one. These scriptures of divine truth had their divine origin back yonder, when "holy men of old wrote as they were moved by the Holy Spirit. With their writings inspiration ceased, and perpetuity was stamped upon the sacred writings. "The word of the Lord endureth forever"—"abideth forever." Now, if this is indeed and in truth the very word of God, it is in the succession. It came down from the first. It may be in many respects like human books; it may be in some respects unlike the original, and unlike other copies and versions, yet the divine marks are on it. We may improve on it as it is; but not as it was. Any change from the original would be a corruption. Its preservation and purity depend on its succession. If you bring me a copy, and claim for it a subsequent yet divine origin, I will try it by this, and if it contradicts any of its statements or doctrines, I will reject it and pronounce it spurious. Many have been thus produced, and tried, and spurned. Bibles don't spring out of the ground, nor do they come up out of the wilderness of man's consciousness, unless inbreathed by the Holy Spirit, who always puts the divine marks upon it. Have men presumed to make Bibles, do you ask? Yes. Their presumption has been displayed in this as well as in church making. And what has man not presumed to do? He has presumed to be the Christ (many will come, saying, I am Christ); to be God—"yea, he has exalted himself above all that is called God or that is worshipped." These christs, and gods and bible-makers, and church-builders are not only presumptuous, but impious. I want neither Bible nor church of man's devising.

TRUE RELIGION.

This is another illustration. The religion we profess is of divine origin. It includes regeneration, recreation and resurrection from a state of moral death. It produces such a change of mind, heart and life as to make all things new. Its origin is divine—the work is of God. The thousand human religions are destitute of the divine marks. They may be imitations, but they are counterfeits. They have other and subsequent origins. God is the author of his own religion, and, like all his works, it is stamped with perpetuity. It is destined to smite the Image and to cover the earth. The law of spiritual propagation is within itself. In the operation of this law, in later times, John—a man "full of the Holy Ghost from his birth," and "sent of God"—says, "Behold the Lamb of God that taketh away the sin of the world." Andrew heard and followed him. He then found his brother Simon and brought him to Jesus. Philip also followed him, and when he found Nathaniel, he said, "Come and see." Then the twelve were sent out, then the seventy. Then he organized his regenerated church, and the gates of hades shall not prevail against it. To this institution he gave the commission to disciple or convert all the nations, immersing them, etc., and the saved through this law of propagation and multiplication "were added to the church;" and when the church was scattered and could not assemble as a church in Jerusalem, the scattered material of the first church, with the converts they made "as they went everywhere preaching the word," were congregated into other churches, and thus "churches were multiplied." But note well: all those churches came out of the first church, at Jerusalem, "which is the mother of us all." Thus we see this first church, "built by the God of heaven," contained seed within itself, and had the command to multiply, to perpetuate itself, by power inherent in its regenerated self, and it had the promise of divine co-operation to the end of time. This law of spiritual propagation we see as clearly as in any of our illustrations. We see this in the law of spiritual genesis today, and, so far as history testifies, it has ever been the law. This church, with these divine marks, is of heaven. Its builder and maker is God. I will build, says the first and the last, and who has all power in heaven and on earth. With omnipotent fiat he stamps his workmanship with perpetuity. He had the keys of death and hades, could shut and none could open, could open and none could shut, and, as a triumphant victor, he declared that the gates that would close on all other institutions should not prevail against his regenerated church. This little stone should ultimately fill the whole earth. So precious did this purchase of his blood appear to his loving eyes, that he calls it his bride, to which he was betrothed with the indissolvable bonds of a divine oath. He calls it his body, of which spiritual connection he is the head. I don't believe he was ever robbed of his body or bereft of his bride. For, if so, the stars would forever have shut their eyes, the moon withheld her light, and the sun turned black as sackcloth of hair. They would have mourned for the bride as they did for the bridegroom who died that she might live forever. He loved his church, and gave himself for it. I am bold to say that every regenerated church of Christ on earth today is in the succession, and all that have not come down this ancestral line are bastards and not sons—are human and not divine. There are many that have not this succession, but many have, or his Word is broken.

But let us revert to the law of spiritual genesis. Rom. 10:13, 15: "Whosoever shall call upon the name of the Lord shall be saved. But how shall they call on him in whom they have not believed, and how shall they believe in him of whom they have not heard, and how shall they hear without a preacher, and how shall they preach except they be sent?"

Now, pray, who will do the sending but previous possessors? Did boards of trade, railroad corporations or turf rings ever send a man to preach the gospel?

Was the commission given to such? The "go ye" was to a special class, to do these things—preach, baptize and teach. They were given all at once, and only once, and that to an elect, called-out and trained body. It was the beginning of authority, to be transmitted; and for anyone to presume to assume such a work is "despising authority."

But, said one, if God had failed to fulfill his promise (and the whole discussion proceeds on this supposition); if he had failed to keep his church in the wilderness, and the world left for a long time without this witness; might we not fall back on chance and accidents? Suppose, says one, that from a passing vessel a few leaves of holy writ should float to a heathen island; might not the idolaters read, and understand, and believe, and obey, and be saved, and start a church?

Begone, ye miserable comforters! Ye would ask me to suck comfort out of God's failure. If God's appointed custodian, whom he solemnly declared he would be with in this work "in all the days," even to the "end of the age," and who, he declared, should testify "to the uttermost parts of the earth;" if this divine scheme had failed, not a floating vessel on all the seas would contain the sacred leaves to float; or, if so, they might spoil in floating; or, if not, the heathen inhabitants might not understand the language; or, if they did, like all natural men, they might not understand the sense; or, if they did, as usual, they might despise the meaning, for it would first convict them of sin; and so, after all, they might reject, since the carnal mind is enmity; or, if not this, they might and probably would "neglect this great salvation." After all that could be said, supposing they would search and enquire for the meaning, to the inquiry, "Understandest thou what thou readest?" the answer would likely be, "How can I except some man guide me?" Then how could he guide except he be sent? And who are to do the sending? If he has put offices "in the church" for its upbuilding, and propagation, and multiplication, and perfection, and if he did this "to the intent that unto principalities and powers in heavenly places might be known by the church the manifold wisdom of God, according to the eternal purposes which he purposed in Christ Jesus our Lord," then my hope is fixed on this.

If God's word, and oath, and promise, and

purpose, which from eternity he purposed in Christ Jesus our Lord, have failed, then tell me not of accidents and chances. If the church of Christ has failed, then why start another out of heathen, self-taught, on an island, with a few leaves?

If Christ's church has not continued; if these promises have all failed, then tell me not about your island, man made—accident churches. I would not join one of them though it had a thousand bibles to teach it and a million gods to back it. If this Bible, with its triune God has failed, then have I failed, now and forever, world without hope and without end. But should a Bible, by providence, fall into the hands of a poor wayfaring man on an island, or elsewhere, and, by reading, he should see in it the Christ a Savior, and should believe on him to the saving of his soul, that same book would show him the great Savior and exemplar, walking all the way from Galilee to the Jordan to be baptized of the only man sent of God to baptize. He would see where this same Lord, long after he ascended to heaven, told the first heathen converts in the house of Cornelius, to send all the way to Joppa for one Simon Peter. He would see, in another place, where this same Christ told another convert, Saul of Tarsus, to go into Damascus and enquire for a certain disciple. He would read where this same Jesus—the Almighty—walking in the midst of the seven golden candle-sticks, girt about the paps with a golden girdle, his hair white as snow, his eyes a flame of fire, his feet like fine brass burning in a furnace, his countenance like lightning—like the sun shining in his strength, in his right hand the seven stars, his voice like many thunders, saying, "I am alive forevermore, and have the keys of death and hades,"—"He that hath ears to hear let him hear what the Spirit saith unto the churches."

Rev. 22:16—"I Jesus have sent mine angel to testify unto you these things in the churches."

If Christ left his churches in charge of his earthly affairs, and if his mind underwent a change in regard to church order, or ordinances, or doctrines, of course he would have affected the change through the churches instead of individuals like Luther, Calvin, Wesley, Campbell, Fox, Joe Smith, etc.

These words were intended for all generations, and especially for the seventh, tenth, sixteenth, eighteenth and nineteenth centuries, when so many presumed to assume authority to set up churches of their own inventions. If these came from the church of God, did he authorize them to divide it into chisms? If not from the church of God, what church authority had they? Can one have church authority without church membership? If Rome was the church of God, then these were schismatic, and if not, they are only the daughters of the woman of Rev. 17:5.

This never-changing Christ, the same yesterday, today and forever, together with this word that liveth and abideth forever, requires every new convert in every place and at every time, to be baptized, which forbids his baptizing himself. Not only so, but it would command him to be baptized at the hands of one authorized to administer it. He who loves righteousness and hates iniquity, could not authorize one to administer it contrary to his faith, and creed, and practice, for that would be sin. No man can get baptism except from one who has received it, who believes it, and who is authorized to administer it; and all of such, after baptism, are taught to be added to the church, a pattern of which was given in Jerusalem. Thus, taught by this book, they would be legitimately connected to another.

I would not belong to a church that is not connected with the wilderness journey, leading through dens and caves of the earth, and through fiery and bloody baptisms of persecution. A church invented by a man and of recent origin could not hold me.

May *man* invent a church? Then *any* man may; and if any man may, *all* men may; and if church invention is a good work, as is supposed, then all men *ought*.

When Paul was converted he was divinely directed to be baptized by a certain disciple. He afterwards joined the church. He then proceeded to beget others through the gospel—God working with him—and these joined the church at Corinth, and other places where he labored. Felix, nor Festus, Agrippa, nor Tertullus ever made a convert to Christ.

Christianity is not sporadic, or indigenous, but exotic. It must come into a man through channels that are sanctified. It did not spring out of me, nor could I have gotten it from an unconverted companion. A believing companion may sanctify the unbelieving one, but the reverse never. We can only give as we have received. What do you think of the idea of God sending a man to beget others through the gospel while he had never been begotten himself; of sending a man to baptize who refused to be baptized himself; of sending a man to put another into the church when he was never in himself? All of this is going on, but not of divine origin or santion. What of a man taking starch, soda, magnesia, etc., and going out to start a corn crop? He must either begin it, or get seed out of the succession. A man can no more start genuine corn than he can start a genuine church. Reason, religion and revelation shut us up to the stream that from the great fountain flowed, and since a stream can not rise above the fountain, what must be the true status of those churches called out of Babylon—the vilest of the vile? God called them out of Rome, but he did not call on them to invent new churches.

But, you ask, was not the church of Christ constituted out of material once bad, such as publicans and harlots? Yes, the God of heaven can set up a perpetuating kingdom out of such material recreated. He did this once, but he did it only once, and if he failed in that, I am sure he would not start another; and I know he never did start but one. Only man is vain and presumptuous enough to attempt a thing that the God of heaven failed in. He also started a perpetuating race out of vivified dust. He did this once, and if this should fail, I don't think the devil would presume to try his hand after God had failed.

But all believe in succession—Catholics, Protestants and Baptists. There is not an ecclesiastical history, we venture to say, in all the world, that does not start out with the ostensible purpose of proving it. The history of the church in the first century, and in the second, third, etc., is the index of all. The only exception to this, outside of infidels, is to be found, and that only recently, among our own people; who, strange to say, have all at once become timid through habits of affiliation. These amphibious, ambidextrous, ambiguous, equivocating brethren display poor skill in trying to dodge the question.

The latest dodge is that Principles have been perpetuated—and if there were none present to make them afraid, they might perhaps, provided you didn't tell anybody, say that Baptist principles have been perpetuated.

I am afraid to ask how kept, lest through fear of being "put out of the synagogue" they answer "in archives." But if they have been kept by men, I will contend that men, keeping Baptist principles, are themselves Baptists, and if Baptists they were church members, hence baptized.

Oh yes, say they, we believe in the perpetuity of the church, but the "invisible church." Now ask them about the invisible church. When was it started? They can't say. What sort of government has it? They can't say. They suppose none. How many ordinances? None. What are its doctrines? It has none. What sort of body is it? It is no body. Where does it meet? Nowhere. Is this the church he built on a rock, and bought with his blood, and that constitutes his body, holding to nothing and meeting nowhere? Then it is invisible. Surely the gates of hades can't prevail against nobody—nothing and nowhere, no, never. This makes the words of Christ true, but why the words?

Our fearful brethren declare that the principles of the gospel have come down, and not the church, and, in saying this, they flatly deny the word of Christ, who said, the gates of hades should not prevail against his church.

Now we propose, in the fear of God, to take a position, to define it, and then, by divine help, to establish it.

The God of heaven set up his kingdom subsequent to Daniel's prophecy. It's nigh approach was announced by John, its presence repeatedly asserted by Christ. Men and women entered it during Christ's ministry, and the violent tried to take it by force. This is the kingdom that should "stand forever," and that should "not be left to other people." It was the Father's good pleasure to give to the little flock this kingdom, and Christ delivered it to them in solemn trust. Daniel had said that, in the end, "the saints of the Most High should take the kingdom, and possess the kingdom forever, even forever and ever. The kingdom and dominion and greatness of the kingdom under the whole heaven should be given to the saints of the Most High," and this kingdom was never to pass away. The dream "was certain and the interpretation of it sure.

This means both perpetuity and continuity. Houses, watches, and the works of men's hands, have perpetuity, but not continuity, and need not. But God's works have both—i. e., perpetuity through continuity—or he could not cease from his labors. God put perpetuating power in his works. Man can not.

This kingdom was to be spread by human effort, by making disciples and baptizing them. These baptized disciples were to co-operate in the extension of this kingdom. Hence, they were to be organized in different places into ecclesiae. These called-out and assembled people must be governed by right principles, for Christ constituted them his executors, or business-doing bodies. The bodies were local, because they were assemblies, and visible because composed of real saints. Christ organized one after which all others were to be patterned. This business-doing body he called his church, and these churches were to multiply themselves, and thus spread the kingdom. Each congregation was complete in itself, and independent of the others, and of civil government. These assemblies were and are distinguishable from all other congregations of men by their divine marks.

CHURCH MARKS.

This spiritual house was to be made up of spiritual stones, to offer up spiritual sacrifices holy and acceptable unto God. No one, however rich, or learned, or honored, could join it until he was born again—must be saved before added to the church; hence they were called saints or holy ones—having been washed, sanctified, justified in the name of the Lord Jesus, and that by the Spirit of our God. All other congregations, assemblies, bodies, churches (?) admit the unsanctified, the unsaved, and hence they are unholy.

The second divine mark is the polity of fraternal equality. No one exercising authority upon, or lording it over the others.

Christ emphatically declared that this should not be so with his disciples. The world never produced such a body, with such a polity, and it never saw but one, and that it hates. Those so-called Congregationalists are counterfeits. They violate the very principle their name indicates, and thus they make void the commandment of Christ by their tradition—infant rantism.

The next mark is—this body is divided into three classes; saints, bishops and deacons, with the saints first in authority, because in majority, and the officers are the servants of the saints by virtue of their office. There is only one business-doing body in this world possessing this peculiarity—the greatest, the slave of all. Equal as a member, but subordinate as an officer.

The mission of this church constitutes another divine mark. Her work is—make disciples—immerse them—teach them all things whatsoever Christ has commanded. There is only one body observing this order, and doing this work, and the work can not be done except in order. The commission of some—most all—reads: Go into all the world, and sprinkle all the babies, and teach the catechism, discipline, etc., and thus disciple them (to our leaders).

Another divine mark of this heavenly kingdom, and hence of the business-doing bodies composing it, is that, like its founder, it disdains all alliance with the kingdoms of this world. The god of this world offered all the kingdoms to Christ, but he spurned the offer. So his kingdom, while in in the world, is not to be of the world, but separate from the world. Among all the aspirants to these honors, mark well the one who, in the faith, has steadfastly refused every such overture.

But the golden mark of all marks is the principle that underlies the actions, and all the actions, of all her subjects. The underlying principle is a vital one, so much so, that no action destitute of it can be acceptable to God. The principle is seen in the following: "First make the tree good, and the fruit will be good." "A corrupt tree can not bring forth good fruit, neither can a good tree bring forth evil fruit." "If ye love me, keep my commandments," "He that loveth is born of God." "Everyone that doeth righteousness is born of God." "Whosoever doeth not righteousness is not of God." "Whether ye eat or drink (or be be baptized or eat the Lord's Supper), or whatsoever ye do, do all to the glory of God." "Herein is my Father glorified, that ye bear much fruit; so shall ye be my disciples."

This divine principle is implanted in regeneration by the Holy Spirit, and is necessary to acceptable obedience. All so-called outward obedience, rendered with a view to obtain forgiveness, salvation, or acceptance with God, is obedience to "another gospel which is not another." It is antipodal to the gospel, and infinitely worse than no gospel. Hence we may expect, under this mark, to find the true church through the past ages denouncing the rite of infant rantism and other acts under the false principle as "inventions of the devil" and subversive of the gospel of Christ.

There are other distinguishing marks, but these are sufficient to identify the true church whenever and wherever found.

Are these marks Scriptural? That has been answered? Are they Reasonable? Let this much suffice. Next, are they Credible and Historical? Read on and see. Have the gates of hades prevailed against it? We will see.

WE ARE GOING ON A CHURCH HUNT.

All writers on Church History of which we have any knowledge, whether Catholic, Protestant or Baptist, have maintained the doctrine of Church perpetuity: but the new phase, bringing the new issue, in this new era, and maintained by a comparitively few of the wise and popular, is Principle perpetuity. That is to say, Baptist principles have been perpetuated, but not by men; or if by men, not Baptist men; or if by Baptist men, not necessarily church men. In this case, Baptist men holding Baptist principles, are not necessarily church members; as if Baptist principles do not, and have not, required church membership. To support this Principle theory, this Scripture is quoted: "Whoso abideth not in the *teaching* of Christ, hath not God; he that abideth in the *teaching*, the same hath both the Father and the Son. If any man cometh to you and bring not this *teaching*, receive him not." And to this is added: [Armittage's History of Baptists] "Pure *doctrine*, as it is found uncorrupted in the word of God, is the only unbroken line of succession which can be traced in Christianity. God has never confided his truth to the personal succession of any body of men; man was not to be trusted with the custody of this very precious charge; but the King of the truth has kept the keys of the truth in his own hand."

How such a conclusion could have been suggested by such a Scripture is marvelous indeed. Read the Scripture again and see if *man* is not as prominent in the text as is *teaching*. *Man* is the actor, agent, nominative to every verb, and then it is added: "If any *man* come to you and bring not this teaching." Baptist principles were committed to Baptist *men*, to be kept by *them*. The commission converts men to principles. Make disciples (of men), baptize THEM, teach THEM to keep safely all things whatsoever I have commanded YOU, and lo! I am with YOU always, even to the end of the world. This is all we claim, but this much we demand. Here is perpetuity of principles, held by MEN in organic capacity, for in no other sense has he, or could he have been with THEM to the end of the world. Evil powers prevailed against individual saints, but the gates of hades have not against his church. Christ came not only to teach principles, but he also built a church. You may boast of blood-bought principles, or blood-bought men, but the word of God tells also of the blood-bought church. For the perfecting of the saints for the work of the ministry and the perpetuity of principles, he puts officers in the church. He is the Savior of the body—the church. The manifold wisdom of God is to be made known unto principalities and powers through the church of God, who had power to raise Christ from the dead and set him at his own right hand, far above all rule and authority and power and dominion, and every name that is named, not only in this age, but in that which is to come, not only gave him to be head over all things to his church, which is his body—the fullness of him that filleth all in all, but he first put all things in subjection under his feet. He is the image of the invisible God, the begotten or Primal cause of all creation; for in him were all things created, in the heavens and upon the earth, things visible and invisible, whether thrones, or dominions or principalities or powers; all things were created through him and unto him; and he is before all things, and, and in him all things hold together. And he is the head of the body, the church, that in all things he might have the pre-eminence. For the whole fullness of God was pleased to dwell in him.

With this almighty Christ at the head, and with all things in subjection at his feet, we are persuaded that he is able, not only to keep and present us, as individuals, holy and unblamable in his sight, but that, having loved the church, and having sanctified and cleansed it with the washing of water in the word, he is also able to present it to himself, a glorious church, not having spot or wrinkle or any such thing. For no man ever yet hated his own flesh, but nourisheth and cherisheth it even as the Lord the church. For we are members of his body, of his flesh and of his bones. For this cause shall a man leave his father and mother, and shall be joined unto his wife, and they two shall be one flesh. "This is a great mystery; but I speak concerning Christ and the church." Wherefore we having received a kingdom which can not be moved, let us have grace whereby we may serve God acceptably with reverence and Godly fear. The Kingdom which Christ, the God of heaven, set up in the days of the Caesars, was never to be destroyed, nor left to other people, but it was to stand forever. His dominion was to be an everlasting dominion, which should not pass away, and his kingdom was not to be destroyed.

In this visible, organic kingdom, the good and the bad were to grow together until the harvest, or end of the world. This is not true of the invisible, for there are none of the bad in that. This visible kingdom, like the net in the sea, is to drag until it is full, and then be brought to shore, and the shore is the end of the world, at which time the wicked are to be severed from among the just, for the kingdom in this state was to gather of every kind, hence, not the invisible. Its perpetuity is also seen in the parable of the leaven, which worked till the whole was leavened; or the mustard seed, which grew to a large tree, or like the stone which the prophet saw till it filled the whole earth.

This infidelity on church perpetuity, which seems to come of the belief, that at one time antiChrist was greater than Christ, is becoming a serious matter. If Christ can save his principles, he can save his people, and if he can save his people, he can save his church; and this is just what is so particularly promised and prophesied. This we would believe in the absence of all history. But histories corroborate the fulfillment of the prophecies and the promises, not in historic detail, but in a fullness and generalness of statement, that confirms the faith in the promises and prophecies. Heaven and earth shall pass away, but my words shall not pass away, says the almighty Head.

A succession of principles assures the succession of Pure Religion. The regenerated beget others.

Dr. T. T. Eaton said:

" If Baptist succession be the bad thing some brethren say, then certainly it ought to be given up. There should be no more of it. The churches now in existence ought to have no succession. When a new church is organized, it should have no sort of connection with other churches, or relations to them. Let churches be organized anywhere, anyhow, by anybody. Just let the people be believers, and let them baptize each other, and start a church. This does away with Baptist succession. And if it be the bad thing that is charged, it ought to be done away with at the earliest moment. Those who oppose Baptist succession have no logical ground to stand on in organizing a church out of material furnished by other churches and with those baptized by regularly ordained ministers. If Baptist succession be sacerdotalism and sacramentalism, then surely we ought not to think of practicing it, and thus keeping up the dreadful isms."

Have not Protestants been instrumental in saving men? Yes, but that is as far as they go, and if not for Baptist influence, all would be christened by a sacrament of damnation. They won't work under the commission as given by Matthew, but against it. Instead of immersing the saved, they aim to sprinkle the unsaved. Instead of teaching all things whatsoever Christ commanded, they would depose and exclude any preacher who did. As soon as Judson and Carey began to follow the commission they were deposed: None of them would allow any of their preachers to preach as Baptists do. I am glad they save some, but sorry they lead all their saved ones astray. They hold enough truth for salvation, but not enough for service.

Any Baptist preacher would be deposed and excluded from any Baptist church if it be known that he believes what preachers of other denominations believe. Other denominations would do the same with their preachers if it were known that they believe as Baptists believe. It was because of these doctrinal differences that they all divided from us and set up churches of their own liking. These are facts. Then on what principle can all be considered as in any sense members of one church? "Is Christ divided?" Paul said that is what the divisions at Corinth meant. Neither Christ nor his church can be divided. "Certain" may go out, but that proves that they were not of us. When this division takes place, it is not the church divided into two or more churches, but those who crept in privily and unawares, and who are in (nominally), but not of the church, going out, make it manifest that they were not all the church. So there must be schisms to make manifest those who are approved. This is true when doctrines fatal to orthodoxy and vital to church life are involved. So those differing and divided can in no sense be thought of as all members of the church of Christ. Schisms may be composed of converted people, but a schism can't be a church, but a cutting off from the church. Among these many claimants, which is the tried and true church?

CHURCH PERPETUITY

IT IS CREDIBLE

SO SAY ALL DENOMINATIONS. WE WILL TAKE, FIRST, THE TESTIMONY OF THE DISCIPLES OF A. CAMPBELL.

To show how Credible and Reasonable and Plausible this Church Perpetuity appears to all unprejudiced minds, we will quote at some length, from the ablest of Mr. Campbell's disciples. They go at it in the right way, and in the right spirit, if they do cut off the limb on which they are perched. "Out of thine own mouth do I condemn thee," would be a righteous sentence in a multitude of instances in this as well as other ages of errors and inconsistencies. The principles they contend for are right, but they err in any and all efforts to apply them to themselves. The superinducing power that had the superscription written on the cross, and that caused the Agnostics to name themselves, may have superinduced the following testimonies:

Mr. David Lipscomb, in the Gospel Advocate, 1867, p. 770, says: "God founded a church that will stand forever; that the gates of hell shall not prevail against it."

Mr. Errett, in his Elements of the Gospel,

p. 40, says: "Here is the setting up of the kingdom. Here is seen the little stone cut out of the mountain without hands, which Nebuchadnezzar saw, and which is yet to become a great mountain and fill the whole earth."

He says again, p. 489: "God did not leave himself without witness during the dark night of persecution." And again: "And so in the moral world, after a long reign of wintry desolation, during which it seemed as if truth had perished, the vernal season of rejoicing came at last, heralded by such warblers as Wyckliff, Huss and Jerome, who, like robins, came with the first gleam of rosy light at the first breath of spring out from the darkness and the cold, sweet harbingers of better times. There was, indeed, a few of God's minstrels who had never ceased to sing. Away in the mountain solitudes of the Alps and the Appenines, hidden in the deserts, caged up in the caves, God gave them songs in the night they never ceased to carol."

T. Fanning, in the Living Pulpit, p. 520, says: "The church was built upon the rock laid in Zion; and she has withstood the rough waves of eighteen centuries, and she will finally triumph over all the principalities and powers of earth."

On p. 535, he says: "The war between Michael and Satan is still raging. The destroyer has diligently labored, but in vain, from the planting of the church, to overthrow the cause, for the protection of which the veracity of the Father's throne is pledged. The deceiver still employs the principalities, powers and expedients of the world to overthrow the kingdom of the Savior. Hence, we can not hope for conflicts to cease until the Lord shall have put the last enemy under his feet."

Mr. Lard, in his Quarterly, 1886, p. 308, says: "It is not the Rock which the unseen is not to prevail against; neither has the church ever become extinct."

Read what Mr. Franklin says, in Living Pulpit, pp. 343, 348-9:

1. A community not founded and established in the right Place is not the church of Christ.

2. A community not founded at the right Time is not the kingdom of Christ.

3. No church can be the true church not founded by the proper persons, Christ and the apostles. . . . p. 348.

1. A community not founded or established in the right Place is not the church of Christ. All agree that in Jerusalem was the place.

"If my hearers desire to know whether the body with which they stand identified is the true church, let them inquire Where it was founded. If it was founded in Jerusalem, it may be the true church; but if it was not founded in Jerusalem, it is most conclusive evidence that it is not the true church. No matter how many good people there are in it, nor how many good things are taught in it, it is not the true church. A difference, then, between any body of people and the body of Christ so striking as originating in Rome, and originating in Jerusalem, or the difference between being founded in Rome, and being founded in Jerusalem, proves that which was founded in Rome, London or Geneva to be counterfeit. The church of Christ was first planted in Jerusalem, and all churches first planted or founded anywhere else are certainly spurious. They are not genuine. Nor is it any matter how many points of resemblance there may be between the genuine and the counterfeit, they are not the same; but the counterfeit is only the more dangerous, and likely to deceive.

"When trying them, to determine which is the true or the genuine church, look for this mark on it: 'In Jerusalem.'

2. A community not founded at the right Time is not the kingdom of God, or body of Christ. This test is a severe one. It is unambiguous. . . p. 350-1.

"When did the church of Rome originate? It did not originate in a day or a year, but gradually subverted the apostles' teachings, and in centuries inaugurated full-grown popery. But there is not a trace of a Pope or universal Father, to say nothing of vice-regents of Christ, or Lord God, the Pope, nor popery, in the first three centuries of the Christian era. Popery was inaugurated too late, by at least three centuries, to be the true or genuine church. It is one of the basest and most impudent counterfeits ever imposed upon the credulity of man. If popery was born too late, or is too young to be the true church, what shall be said of those communities born in the last three centuries? They are all too young by largely more than a thousand years. No church that came into existence since the death of the apostles can be the church of the living God. No church can be the true church that was not founded by Christ and the apostles. Churches founded by other persons, or originating with other persons, are simply not the church of Christ. All books, all parties, and all men agree that Christ and the apostles founded the community called "the body of Christ"—the "one body of Paul." What shall we then say of a church that traces its history to George Fox, and finds not a trace of its existence beyond him?

"There never was a Quaker before George Fox, nor a Quaker church. The history of the world does not refer to the existence of a Lutheran, or a Lutheran church, before Martin Luther lived. The Lutheran church originated with Luther. The body of Christ existed from the apostolic day till the time of Luther, before there was any Lutheran church. The Presbyterian church originated with John Calvin. Before the time of Calvin there never was a Presbyterian, nor a Presbyterian church. The church, or body of Christ, existed from the time of the apostles till the time of Calvin, and consequently could not have been established by Calvin. Presbyterianism was therefore born many long centuries too late to lay any claims to Christianity. It may have incorporated some Christianity in it, but it is carefully and very justly labeled Presbyterianism.

"The Methodist church originated with John Wesley. Before the time of John Wesley there never was a Methodist church or a Methodist. But the church of Christ existed from the time of the apostles till the time of Wesley. Hence, Methodism originated with the wrong person to be the church of Christ. The body of Christ originated with Christ and his apostles, and not with Wesley. Any body or community that did not originate with Christ and his apostles, but with some more modern person or persons, is manifestly not the body of Christ."

If we can now prove by these witnesses that their church (?) started at some other time, and in some other place, by some other persons, then our case is made out. Of course, all other witnesses in the world would laugh at the idea that this modern movement is the church described above and below, but we will take also some first-class testimony from these self-same witnesses as to their own origin, and then as to the Baptists.

R. Milligan, in Living Pulpit, p. 381, testifies against his so-called church, that begun in this country and in this century, and could not have been the church driven into the wilderness. **He** says:

"The church was driven like a poor, disconsolate widow, into the wilderness for the long period of one thousand two hundred and sixty years. And at the close of this period, in A. D. 1793, when the persecuting power of the Man of Sin was broken by means of the French Revolution, there really seemed to be but little of pure Christianity left in the world, except in the valleys, hidden."

Living Pulpit—Introduction pp. 13-14, by W. L. Moore, we see this so-called church-body beginning in this century, and where, and by whom, and for what, and from what. Read and decide if this is the church that Christ built upon a rock, that the gates of hades should not prevail against.

"This was the work proposed by the Reformation of the Nineteenth Century. A few words concerning the origin and character of this movement are necessary at this point. In the year 1807, Thomas Campbell, a Presbyterian minister from the north of Ireland, arrived in the United States. He had not been in this country long when he conceived a plan of Christian Union upon the basis of the Bible, and the Bible alone. Discarding all human creeds and confessions of faith, a society was formed in Washington, Pa., for the purpose of propagating these sentiments. 'Soon after, two churches were organized.'

. . . .

"This was the beginning of the great reformatory movement known as the Reformation of the Nineteenth Century. But Thomas Campbell, and those who operated with him in Western Pennsylvania and Western Virginia, were not alone in these efforts at a reformation of Primitive Christianity. In Kentucky and Tennessee, Stone, Marshall, Thompson, Dunlevy and others, were zealously advocating the same principles. Under the influence of these movements, which had no well-defined organization, a latent force was excited, which had taken the body and form of what is now known as the Christian Church or Disciples of Christ."

On p. 47, Burnett says, this so-called church started within the last fifty-five years, and started from zero. He says: "Surrounded by a multitude of religious denominations, within the last fifty-five years, a community has grown from zero to a half million, without a denominational aspect, and stands today unmarked by a human formula. It is founded upon the good confessions that Jesus Christ is the Son of the living God."

But that "good confession" found in Acts 8:38 is spurious. It is not found even in their own translations. The devils believe all that is said about him. Yea, they said they knew him to be the holy one of God, and they obeyed his every commandment; but their faith and knowledge and obedience were not from a good heart, nor did it, nor could it, make the heart of men or devils right in the sight of God. Simon Magus, I am sure, made a better confession than that, and was baptized, but he was "in the gall of bitterness and in the bond of iniquity," and "his heart was not right in the sight of God." Both Catholics and Protestants have a better creed than the above, and yet by these they are shut out of the kingdom of heaven, because they have not immersion and succession. Thus the lesser things are put above the greater.

This great, great granddaughter of Rome—more like its mother than any of her wayward daughters, did not provoke a single one of those popish fulminations that drove the woman into the wilderness. Let us try a few of the canons of the Council of Trent, and see if they aimed at this so-called church, born out of due time, and at the wrong place, and set up by the wrong persons. One canon says:

"Whosoever shall affirm that men are justified solely by the imputation of the righteousness of Christ . . . or that the grace in which we are justified is only the favor of God, let him be accursed."

Another canon says: "Whosoever shall affirm that justifying faith is nothing else but confidence in the divine mercy, by which sins are forgiven for Christ's sake, or that it is that confidence only by which we are justified, let him be accursed."

"Whosoever shall affirm that the ungodly is justified by faith only, so that it is to be understood that nothing else is to be required to cooperate therewith in order to obtain justification, and that it is on no account necessary that he should prepare and dispose himself by the effect of his own will, let him be accursed."

The fourth canon said: "Whosoever shall affirm that the sacraments of the new law are not necessary to salvation . . . . or that men may obtain the grace of justification by faith only, without the sacraments . . . . let him be accursed."

The fifth canon said: "Whosoever shall affirm that the sacraments of the new law do not contain the grace which they signify, or that they do not confer that grace on those who place no obstacle in its way, as if they were only the external signs of grace and righteousness received by faith and marks of Christian progression, whereby the faithful are distinguished from unbelievers, let him be accursed."

Canon seven said: "Whoever shall affirm that grace is not always conferred by those sacraments, and upon all persons, as far as God is concerned, if they be rightly received, but it is only bestowed some times and upon some persons, let them be accursed."

If this little modern so-called church had been the only opposition to this anti-Christian persecuting power, would not the old mother have taken its little grandbaby in its arms and kissed it to death, saying, "so much like its old mother, bless its little heart." Indeed, these fulminations sound just like the one from its offspring of recent date. The language of the two is so similar, that we can safely say: "Thy speech betrayeth thee." Read more of the origin of this sect:—

MR. SEGAR'S TESTIMONY.

Mr. Charles V. Segar (Life of A. Campbell, p. 25), says: "Alexander Campbell soon became chiefly and prominently known as the recognized head of a new religious movement, the object of which was to restore primitive Christianity in all its simplicity and beauty. Out of this movement has grown a people, who choose to call themselves Christians, or Disciples, now numbering not less than five hundred thousand members in the United States."

In the Rice-Campbell Debate, p. 473, we find

the following language by Alexander Campbell: "Here is the Presbyterian Church with its eighty ministers, its eight thousand and less members after the labors of more than a half century. In one-third that time the cause we plead, notwithstanding our feebleness, and all the errors and accidents incident to a new commencement, and without colleges and schools of learning, guided, aided and blessed from nothing, have in less than twenty years outnumbered this old-learned and well-disciplined host some five to one."

So it appears that the organization with which Campbell was identified started from nothing twenty years previous to the debate, which was held in 1843. This dates the establishment of said organization between 1823 and the date of the debate. We should like to know if that was the organization which Campbellites call "The Church of Christ?"

Professor Hinsdale, principal Hiram College, Ohio, a Disciple college, in laying the cornerstone of the Garfield Memorial Church, gave a history of the church from its organization, at Washington, Pa., to the present time.

HENRY CLAY'S TESTIMONY.

Mr. Campbell, in the year 1847, made a tour to Europe, and on going, he received a letter of recommendation from Henry Clay, the well-known statesman of Kentucky. In that recommendation we have the following language (vol. 2, p. 547 of Memoirs of Mr. Campbell): "Dr. Campbell is among the most eminent citizens of the United States, distinguished for his great learning and ability, for his successful devotion to the education of youth, for his piety, and as the head and founder of one of the most important and respectable religious communities in the United States."

The above is a correct statement. But if it is false, then Mr. Campbell used a falsehood to deceive the nobles of England in order to get favors.

Professor R. Richardson, of Bethany College, in Religious Denominations, p. 224, says: "The Religious Society, designated in different sections as 'Baptists,' 'Reformed Baptists' and 'Campbellites,' had its origin in an effort made a few years since, to effect the union of the pious of all parties."

L. P. Haley, St. Louis, on the origin of his church, said: "Mr. Campbell made a statement of his new doctrine, which appeared to many as a new revelation. It was from this moment that these significant words were uttered and accepted; the more intelligent ever afterward dated the formal commencemens of the Current Reformation, which has been styled Campbellism."

F. D. Power, Washington City pastor, in Shaffe-Herzog Encyclopedia, p. 644, says: "As a distinct body of believers, they date from the early part of the present century . . . But as long before as 1811, he had publicly advocated the principles already stated, and had organized the first regular organization at Bush Run, Pa., May 4, 1811, with thirty members. . . . In 1813 the Bush Run church united with the Red Stone Baptist Association, and ten years later with the Mahoning Association in the Western Reserve of Ohio. In 1827 the Baptist churches withdrew fellowship from them, and the followers of Campbell organized themselves anew."

So say their own chosen witnesses, and it is all

we want them to say. They got in unlawfully and got out scripturally.

They have candidly said all we could wish on the general principle of Church Perpetuity. That the true church begun in Jerusalem, over 1800 years ago, and that by Christ and his apostles, and that it has continued hrough persecutions to the present time, and is never to be overthrown. They also candidly confess that their church started less than 100 years ago, May 4, 1811, by Thos. and Alex. Campbell—the wrong persons, the wrong time, and the wrong place. Now, are they candid enough to say, that the Baptist church fills the bill in all the particulars they have named? WONDERFUL!!!!

Read and see How Conclusive is Baptist Perpetuity. This will come after the Historical.

But it is said that Baptists generally have abandoned their church perpetuity doctrine. I will add the following:

The American Baptist Publication Society some years since brought out a book on the following subject, from the Preface and Appendix of which I make the following quotations:

THE BOGOMILS OF BULGARIA AND BOSNIA—
PREFACE.

"The belief that there had existed through all the ages since the Christian era churches that adhered strictly to scriptural doctrines and practice, churches which were the true successors in faith and ordinances of those founded by the apostles, and had never paid homage to Greek patriarch or Roman pope—was firmly impressed upon the minds of the Baptist church historians of the first fifty years of the present century.

"To the writer it has seemed to be a matter of great consequence to be able to demonstrate that there were churches of faithful witnesses for Christ who had never paid homage or given in their allegiance to the anti-Christian churches of Constantinople or Rome.

"It was true that both Greek and Roman churches had put the brand of heresy on every sect which had dared to deny their dogmas; but might it not be that beneath that brand could be discovered the lineaments of the Bride of Christ?

"In the Christian churches of Armenia, Bulgaria and Bosnia, I believed, were to be found the churches which from the fifth to the fifteenth century were the true successors of the churches founded by the apostles, in all matters of faith and practice. The 'Historical Review of Bosnia,' contained in the second edition of Mr. Arthur J. Evans' work on Bosnia, in 1876, first opened my eyes to the wealth of the new historical discoveries thus brought to light in Bosnia and Bulgaria. Mr. Evans is a member of the Church of England, an eminent scholar, thoroughly devoted to archeological investigations, and had made very patient and successful researches on this very subject.

"Among these I have found, often in unexpected quarters, the most conclusive evidence that these sects were all, during their earlier history, Baptists, not only in their views on the subjects of baptism and the Lord's Supper, but in their opposition to Pedobaptism, to a church hierarchy, and to any worship of the Virgin Mary or the saints, and in their adherence to church independence and freedom of conscience in religious worship. In short, the conclusion has forced itself upon me that in these "Christians" of Bosnia, Bulgaria and Armenia we have an apostolic succession of Christian churches, New Testament churches, and Baptist churches, and that as early as the twelfth century these churches numbered a converted, believing membership as large as that of the Baptists throughout the world to-day.

APPENDIX II.

"Were the Paulician and Bogomil churches Baptist churches?

"Within the last two years a Baptist newspaper of large circulation and conducted with great ability has asserted editorially that 'there was no evidence at present attainable which justified a belief in the existence of Baptist churches during the period between the fourth and eleventh and twelfth centuries.'

"The writer did not deny, although he did not assert, that there might have been during that period individuals who held to Baptist doctrines.

"But great men are not always wise, and their dicta are not always infallible. It happened, at the very time that this statement was made, that there was evidence obtainable that during the period specified Baptist churches as pure as any now in existence were maintained and their membership during a part of that time was as large as, and perhaps larger than, that of the Baptist churches throughout the world at the present day.

"In our Demonstration on this point, it may be well to define what are and have been in all ages the distinguishing characteristics of Baptist churches.

"But there is one fact which should be kept in mind — the Bogomils, and, earlier, the Paulicians, as well as the churches which affiliated with them in western Europe, refused to be called reformers, or even Protestants, if by that term there should be any implication that they were originally seceders from either the Roman or the Greek churches. They said uniformly and boldly, 'We have never had any connection with those corrupt churches; we have no belief that they can ever be reformed into churches of Christ.'

"This is just the position that the Baptist churches, and they only, have always occupied. They did not come out of Rome, for they never belonged to it. They sympathize, indeed, with what is good in the work of the Reformation, and with the churches which cannot go farther back than Luther or Calvin or Zwinglius for their origin; yet all of these churches retain, in their ordinances, their infant baptism, and their profession has still some stains upon it. The Baptist churches, on the other hand, trace their spiritual lineage back in an unbroken line through myriads of white-robed martyrs who never were defiled by contact with Rome to the days of the apostles, and reckon as among their earliest elders and preachers the names of Paul and Peter and John, of Stephen and Philip and Barnabas, of Silas and Timothy and Titus; and the only priest they know is the Great High Priest who is passed into the heavens, the Shepherd and Bishop of Souls.

"In this noble position we stand as a denomination alone."

The above book was not printed in the "Southwest," but in the Northeast, in Philadelphia, by the American Baptist Publication Society. In their catalogue I find also the following: "Lectures on Baptist History," by William R. Williams, D.D., New York; "The Origin, Continuity, Principles, Spirit and Polity and Position of the Baptists," by T. G. Jones, D.D.; "The Church in the Wilderness, or the Baptists Before the Reformation," by W. W. Everets, D.D., Chicago; "Origin of the Baptists," by S. B. Taylor, D. D.; "Baptist History from the Foundation of the Christian Church to the Close of the Eighteenth Century," by J. M. Cramp, D.D. So you see "The Credibility" of this doctrine is not confined to the Southwest. I have about a dozen histories by Baptists, and I wish every one had them. Most of them go into details. I like that, but I thought I would offer one that would carry you down the line swiftly, but surely. I get my testimony from those not Baptists.

Under the last head, "It Is Conclusive," we will let those not Baptists give the concluding and conclusive testimony. I hope to make it clearly and convincingly conclusive.

IT IS HISTORICAL.

The great ecclesiastical histories undertake to give the history of all the schisms and sects disgracing the Christian religion, and this makes so great the amount of reading and rubbish that but few will undertake to read through them. So I have tried to do this for the reader, and have culled some things about Baptist History. I have aimed to give just enough to identify the Baptists with the true line of witnesses through the dark ages of Papal persecutions. The great Apostasy that departed from the faith, persecuted those who tried to hold to the faith. Who were they? We will first

EPITOMIZE MOSHEIM ON BAPTIST HISTORY.

Referring to the Schaff-Herzog Encyclopedia, Vol. III, pp. 1586-7, and to Encyclopedia Brittanica, Vol. V, p. 765, I find that J. L. Mosheim is put at the head of ecclesiastical historians.

I will only give a few items with characteristic pointers from the nineteenth, eighteenth and seventeenth centuries, as their history during that time is not in dispute. Turning to page 729, the Baptists are referred to as "The Baptists or Anabaptists."

There were some irregularities, yet there were orderly representatives of these peoples. The peculiarities of these peoples, in the main, were organically preserved. We must never trust the controversial opponents of any people to state their doctrines.

If so, their statements always should be received with many grains of allowance. A good illustration of this is given by these historians themselves. I use the plural because Maclaine, in his Introduction, confesses the liberty he takes in his translation which clearly makes it the history in part of two men. (Maclaine was an Episcopalian and Mosheim a Lutheran.) On page 203, speaking of the injustice done the Paulicians by the Greek writers in stating their doctrines, the Greek writers say the Paulicians "treated contemptuously the Virgin Mary;" and then the historians add: "That is to say . . . they refused to adore and worship her." The Greeks said the Paulicians loaded the cross of Christ with contempt and reproach, and the historians add:

"By which we are only to understand that they refused to follow the absurd and superstitious practice of the Greeks, who paid to the pretended wood of the cross a certain sort of religious homage." Hence we will not appeal to these historians for an exact statement of Baptist *doctrine* through the past centuries, but we seek their testimony concerning our *history*—our existence as an anti-Catholic people, being persecuted by that anti-Christian power according to prophecy, and as the true church, according to prophecy, was to be persecuted, we shall try to identify ourselves with the persecuted people under the various names given them. And as an illustration of this variety of names given to the same people, we find on page 257 this explanation concerning these same Paulicians: "In Italy they were called Paterini and Cathari, or rather Gazari, which latter appellation the Germans have preserved, with a small alteration only, which is proper to adapt it to the genius of their language. In France they were called the Albigenses from the town of Albi, and Bulgarians, because they came from Bulgaria; . . . also Publicans, which was probably a corrupt pronunciation of Paulicians, and Boni Homines, or 'Good Men,' with several other titles and epithets."

So, don't become confused by a change of names. Should you attempt to trace the history of the name of the Deity, you would find it changing with all the languages and dialects of earth, and often with more than one name in the same language. In thirteen languages and dialects the name of Deity is spelled with two letters; in twenty-one it is spelled with three letters, the Irish Druids having the longest, "Joabulion." Let there be no confusion, then, about false statements of doctrines and change of names. Our object is not merely to prove but to *trace* Baptist History. So, being called Baptists or Anabaptists on page 749 in the nineteenth century, we turn now to page 728 in the eighteenth century, and we read: "The Baptists, Anabaptists, or Antipedo Baptists, were then gaining ground in this century." After stating their belief in immersion of adult believers only, the doctrine of the Millenium, Intermediate State, and baptism of those who had received the rite in infancy, they add: "They admitted that mere baptism without proofs of faith and spiritual conversion, would be insufficient to save adults. Faith, they said, would operate in that respect without good works; yet the effect of true faith and of God's grace would appear in the performance of just, virtuous and benevolent acts." These are good Baptist earmarks.

Now turning to the seventeenth century, page 637, in chapter 5, we quote another remark concerning the Mennonites or Anabaptists: "All matters of importance are proposed, examined and decided in the meetings of the brethren. By their suffrages the ministers are elected to their holy office, and are all, the deacons excepted, installed by public prayers, attended with imposition of hands."

Now turning to page 615 in the seventeenth century, we find this remarkable marginal note. I copy it in large capitals: "WE ARE NOT TO IMAGINE BY THE TERM HOT-HEADED

(FURIOSI) THAT THE ANABAPTISTS RESEMBLED THE FURIOUS FANATICS OF THAT NAME WHO FORMERLY EXCITED SUCH DREADFUL TUMULTS IN GERMANY, AND MORE ESPECIALLY AT MUNSTER. THIS WAS BY NO MEANS THE CASE; THE ENGLISH ANABAPTISTS DIFFERED FROM THEIR PROTESTANT BRETHREN ABOUT THE SUBJECT AND MODE OF BAPTISM ALONE, CONFINING THE FORMER TO GROWN CHRISTIANS AND THE LATTER TO IMMERSION OR DIPPING."

Those rGeman Anabaptists so-called were no kin of ours. Like some Campbellites in Texas, they rebaptized, and were thus called "Anabaptists," but the Anabaptists of the time denounced them, and all historians of note that I know testify as above. We have stronger vindication in another place than the above. Notice how strong they put it: "THIS WAS BY NO MEANS THE CASE."

Dr. Mosheim, with all of his superabounding facilities and with all of his animosity toward the Baptists, assisted by his antibaptist translator, Archibald Maclaine, was unable to sustain such a charge. No one, with the testimony that I have, will believe that the madmen of Munster were Baptists, and those who assert it are ignorant slander-mongers. They bear false witness against the martyr witnesses of Jesus Christ.

So we trace our history, not through the "mad men of Munster," nor through the sprinkling or Pedobaptist schisms from the true Anabaptists or Mennonites, for in those days as now, there were frequent defections from the faith, brought about by the want of courage to withstand the oppressive opposition. I believe all of our people to-day would stand unflinchingly on Baptist history, and church constitution, and definition, and administration of ordinances, etc., if they had the courage of martyrs. But for lack of this, many wither before ridicule, the most cruel weapon now used against us, and hence their yielding of this point and that, in order that all may be churches alike, and all ministers alike, and all authority alike to officiate in the ordinances of the church. If Christ built his own church, after his own model, and has preserved it through ten thousand baptisms of fire and blood till now, then that church after that model still exists, and all others are the churches of men, and some of them the most unholy of men. But who has the courage to say it? How many believe it privately, but publicly contradict it? If Baptist churches originated like others—set up and modeled by men, then it is no more the church of Christ than others. Here is the issue and the rub. If this be not true, then I prefer membership in one of the more p o p u l a r "branches." But is it true? That is the question.

BAPTISTS IN THE SIXTEENTH CENTURY.
CHAPTER II.

We want to know what Mosheim says about Baptists of the sixteenth century, and especially about the Baptists of England practicing immersion in this century, and yet some fix their origin in the seventeenth century, and make the wonderful discovery that they invented immersion one hundred years after Mosheim credits them with "dipping only once," and "adults only," and regarded themselves as the "only true church." But see the quotation concerning English Baptists further on. Page 490-1, chap. III, is headed: HISTORY OF THE ANABAPTISTS OR MENNONITES (and so on the top of every page to 501). Having previously connected the Baptists with the Anabaptists and now with the Mennonites, he proceeds to connect them with the Waldenses and other ancient sects.

"The true origin of that sect which acquired the denomination of Anabaptists by their administering anew the rite of baptism to those who came over to their communion, and derived that of Mennonites from the famous man to whom they owe the greatest part of their present felicity, is hidden in the depths of antiquity, and is of consequence, extremely difficult to be ascertained. . . . The modern Mennonites not only consider themselves as the descendants of the Waldenses, who were so grievously oppressed and persecuted by the despotic head of the Romish church, but pretend, moreover, to be the purest offspring of these respectable sufferers, being equally averse to all principles of rebellion, on the one hand, and all suggestions of fanaticism on the other. . . . It may be observed, in the first place, that the Mennonites are not entirely in an error when they boast of their descent from the Waldenses, Petrobrusians and other ancient sects, who are usually considered as witnesses of the truth, in times of general darkness and superstition. Before the rise of

Luther and Calvin, there lay concealed, in almost all the countries of Europe, particularly in Bohemia, Moravia, Switzerland and Germany, many persons who adhered tenaciously to the following doctrine, which the Waldenses, Wickliffites and Hussites had maintained, some in a more disguised, and others in a more open and public manner, viz: 'That the kingdom of Christ, or the visible church which he established upon earth, was an assembly of true and real saints, and ought, therefore, to be inaccessible to the wicked and unrighteous, and also exempt from all those institutions which human prudence suggests, to oppose the progress of iniquity, or to correct and reform transgressors.'"

Page 493: "The conduct of the Anabaptists, under the pressure of persecution, plainly showed the extreme difficulty of correcting or influencing, by the prospect of suffering, or even by the terrors of death, minds that are . . . firmly bound by the ties of religion. In almost all the countries of Europe, an unspeakable number of these unhappy wretches preferred death, in its worst form, tc a retraction of their errors. Neither the view of the flames that were kindled to consume them, nor the ignominy of the gibbet, nor the terrors of the sword, could shake their invincible, but ill-placed constancy, or make them abandon tenets that appeared dearer to them than life and all its enjoyments. The Mennonites have preserved voluminous records of the lives, actions and unhappy fate of those of their sect who suffered death for the crimes of rebellion or heresy, which was imputed to them. Certain it is that they were treated with severity, and it is much to be lamented that so little distinction was made between the members of this sect, when the sword of justice was unsheathed against them. Why were the innocent and guilty involved in the same fate? Why were doctrines purely theological, or at worst fanatical, punished with the same rigor that was shown to crimes inconsistent with the peace and welfare of civil society? Those who had no other marks of peculiarity than their administering baptism to adult persons only, and their excluding the unrighteous from the external communion of the church, ought undoubtedly to have met with milder treatment. . . . Many suffered for errors which they had embraced with the most upright intentions, seduced by the eloquence and fervor of their doctors, and persuading themselves that they were contributing to the advancement of true religion. . . . It is true that many Anabaptists suffered death, not on account of their being considered as rebellious subjects, but merely because they were judged to be incorrigible heretics; for in this century the error of limiting the administration of baptism to adult persons only, and the practice of rebaptizing such as had received that sacrament in a state of infancy, were looked upon as most flagitious and intolerable heresies.''

Page 494: "While the terrors of death in the most dreadful forms were presented to the view of this miserable sect, and numbers of them were executed every day without a proper distinction being made between the innocent and the guilty, those who escaped the severity of justice were in the most discouraging situation that can well be imagined.''

Page 495: "Menno retained, indeed, the doctrines commonly received among the Anabaptists in relation to the baptism of infants, the Millenium or thousand years' reign of Christ upon the earth, the exclusion of magistrates from the Christian church, the abolition of war, and the prohibition of oaths enjoined by our Savior.''

Marginal note.—"Many of these ancient Anabaptists abstained religiously from all acts of violence and sedition, followed the pious examples of the ancient Waldenses, Henricians, Petrobrusians, Hussites and Wickliffites. . . . All this will be allowed without hesitation. . . . Nothing can be more certain than this fact, viz: that the first Mennonite congregations were composed of the different sorts of Anabaptists already mentioned of those who had been always inoffensive and upright."

Page 497: "The opinions entertained by the Mennonites in general, seem to be derived from this leading and fundamental principle, that the kingdom which Christ established upon earth is a visible church or community, into which the holy and just are alone to be admitted, and which is consequently exempt from all those institutions and rules of discipline that have been invented by human wisdom for the correction and reformation of the wicked." . . .

Page 498: "Notwithstanding all this, it is manifest beyond all possibility of contradiction, that the religious opinions which still distinguish the Mennonites from all other Christian communities, flow directly from the ancient doctrine of the Anabaptists concerning the *nature of the church*. It is in consequence of this doctrine that they admit none to the sacrament of baptism but persons who are come to the full use of their reason; because infants are incapable of binding themselves by a solemn vow to a holy life, and it is altogether uncertain whether, in mature years, they will be saints or sinners."

Now for Mosheim, concerning the Baptists of England.

Page 500: "The sectaries in England who reject the custom of baptizing infants, are not distinguished by the title of Anabaptists, but that of

Baptists. It is, however, probable that they derive their origin from the German or Dutch Mennonites, and that in former times they adopted their doctrine in all its points. . . . They (the General Baptists) agree with the Particular Baptists in this circumstance, that they admit to baptism adult persons only, and administer that sacrament by dipping or total immersion. . . . After the manner of the Ancient Mennonites, they look upon their sect as the only true Christian church, and consequently shun, with the most scrupulous caution, the communion of all other religious societies. They dip only once. . . . the candidates for baptism." (This was 100 years before the "invention of immersion.")

Page 501: "They adopt the doctrine of Menno with respect to the millenium or the reign of the saints with Christ upon the earth for a thousand years."

Page 505: "There were certain sects and doctors against whom the zeal, vigilance and severity of Catholics, Lutherans and Calvinists were united, and in opposing whose settlement and progress these three communions, forgetting their dissensions, joined their most vigorous counsels and endeavors. The object of their common aversion was the Anabaptists. . . . To avoid the unhappy consequences of such a formidable opposition, great numbers of both classes retired into Poland, from this persuasion, that in a country whose inhabitants were passionately fond of freedom, religious liberty could not fail to find a refuge." In the face of all this history of the Baptists in the sixteenth century, what shall we say of that "discovery," that "immersion was invented by the English Baptists in 1641," and that the Baptists had their beginning in 1610-11. Let us follow this history back into other centuries "before the rise of Luther and Calvin."

CHAPTER III.

I last gave the history of "the Baptists, Anabaptists or Mennonites" in the sixteenth century according to Mosheim. This was one hundred years prior to their origin, according to some. Now notice some linking words that I shall italicize. Mosheim said, the origin of the Anabaptists or Mennonites was hid in the depths of antiquity; that they considered themselves the *descendants* of the Waldenses; the *offspring* of those respectable sufferers. His own testimony is, that they are not in error when they boast of their *descent* from the Waldenses, Petrobrusians and other ancient sects—the witnesses of the truth in the times of general darkness and superstition. So far from being a branch of the Reformation, and more modern than some of them, he says: "Before the rise of Luther and Calvin there lay concealed in almost all the countries of Europe, persons who tenaciously held to the doctrine of the Waldenses, Wickliffites," etc., and the particular doctrine stated is the prime plank in the Baptist platform.

The *linking* words "descend," "descendants," "offspring," etc., show continuity, or what is improperly and unfortunately called succession. They forbid the idea that this system of doctrine which characterized them as the witnesses of the truth, was invented by different men at different times and places, but was handed down from generation to generation; and while no two historians will agree in a statement of this doctrine, yet we know that the word of God is true. War was made against them, "because they kept the commandments of God and had the testimony of Jesus Christ."—Rev. 12:17. "Here is the patience of the saints; here are they that keep the commandments of God and the faith of Jesus Christ."—Rev. 14:12. "For the gospel's sake" they should be persecuted by all nations. My scope will not allow me to *discuss* doctrinal and historical issues, but only to show the *existence* of the persecuted church, wearing these various names. These indissoluble linking words give us an unquestionable passport into the preceding centuries. Let us assure ourselves of the existence of these witnesses of the truth in the fifteenth century.

481: Marginal note.—"One church was not entitled to exercise jurisdiction over another, but each might give the other counsel or admonition, if its members walked in a disorderly manner, or abandoned the capital truths of religion, and if the offending church did not receive the admonition, they were allowed to disown it publicly as a church of Christ. On the other hand, the powers of the church officers were confined within the narrow limits of their own society. The pastor of the church might not administer baptism or the Lord's Supper to any but to those of his own communion. . . . The church at Leyden, where Robinson had fixed the standard of interdependence, about the year 1595, was dispersed; and it is very remarkable that some members of this church, transplanting themselves into

America, laid the foundation of the colony of New England."

Surely they were Baptist churches.

Page 373: "In England and Scotland the disciples of Wickliffe, whom the multitude had stigmatized with the odious title of Lollards, continued to inveigh against the despotic laws of the pontiffs, and the licentious manners of the clergy. The Waldenses, though persecuted and oppressed on all sides, raised their voices even in the remote valleys and lurking places, whither they were driven by the violence of their enemies, and called aloud for succor to the expiring cause of religion and virtue. Even in Italy, many, and among others the famous Savanarola, had the courage to declare that Rome was become the image of Babylon; and this notion was soon adopted by multitudes of all ranks and conditions. But the greatest part of the clergy and monks, persuaded that their honors, influence and riches would diminish in proportion to the increase of knowledge among the people, and would receive inexpressible detriment from the downfall of superstition, vigorously opposed everything that had the remotest aspect of a reformation, and imposed silence upon these importunate censors by the formidable authority of fire and sword."

These "remote valleys and lurking places" were the places prepared of God for the safe keeping of his church. They were to be "driven" into them by the "sword and fire" of persecution. So far history confirms prophecy. So we see the Baptists, Anabaptists, Mennonites or Waldenses "lived and moved and had their being" in the fifteenth century. Can we find any trace of them in the *fourteenth* century?

Page 355: "In the Latin church the inquisitors, those active ministers and executioners of papal justice, extended their vigilance to every quarter, and most industriously hunted out the remains of those sects who opposed the religion of Rome, even the Waldenses, the Catharists, the Apostolists, and others; so that the history of these times abounds with numberless instances of persons who were burned or otherwise barbarously destroyed by those unrelenting instruments of superstitious vengeance."

We find an important item concerning the Wickliffites in this fourteenth century."

Page 345 : " The event was, that of the twenty-three opinions for which Wickliffe had been prosecuted by the monks, ten were condemned as heresies, and thirteen as errors. . . . He left many followers in England and other countries, who were styled Wickliffites and Lollards. . . . Wherever they could be found they were terribly persecuted by the inquisitors, and other instruments of papal vengeance. In the council of Constance, in 1415, the memory and opinions of Wickliffe were condemned by a solemn decree; and about thirteen years after his bones were dug up and publicly burned."

Can we now find the existence of this line of witnesses in the thirteenth century?

Page 327: " During the whole of this thirteenth century, the Roman pontiffs carried on the most barbarous and inhuman persecution against those whom they branded with the denomination of heretics: *i. e.*, against all those who called their pretended authority and jurisdiction in question, or taught doctrines different from those which were adopted and propagated by the church of Rome. For the sects of the Cathari, Waldenses, Petrobrusians etc., gathered strength from day to day, spread imperceptibly throughout all

Europe, assembled numerous congregations in Italy, France, Spain and Germany, and formed, by degrees, such a powerful party as rendered them formidable to the pontiffs, and menaced the papal jurisdiction with a fatal revolution. To the ancient sects new factions were added, which, though they differed from each other in various respects, unanimously agreed in this point: "That the public and established religion was a motley system of errors and superstition, and that the dominion which the popes had usurped over Christians, as also the authority they exercised in religious matters, were unlawful and tyrannical." Such were the notions propagated by the secretaries, who refuted the superstitions and impostures of the times by arguments drawn from the holy Scriptures, and whose declamations against the power, the opulence, and the vices of the pontiffs and clergy, were extremely agreeable to many princes and civil magistrates, who groaned under the usurpations of the sacred order. The pontiffs, therefore, considered themselves as obliged to have recourse to new and extraordinary methods of defeating and subduing enemies, who, both by their number and their rank, were every way proper to fill them with terror."

The Albigenses constitute an important link in this chain of witnesses, according to our great historian.

Page 329: "In 1209, a formidable army of cross-bearers commenced against the heretics (who were comprehended under the general denominations of Albigenses) an open war, which they carried on with the utmost exertions of cruelty, though with various success, for several years." On page 329, in a marginal note, the Albigenses are divided into various sects, not that they were schisms from each other, but all called sects because they did not affiliate with Rome. Among these Albigensian sects the Waldenses are mentioned as "the least pernicious." So these are sister sects, and sisters to the one mentioned in Acts 28:22.

CHAPTER IV—TWELFTH CENTURY.

I would now ask, even "the slow of heart to believe," if we have not reached the twelfth century with Baptist history fairly? Did not our great historian call us Baptists or Anabaptists and then Anabaptists or Mennonites, and in his ample account of them in the sixteenth century did he not, speaking of them in that century, say that their "origin was hid in the depths of antiquity?" Did not the Anabaptists or Mennonites of the sixteenth century claim their descent from the ancient Waldenses, and did not our historians concede that they were not in error in claiming this descent? Did they not concede this claim of being the purest offspring of those ancient sects who are usually considered as witnesses of the truth in times of general darkness and superstition—long before the rise of Luther and Calvin? Am I perverting or even straining this history to make my point? Now will you not follow me into preceding centuries, and for the present, especially into the twelfth century? Let us not weary, for we are on the road to Jerusalem which is the mother of Baptist churches. This road runs through mountains and dens and caves of the earth, and is marked most of the way with the martyr blood of its pilgrims. The way of Catholics and Protestants runs through the highways of the kingdoms of the world, but it runs into Rome and not Jerusalem. We are now tracing Baptist history under various denominational names. When we are through with this historical argument, let us discuss the continuity of Bapitst churches, which requires a diferent kind of argument. Here is what Mosheim says about the Waldenses in the twelfth century:

Page 290. "This sect was known by different denominations" . . . Page 291. "They accordingly formed religious assemblies, first in France, and afterward in Lombardy, whence they propagated their sect through the other provinces of Europe with incredible rapidity, and with such invincible fortitude that neither fire, nor sword, nor the most cruel inventions of merciless persecution, could damp their zeal or entirely ruin their cause.

' The attempts of Peter Waldus and his followers were neither employed nor intended to introduce new doctrines into the church, nor to propose new articles of faith to Christians. All they aimed at was to reduce the form of ecclesiastical government, and the lives and manners both of the clergy and people to that amiable simplicity, and that primitive sanctity, which had characterized the apostolic age, and which appear so strongly recommended in tbe precepts and injunctions of the divine author of our holy religion. In consequence of this design they complained that the Roman church had degenerated, under Constantine the Great, from its primitive purity and sanctity. They denied the supremacy of the Roman pontiff. . . . . They considered every Christian as in a certain measure qualified and authorized to instruct, exhort and confirm the brethren in their Christian course and demanded the restoration of the ancient penitential discipline of the church; i. e., the expiation of transgression by prayer, fasting and alms, which the new invented doctrine of indulgences had nearly abolished. . . . They maintained that the power of delivering sinners from the guilt and punishment of their offenses belonged to God alone, and that indulgences, in consequence, were the criminal inventions of sordid avarice. They looked upon the prayers and other ceremonies that were instituted in behalf of the dead as vain, useless and absurd." Here follows a marginal note of great importance. Some have labored to make Peter Waldus the founder of the Waldenses, and have thus given them a human founder like all others have. "But their rock is not our rock, our enemies themselves being judges." Wesley says on Rev. 13:7, that about 1160 "the Papists changed the name Vallenses into Waldenses on purpose to represent them as of modern origin." He says "they were much more ancient than him."

We could introduce much proof, yea, overwhelming proof to this end, but must confine our investigations at present mainly to this history. Read, remember, rehearse and oft repeat the following testimony of the origin of the Waldensian Baptists.

Marginal note. "Certain writers give different accounts of the origin of the Waldenses, and suppose they were so called from the valleys in which they had resided for many ages before the birth of Peter Waldus. . . . There were in the valleys of Piedmont, long before this period, a set of men who differed widely from the opinions adopted and inculcated by the church of

Rome. . . for it seems evident from the best records that Waldus derived his name from the true Valdenses of Piedmont, whose doctrine he adopted and who were known by the names of Vaudois and Valdenses, before he or his immediate followers existed. If the Valdenses had derived their name from any eminent teacher, it would probably have been from Valdo, who was remarkable for the purity of his doctrine, in the ninth century, and was the contemporary and chief counselor of Berengarius . . . . The bloody inquisitor, Reinerus Sacco, who exerted such a furious zeal for the destruction of the Waldenses, lived but about eighty years after Valdus of Lyons, and must, therefore, be supposed to have known whether he was the real founder of the Valdenses or Leonists; and yet it is remarkable that he speaks of the Leonists . . . as a sect that had flourished above 500 years, and even mentions authors of note, who make their antiquity remount to the apostolic age. See the account given of Sacco's book by the Jesuit Gretser, in the Bibliotheca Patrum. . . . . Whoever will be at the pains to read attentively the second, twenty-fifth, twenty-sixth and twenty-seventh chapters of the first book Leger's Historie Generale des Eglises Vaudoises will find this distinction entirely groundless. When the Papists ask us where our religion was before Luther, we generally answer, in the Bible; and we answer well. But to gratify their taste for tradition and human authority, we may add to this answer, and in the valleys of Piedmont." In another note on same page we read: "Though these writers are not . . . perfectly agreed about the number of doctrines . . . yet they are nearly unanimous in acknowledging the sincere piety and exemplary conduct of the Waldenses."

When we are through with the historical proof we may give the *doctrine* of the Waldenses, etc. But the witnesses of the truth were called by other names in this century. So turning to page 288 we read: "Among the sects that troubled the Latin church during this century, the principal place is due to the Cathari or Catharists whom we have already had occasion to mention." (A marginal note here refers to the third century and especially to the ninth. So our passport to further antiquity is indisputable.) "This numerous faction leaving their first residence, which was in Bulgaria, spread themselves throughout almost all the European provinces, where they occasioned much tumult and disorder; but their fate was unhappy, for wherever they were found they were put to death with the most unrelenting cruelty."

On page 289 we find this concerning the doctrine of the Petrobrussians: "That no persons were to be baptized before they had full use of their reason. That God would accept a sincere worship wherever it is offered; that crucifixes, as instruments of superstition, deserved to be destroyed; that the real body and blood of Christ were not exhibited in the Eucharist, but were merely represented in that holy ordinance by figures and symbols; and lastly, that the oblations, prayers and good works of the living could in no respect be advantageous to the dead." These are Baptist ear marks, and prove clearly that so far as we have gone there is not a doubt to be entertained that we are on the plain, strait and narrow way that leads to Jerusalem. Let us not weary in the journey.

CHAPTER V.
ELEVENTH CENTURY.

Page 248. After drawing at some length the "hideous portrait of the religion of this age" with "features full of deformity" and "its guardians equally destitute of knowledge and virtue," "holding forth in their conduct scandalous examples of the most flagitious crimes," with "people sunk in the grossest superstition and employing all this zeal in the worship of images and relics," with a "trifling round of ceremonies imposed by the tyranny of a despotic priesthood"—in the midst of this blackness of moral darkness the historian, of course, and of necessity, must mention that small remnant of the elect which God always reserves unto himself, "those chosen spirits who had escaped the general contagion, who lay too much concealed and had, therefore, too little influence to combat with success the formidable patrons of impiety and superstition, who were very numerous in all ranks and orders, from the throne to the cottage." The historian then proceeds with this remarkable testimony:

"Notwithstanding all this, we find, from the time of Gregory VII, several proofs of the zealous effort of those who are generally called by the Protestants the witnesses of the truth—by whom are meant such pious and judicious Christians as adhered to the pure religion of the gospel and remained uncorrupted amidst the growth of superstition, who deplored the miserable state to which Christianity was reduced by the alteration of its divine doctrines and the vices of its profligate ministers; who opposed with vigor the tyrannic ambition, both of the lordly pontiff and the aspiring bishops, and in some provinces privately, in others openly, attempted the reformation of a corrupt and idolatrous church and of a barbarous and superstitious age. This was, indeed, bearing witness to the truth in the noblest manner, and it was principally in Italy and France that the marks of this heroic piety were exhibited. . . . 249: They had also formed to themselves a notion that the primitive church was to be the standing and perpetual model, according to which the rites, government and worship of all Christian churches were to be regulated in all the ages of the world; and that the lives and manners of the holy apostles were to be rigorously followed, in every respect, by all the ministers of Christ.''

What weighty words are these! How suitable to the cause I am pleading! I now quote the following words, which will lead me to say something about doctrine in this chapter.

Page 258: "It is difficult to come to a fixed determination with respect to the character and doctrine of these secretaries; for when we examine matters attentively, we find that even their enemies acknowledged the sincerity of their piety, that they were blackened by accusations which were evidently false, and that the opinions for which they were punished differ widely from the Manichaean system. . . . Their particular tenets may be reduced to the following heads: (1) They rejected baptism, and in a more especial manner the baptism of infants as a ceremony that was in no respect essential to salvation. (2) They reject, for the same reason, the sacrament of the Lord's Supper.''

Marginal note.—"We shall have occasion to give a more copious account of these fanatics in the history of the thirteenth century, in which they were first drawn from their obscurity and condemned by many councils; and especially in Germany. It is, however, certain that they had a clandestine existence long before that period, and that they propagated their tenets secretly in several places."

In the above I give two statements out of sixteen concerning the doctrine of these sects "everywhere spoken against." It is evident that every statement is a misstatement. They rejected neither baptism nor the Lord's Supper, but they rejected them "as necessary to salvation." It is clearly an anti-catholic creed, misstated as our creed is to this day. I have often heard with my own ears that Baptists believe "there are infants in hell not a span long," "that no one can be saved without immersion," "that there are no Christians but Baptists," etc. The Baptists are further from such beliefs than any of their accusers.

Let me suppose that I have at least one critical reader who is trying to file objections to the course I am pursuing.

I have said that my present purpose is to trace a continuity of witnesses, suffering even unto death for their anti-catholic doctrines rather than to define or defend those doctrines. But I imagine my fault-finding critic in impatience is saying, "Aha! aha! Can people be Baptists who believe such doctrines?" What doctrines? I know they are accused of every heresy, but as in the case of their Lord, the false witnesses do not agree. Such evidence never justly gained a case.

It is false and full of malice. God preserved his people that they might preserve his truth. The persecution of his church was to be "for the gospel's sake," for "keeping the commandments of God and holding to the faith of Jesus Christ." This is God's testimony concerning the orthodoxy of his persecuted saints. If they had not differed and disputed with anti-christian teachers, they need not have died. They differed from "the lying christs, and lying prophets, and lying teachers which should arise, and, if possible, deceive the very elect," "whose coming was after the working of Satan, with all power and signs and lying wonders, and with all deceivableness of unrighteousness," to whom "God sent strong delusion that they should believe a lie, that they all might be damned who believed not the truth." Such is the testimony of God concerning both them and their adversaries. We can see from history that God's testimony is true, and all who differed from him were liars. These liars wrote most of our history, and to justify themselves in the death of the martyrs they accused them of every "damnable and intolerable heresy." No one can candidly read a dozen of these histories with their abounding contradictions without throwing their testimony out of court. Maclaine says that Mosheim was often misled by these lying historians. At one time the Manicheans were the most detestable to the Catholics. They were charged with most any false doctrine, and all others who opposed the Catholics were called Manicheans. Hence, the Paulicians of the time were called Manicheans or "a branch of the same." Now what is the most rational conclusion in this and in similar cases? Note this point that commends itself to every one's judgment. When adverse testimony is from enemies, it is probably false, especially if they are known as malicious liars. But when the testimony is favorable it is probably correct, because in spite of the enmity of the heart and untruthfulness of the tongue, the evidence is so strong as to compel the truth against their evil dispositions. Let me now illustrate the general subject.

Protestants are opposed to Catholics. Baptists are also opposed to Catholics, hence Baptists are called Protestants. Indeed, many indiscreet Baptists call themselves Protestants. Hence, the future historian will so write it, and Baptists of to-day will be charged with Protestant doctrines, such as sprinkling and pouring for baptism. One of us, the most highly honored among Southern Baptists, has even now done worse than this, and that in the face of as much contrary evidence as the future historian will have. Take another illustration. Baptists are called Calvinists—many call themselves Calvinists; hence, they are said to be like the Presbyterians on the doctrines of grace. Many Baptists say so. But when we come to apply and practice these doctrines, we are the poles apart. I do not mean poles terrestrial, but poles celestial; and if there be poles yet further apart, I refer to them. As far as the uttermost east is from the uttermost west, so far are Presbyterians and Baptists apart on the application and practice of the doctrines of grace. The Presbyterians put this construction on the covenant of grace: "The promise is to you and your children," that is, natural offspring, so that if even one parent is a believer (even professor) the children are born holy and are entitled to the seal of the covenant. They put the "seal" upon the infant of one professed believer, "counting it for the seed," and then claim by the seal that the promise is sure to all such as the seed. They educate in the catechism these once born holy (?) seed, and claim they will persevere through grace to glory. They believe that is sufficient for the natural seed of one believing parent, and that is all they offer them. But Baptists believe that all such seed will be damned. Like their Master, they say, "except ye be born AGAIN ye can not see the kingdom of God."

"That which born of flesh is flesh," etc. Nay, make if stronger yet. Let both parents be saints, Baptist saints, descended from a long line of pious Baptist ancestry; let the unfeigned faith be not only in the mother and grandmother, but in the other parents as well; and if a son Timothy has the same faith, it is not because of his birth, nor can the Holy Scriptures make him thus wise unto salvation, $i.\ e.$, by birth, but only through personal faith in Christ Jesus. Nay, let this holy (?) seed be dipped once or thrice; let them be taught all the Baptist songs of Zion, trained up in Spurgeon's catechism and graduated in Boyce's theology; nay, let them speak with the tongues of men and angels, and have the gift of prophecy, and understand all mysteries and all knowledge, and let them have all faith so that they can remove mountains, and let them morsel out all their goods to feed the poor, and then give their bodies to be burned, and it all may profit them nothing. "One thing they would lack," say all Baptists, and to the united Presbyterian claim, they would give their united denial with voices louder than the seven apocalyptic thunders. And yet Baptists are called Calvinists, and are said to be like the Presbyterians on the doctrines of grace. If it is so hard to tell what Baptists now believe, what of the dark ages, when their enemies were trying in every way to do them hurt, and thus bring to naught the promises of Christ through these traditions and traductions? Then, for the present, let us proceed with the history of the people of God, and after that study their doctrines.

CHAPTER VI.

TRACED FROM THE BEGINNING THE OTHER WAY.

We have traced the Baptists, Anabaptists, Mennonites, Waldenses, etc., back to A. D. 1000. Here they are in the valleys of Piedmont and in their mountain fastnesses, the places prepared of God. They had trials of cruel mockings and scourgings, yea, moreover, of bonds and imprisonment; they were stoned, sawn asunder, tempted, slain with the sword; they wandered about in sheepskins and goatskins; being destitute, afflicted, tormented, whom the world hated, and of whom the world was not worthy; they wandered in deserts and in mountains and in dens and caves of the earth—the true and persecuted witnesses holding the faith of Jesus Christ. This path of thorns and fire and blood was trod these eight hundred years, not by Protestant, but by Baptist feet. The Protestants came out of Rome, and not out of the mountains and dens and caves of the earth. The next four hundred years backward, *i. e.*, from the eleventh to the seventh century, our historian was mainly occupied with the Roman and Greek controversy, and not so full on Baptist history as during the first seven hundred, and the last eight hundred years. Those intermediate four hundred years are considered the hardest to bridge over, hence I desire to put my best efforts on that. But I purpose to bridge that chasm. But in order to do this, let us begin now at the other end, and come up to the wilderness from that side. The man who says the Catholics are older than the Baptists is an ecclesiastical ignoramus. I have proved that those were Baptists who came out of the wilderness. Now, let me prove those were Baptists who went into the wilderness, and lastly, those were Baptists while in the wilderness. We now begin at the first. We get a very significant forecast of what is coming from the introduction:

Page 10: "When we look back to the commencement of the Christian church, we find its government administered jointly by the pastors and the people. But, in process of time, the scene changes, and we see these pastors affecting an air of pre-eminence and superiority, trampling upon the rights and privileges of the community and assuming to themselves a supreme authority; both in civil and religious matters. This invasion of the rights of the people was at length carried to such a height that a single man administered, or at least claimed a right to administer, the affairs of the whole church with an unlimited sway."

Note.—It was not so in the beginning, but gradually became so in process of time," *i. e.*, from the second to the seventh centuries. See if the following testimony during these centuries does not confirm this. How was baptism administered at first? Like Catholics do now or Baptists?

Century 1. Page 10: "Those who, moved by solemn admonitions, had formed the resolution of correcting their evil dispositions and mending their lives, were initiated into the kingdom of the Redeemer by the ceremony of immersion or baptism. Christ himself, before he began his ministry, desired to be solemnly baptized by John in the waters of the Jordan."

This is a Baptist ear-mark. They had it all their own way for a while. But soon some began to pervert ordinances, officers, government and doctrines, until the apostasy culminated and separated. "Of your own selves shall men arise, speaking perverse things, to draw away disciples after them." "They went out from us," "departed from the faith." Were the first churches Baptist in polity, or Catholic? Read on and see.

Page 20: "If it be true that the apostles acted by divine inspiration, and in conformity with the commands of their blessed Master, (and this no Christian can call in question), it follows, that the form of government which the primitive churches borrowed from that of Jerusalem, the first Christian assembly established by the apostles themselves, must be esteemed as of divine institution. . . . In those early times every Christian church consisted of the people, their leaders and the ministers or deacons." Paul addressed them as "saints, bishops and deacons."

Were the first churches officered according to Baptist rule? I mean officers both in name and in character.

Page 21: "The people were undoubtedly the first in authority; for the apostles showed, by their own example, that nothing of moment was to be carried on, or determined, without the consent of the assembly. It was, therefore, the assembly of the people which chose rulers and teachers. The same people rejected or confirmed, by their own sufferages, the laws that were proposed of the assembly; ex-communicated profligate and unworthy members of the church; restored the penitent to their forfeited privileges; passed judgment upon the different subjects of controversy and dissension that arose in their community; examined and decided the disputes which happened between elders and deacons; and, in a word, exercised all that authority which belongs to such as are invested with sovereign power. There reigned among the members of the Christian church a perfect equality. Nor in this first century was the distinction made between Christians of a more or less perfect order, which took place afterwards. Whoever acknowledged Christ as the Savior of mankind and made a solemn profession of his faith in him, was immediately baptized and received into the church.

Those who had been solemnly admitted into the church by baptism, were authorized to vote in the ecclesiastical assemblies. Presbyters or bishops were titles in the New Testament, undoubtedly applied to the same order of men. The church was undoubtedly provided from the beginning with inferior ministers or deacons."

Now, say, gentle reader, is Mosheim describing A Baptist Church, or The Catholic Church? Let all those be treated for mental imbecility that can't decide so simple a question as that. This is the one and only way back. The road has not forked yet. That is several hundred years ahead.

Page 22: "All the other Christian churches followed the example of that of Jerusalem, in whatever related to the choice and office of the deacons. . . . . The church of Jerusalem, grown considerably numerous, and deprived of the ministry of the apostles, who were gone to instruct the other nations, was the first which chose a president or bishop. . . . The other churches followed by degrees such a respectable example. Let none, however, confound the bishops of this primitive and golden period of the church with those of whom we read in the following ages; for though they were both distinguished by the same name, yet they differed in many respects. A bishop during the first and second centuries was a person who had the care of one Christian assembly, which, at that time, was generally speaking, small enough to be contained in a private house. In this assembly he acted, not so much with the authority of a master as with the zeal and diligence of a faithful servant. . . .
The churches, in those early times, were entirely independent, none of them being subject to any foreign jurisdiction, but each governed by its own

rules and its own laws; for though the churches founded by the apostles had this particular deference shown to them, that they were consulted in difficult and doubtful cases, yet they had no judicial authority, no sort of supremacy over the others, nor the least right to enact laws for them. Nothing, on the contrary, is more evident than the perfect equality that reigned among the primitive churches; nor does there even appear, in this first century, the smallest trace of that association of provincial churches, from which councils and metropolitans derive their origin."

Say, reader, is this the history of Baptists or Catholics? Of course, Protestants were not born till fifteen hundred years later. But Christ built a pattern church that was to be *multiplied* and *perpetuated*. Have Baptists or Catholics the right of way in the first century, say, reader?

Page 25: "Then baptism was administered to *none* but such as had been previously instructed in the principal points of Christianity, and had also given satisfactory proofs of pious dispositions and upright intentions." In the preceding sentence, Dr. Mosheim says this custom was afterward "changed for the wisest, most solid reasons." In heart, he seemed always to be on the Catholic side. Note the next pointer.

Page 26: "One of the circumstances which contributed chiefly to preserve, at least, an external appearance of sanctity in the Christian church, was the right of excluding from it and from all participation of the sacred rites and ordinances of the gospel, such as had been guilty of enormous transgressions, and to whom repeated exhortations to repentance and amendment had been administered in vain. This right was vested in the church from the earliest period of its existence by the apostles themselves, and was exercised by each Christian assembly upon its respective members." Do Baptists or Catholics follow this custom to-day? Is he describing the Catholic church of to-day or a Baptist church of to-day? The question answers itself to every man's conscience. Now on the same page, concerning rites and ceremonies:

"The rites instituted by Christ himself were only two in number, and these were intended to continue to the end of the church here below, without any variation. These rites were baptism and the Lord's Supper, which are not to be considered as mere ceremonies, nor yet as symbolic representations only, but also as ordinances accompanied with a sanctifying influence upon the heart and the affections of true Christians." Yes, of "true Christians," and not of sinners to make them Christians. Read that paragraph over again and ask yourself: Were these Baptists or Catholics? There is but one answer. Does the following quotation favor the Baptists or Catholics?

Page 28: "The holy supper was distributed by the deacons. . . . The sacrament of baptism was administered in this century without the public assemblies, in places appointed and prepared for that purpose, and was performed by an immersion of the whole body in the baptismal font." The Mississippi river has a very small beginning, but it grows at length into a mighty stream. The next quotation gives us the beginning of that great stream of the corrupt apostasy which will grow rapidly as we proceed.

Page 28: "The Christian church was scarcely formed, when, in different places, there started up certain pretended reformers, who, not satisfied with the simplicity of that religion which was taught by the apostles, meditated changes of doctrine and worship, and set up a new religion drawn from their own licentious imaginations."

Thus ends the first century. We have forecastings of the Catholic church in the first and last quotations, but we have not a word of its history, for it had no existence in the first century. These writers were in sympathy with the Catholics, and time and again justified changes, and their cruel treatment of the Baptists, generally, as now, called heretics, but neither they or others have been able to write a history of the Catholics in the first century, for the very good reason that there were none. But we will see when they begun and how and for what. "But if a man be ignorant let him be ignorant," for on on this subject it is without the shadow of excuse.

CHAPTER VII—SECOND CENTURY.

According to Mosheim, ecclesiastical history, during the first century, was the history of Baptist churches. No more need be said for that century. Nothing like Catholicism or Protestantism had any show of existence in the first century. Had the Baptists? Say, candid reader. Now for the second century.

Page 41: "The form of ecclesiastical government, whose commencement we have seen in the last century, was brought in this to a greater degree of stability and consistence. One inspector or bishop presided over each Christian assembly, to which office he was elected by the voices of the whole people. . . . During a greater part of this century the Christian churches were independent with respect to each other; nor were they joined by association, confederacy or any other bonds than those of charity. Each Christian assembly was a little state, governed by its own laws, which were either enacted, or, at least, approved by the society. But in process of time all the Christian churches of a province were formed into one large ecclesiastical body, which, like confederate states, assembled at certain times in order to deliberate about the common interest of the whole." Note the words: "In process of time." This did not occur in the first or second centuries, but subsequent to that time. But read further about this future departure from the faith. "To these assemblies, in which the deputies or commissioners of several churches consulted together, the names of synods was appropriated by the Greeks, and that of councils, by the Latins; and the laws that were enacted in these general meetings were called canons, $i.\ e.$, rules." The apostasy looms up on the future horizon. Read on. "These councils, of which we find not the smallest trace before the middle of this century, changed the whole face of the church, and gave it a new form; for by them the ancient privileges of the people were considerably diminished, and the power and authority of the bishops greatly augmented. The humility, indeed, and prudence of these pious prelates prevented their assuming all at once the power with which they were afterward invested. At their first appearance in these general councils, they acknowledged that they were no more than the delegates of their respective churches, and that they acted in the name and by the appointment of their people. But they soon changed this humble tone, imperceptibly extended the limits of their authority, turned their influence into dominion and their counsels into laws; and openly asserted, at length that Christ had empowered them to prescribe to his people authoritative rules of faith and manners. Another effect of these councils was the gradual abolition of that perfect equality which reigned among all bishops in the primitive times." These are forecastings of the coming apostasy. These things did not occur in the second century. See next how baptism was administered in the second century. Sprinkling and pouring not yet invented by the "Man of sin and son of perdition."

Page 49: The persons that were to be baptized, after they had repeated the creed, confessed and renounced their sins, and particularly the devil and his pompous allurements, were immersed under water, and received into Christ's kingdom by a solemn invocation of Father, Son and Holy Ghost, according to the express command of our blessed Lord. . . . Adult persons were prepared for baptism by abstinence, prayer and other pious exercises."

Now the leaven of iniquity begins to work. But the whole was not leavened. God reserved unto himself his elect and chosen witnesses who stood fast and contended earnestly for the faith. Watch that point. That is the point at issue. Did the apostasy swallow up all, or was a remnant there for a final separation and persecution? If so, the true church was separated from by the false. We now enter the THIRD CENTURY.

Page 63: "The face of things began now to change in the Christian church. The ancient method of ecclesiastical government seemed, in general, still to subsist, while at the same time, by imperceptible steps, it varied from the primitive rule, and degenerated toward the form of a religious monarchy; for the bishops aspired to higher degrees of power and authority than they had formerly possessed, and not only violated the rights of the people, but also made gradual encroachments upon the privileges of the presbyters; and that they might cover these usurpations with an air of justice, and an appearance of reason, they published new doctrines concerning the nature of the church and of the Episcopal dignity, which, however, were in general so obscure, that they themselves seemed to have understood them as little as those to whom they were delivered. One of the principal authors of this change, in the government of the church, was Cyprian, who pleaded for the power of the bishops with more zeal and vehemence than had ever been hitherto employed in that cause, though not with an unshaken constancy and perseverance; for in difficult and perilous times, necessity sometimes obliged him to yield, and to submit several things to the judgment and authority of the church. This change, in the form of ecclesiastical government, was soon followed by a train of vices which dishonored the character and authority of those to whom the administration of the church was committed; for, though several yet continued to exhibit to the world illustrious examples of primitive piety and Christian virtue, yet many were sunk in luxury and voluptuousness, puffed up with vanity, arrogance and ambition, possessed with a spirit of contention and discord, and addicted to many other vices that cast an undeserved reproach upon the holy religion, of which they were the unworthy professors and ministers. This is testified in such an ample manner, by the repeated complaints of many of the most respectable of this age, that truth will not permit us to spread the veil, which we should otherwise be desirous to cast over such enormities among an order so sacred. The bishops assumed, in many places, a princely authority, particularly those who had the greatest number of churches under their inspection, and who presided over the most opulent assemblies. They appropriated to their evangelical function the splendid ensigns of temporal majesty; a throne surrounded with ministers, exalted above his equals the servant of the meek and humble Jesus; and sumptuous garments dazzled the eyes and the minds of the multitude into an ignorant veneration for this usurped authority." This love of pre-eminence, rebuked by Christ and Paul and Peter and John, has now grown into overgrown bishops, and this will continue to grow until the papacy is reached, and this will "exalt itself above all that is called God or that is worshipped." Watch the preservation of the church amidst the growing evils. The following is also a Baptist earmark:

Page 68: "The most famous controversies that divided the Christians during this century were, concerning the millennium, or reign of a thousand years; the baptism of heretics, and the doctrine of Origin. Long before this period an opinion had prevailed that Christ was to come and reign a thousand years among men, before the entire and final dissolution of this world. This opinion had hitherto met with no opposition." This is in the middle of the third century. The mystery of iniquity is now working. Will Christ preserve his saints, his truth and his church? He said he would.

CHAPTER VIII—THIRD CENTURY

The true witnesses of Christ began in the third century to separate themselves from the corrupt churches. This good work begun in Rome and spread rapidly everywhere. The corrupt party left in the Church of Rome constituted the seed out of which grew the Roman hierarchy. There were no national bishops yet, and no pope for several hundred years. A metropolitan bishop, lording it over God's heritage, was the embryo pope of this and the next three centuries. But watch the development of the apostasy and the persecution and preservation of the church by flight into the wilderness.

Page 68: "In this century the Asiatic Christians came to a determination in a point that was hitherto, in some measure, undecided; and in more than than one council established it as a law, that all heretics were to be rebaptized before their admission to the communion of the true church. When Stephen, bishop of Rome, was informed of this determination, he behaved with the most unchristian violence and arrogance toward Asiatic Christians, broke communion with them, and excluded them from the communion of the church of Rome." Thus the churches of Asia claimed to be the true churches, and the separation was the occasion of their becoming Anabaptists, and this rebaptism, as it is called, continued to the present day. And now we come to alterations and perversion of ordinances.

Page 70: "Several alterations were now introduced in the celebration of the Lord's Supper by those who had the direction of divine worship. . . . Those who were in a penitential state, and those also who had not received the sacrament of baptism, were not admitted to this holy supper. . . . It was also more frequently repeated in some churches than in others; but was considered in all as one of the highest importance, and as essential to salvation; for which reason it was even thought proper to administer it to infants." Sacraments, as the ordinances were then called, being considered necessary to salvation, and infants needing salvation, therefore infants needed the sacraments. Thus came in also infant baptism, so-called. "There were, twice a year, stated times when baptism was administered to such as, after a long course of trial and preparation, offered themselves as candidates for the profession of Christianity. . . . The remission of sin was thought to be its immediate and happy fruit." Baptism being necessary to salvation, as the apostates thought, was necessary for both infants and adults, and hence it was necessary to the remission of sins. This is the first time in history this doctrine is found, and it was the foundation of the "apostasy," "the Man of Sin and Son of Perdition."

Page 74: "Among the sects that arose in this century, we place that of the Novatians. . . . Novatian separated himself from the jurisdiction of Cornelius, who, in turn, called a council at Rome, in the year 251, and cut off Novation and his partisans from the communion of the church." From now on it is the custom of Catholics and Protestant historians to call the true witnesses after the name of some leader or learned one who championed the cause of truth against the apostasy now called Catholics. When this new name is applied to the "sect everywhere spoken against," it is said to "originate," but it was only the new name that originated. When this matter is studied in the light of many witnesses, it is clear enough, but for the present we are confined to one witness, Dr. Mosheim. Read what he says:

Page 74: "There was no difference, in point of doctrine, between the Novatians and other Christians. What peculiarly distinguished them was their refusing to re-admit to the communion of the church those who, after baptism, had fallen into the commission of heinous crimes, though they did not pretend that even such were excluded from all possibility or hopes of salvation. They considered the Christian church as a society where virtue and innocence reigned universally, and none of whose members, from their entrance into it, had defiled themselves with any enormous crime, and, in consequence, they looked upon every society which re-admitted heinous offenders to its communion as unworthy of the title of a true Christian church. For that reason they assumed the title of Cathari, *i. e.*, pure; and what showed a still more extravagant degree of vanity and arrogance, they obliged such as came over to them from the general body of Christians, to submit to be baptized a second time, as a necessary preparation for entering into their society. . . . They considered the baptism administered in those churches, which received the lapsed into their communion, as absolutely divested of the power of imparting the remission of sins."

I have investigated this matter in the

light of eight or ten other historians, such as Neander, Waddington, Butler, Ruter, Geissler, Robinson, Summerbell, etc., and nearly as many Baptist writers on the subject, and I see clearly that the combined testimony of those non-Baptist writers justifies the following conclusions: Novatian was a member of the Church of Rome, planted by Paul, but now so corrupt, that a separation is necessary to preserve the faith. The church, like most metropolitan churches in all ages, got rich and greedy of filthy lucre, opened wide its doors for the admission of members of most any sort, especially the rich; and, as they did not like to lose any, they invented the doctrine of church salvation, *i. e.*, without baptism no remission of past sins, and without church membership no future salvation; so that if public or private sentiment compelled them to exclude, they easily and quickly restored them again. But Novatian, with the true and faithful in the church, was in favor of keeping the church pure by strict discipline, and such as were guilty of enormous crimes, and especially those who, in the face of persecution (from the emperors of Rome, for there was yet no pope) such as denied their Lord and embraced heathenism to save their lives, that all such fell either under Heb. 6:6 or 1 John 2:19, and should be promptly and forever excluded from the church. He contended that this would not debar them from salvation, which was of the Lord, by grace through faith. This doctrine had been taught and held in that church from the beginning, but the corruption had crept in, and the corrupters were in power, and the Novation party, as it was called, whether in majority or minority, when they separated themselves, they constituted the true church of God at Rome. "They came out from among them" at the voice of God. So a council of over forty decided in a similar case in Texas. Novatian became the pastor of the separated church, and his example inspired the pure and faithful far and wide, who also separated themselves from their corrupt churches, following this worthy example in Rome. As Butler says, page 167: "The Novatians considered themselves as the only pure communion, and unchurched all churches which defiled themselves by re-admitting the lapsed or other gross offenders. They rejected heretical baptism and rebaptized all who joined their communion. While they admitted the possibility of mercy to a mortal sinner, they denied the right of the church to absolve him. . . . Both parties quoted the recognition of the church abroad. . . . But this Novatian sect propagated itself in the West and East down to the fifteenth century." Robinson says, Researches, page 126: "A tide of immorality pouring into the church, Novatian withdrew, and a great many with him. . . . Great numbers followed his example, and all over the empire Puritan churches were constituted and flourished through the succeeding two hundred years. Afterwards, when penal laws obliged them to lurk in corners, and worship God in private, they were distinguished by a variety of names, and a succession of them continued till the Reformation." (And we may add till now.) This is what some in these "last days" laugh at. They make sport of those who believe and say they can prove that there has been a continuity of Baptist principles, Baptist people, and Baptist churches.

But, you may ask, what of Novatian's circumfusion? I answer nothing, even if it be true, and of which there are doubts. Who knows but he was properly baptized after his restoration to health, for public sentiment at that time required it. We don't know even how he died, whether a martyr or not. Granting all, his was an isolated case. He neither began or propagated a sect. Others followed his example in separating from the corrupt churches, and thus followed the divine command, and thus their walk was orderly. The disorderly constituted the apostasy.

But there were true churches in all countries that came down from Jerusalem, and other churches that were never connected with Rome. Many of these fellowshipped this Novatian church, and others divided over it. All true churches did not all come down from Rome. Some descended from the churches of Judea, Asia, Greece, etc.

I trust my readers are not weary with these historical verifications of the promises of Christ. Recent utterances, disdaining historical testimony, and "appealing alone to the Scriptures," were made by those whom, it is feared, have abandoned the doctrine of church perpetuity. Let us search both Scripture and History.

Page 86: "The people continued, as usual, to choose freely their bishops and their teachers. The bishops governed the church and managed the ecclesiastical affairs of the city or district, where he presided in council with the presbyters, not without a due regard to the suffrages of the whole assembly of the people. . . . Even the bishops themselves, whose opulence and authority were considerably increased since the reign of Constantine, began to introduce innovations into the forms of ecclesiastical discipline, and to change the ancient government of the church. Their first step was an entire exclusion of the people from all parts in the administration of ecclesiastical affairs."

Congregationalism, or "suffrages of the whole assembly," was the original model of church government. But it gradually degenerated into presbytery, episcopacy, and finally papacy. Those who contended earnestly for the original pattern were called in some countries Novatians, and in others Donatists. These men did not originate sects, but separated from the growing apostasy and perpetuated the true churches.

Page 100: "The Donatists brought this controversy before Constantine, the prince, in the year 313, commissioned Melchiades, bishop of Rome, to examine the matter, and named three bishops of Gaul to assist him in this inquiry. . . . Here again the Donatists lost their cause, but renewed their efforts by appealing to the immediate judgment of the emperor, who condescended so far as to admit their appeal; and, in consequence thereof, examined the whole affair himself in the year 316, at Milan, in presence of the contending parties. The issue of this third trial was not more favorable to the Donatists than that of the two preceding councils, whose decisions the emperor confirmed by the sentence he pronounced. Hence, this perverse sect loaded Constantine with the bitterest reproaches."

Marginal note. — "Certain it is that, at this time, the notion of a supreme judge set over the church universal, by the appointment of Christ, never had entered into any one's head." As the world hated and persecuted Christ, so it hated and persecuted his true followers. The true witnesses must be driven into the wilderness, and we see the driving has commenced. "The emperor, animated with a just indignation at such odious proceedings, deprived the Donatists of their churches in Africa, and sent into banishment their seditious bishops; and he carried his resentment so far as to put some of them to death, probably on account of their intolerable petulance and malignity they discovered both in their writing and in their discourses. Hence, arose violent commotions and tumults in Africa, as the Donatists were exceedingly powerful and numerous in that part of the empire."

Notice the language of these historians. It betrays as much malignity and intolerance as the persecutors themselves had. It shows the spirit of Protestantism at the time this history was written.

Page 101: "After the death of Constantine the Great, his son Constans, to whom Africa was allotted in the division of the empire, sent Macarius and Paulus into the province, with a view to heal this deplorable schism, and to engage the Donatists to conclude a peace. . . . Macarius no longer used the soft voice of persuasion to engage them to an accommodation, but employed his authority for that purpose. A few submitted; the greatest part saved themselves by flight; numbers were sent into banishment, among whom was Donatus the Great; and many of them were punished with the utmost severity. During these troubles, which continued nearly thirteen years, several steps were taken against the Donatists which the equitable and impartial will be at a loss to reconcile with the dictates of humanity and justice; nor, indeed, do the Catholics themselves deny the truth of this assertion. Such treatment naturally excited, among the Donatists, loud complaints of the cruelty of their adversaries."

These Protestant historians call one party Catholics, and the others they call by various titles, but generally styled heretics and schismatics. But the heretics and schismatics were all on the other side.

Page 101: "The doctrine of the Donatists was conformable to that of the church, as even their adversaries confess; nor were their lives less exemplary than those of other Christian societies. . . . The crime, therefore, of the Donatists lay properly in the following points: in their declaring the church of Africa, which adhered to Cæcilianus, fallen from the dignity and privileges of a true church and deprived of the gifts of the Holy Ghost, on account of the offenses with which the new bishop, Felix, who had consecrated him, were charged; in their pronouncing all the churches, which held communion with that of Africa, corrupt and polluted; in maintaining that the sanctity of their bishops gave their community alone a full right to be considered as the true, the pure and holy church; and in their avoiding all communication with other churches from an apprehension of contracting their impurity and corruption. This erroneous principle was the source of that most shocking uncharitableness and presumption which appeared in their conduct to other churches. Hence, they pronounced the sacred rites and institutions void of all virtue and efficacy among those Christians who were not precisely of their sentiments, and not only rebaptized those who came over to their party from the other churches, but even with respect to those who had been ordained ministers of the gospel, they observed the severe custom either of depriving them of their office, or oblige them to be ordained the second time."

Thus closes the fourth century. Now, reader, do you not recognize two parties, one departing from the faith and from the spirit of Christianity, corrupting the doctrine and persecuting the saints? Well, in this don't you see the historical verification of the prophets? Did not the obedient comply with the Scripture to "mark those which cause divisions and offenses contrary to the doctrine they received, and avoid them." (Rom. 16:17.) And also this: "Wherefore come out from among them and be ye separate, saith the Lord, and touch not the unclean, and I will receive you and will be a father unto you, and ye shall be my sons and daughters, saith the Lord almighty."—2 Cor. 6:17, 18. Also 2 Thes. 2:15 and 3:6, etc. But you see another thing, dear reader, that I want you to note. After separating themselves, they claimed to be the only true churches of Jesus Christ, and refused to recognize the other so-called church or churches, and also refused to receive their administration of ordinances and ordinations. This the few and faithful continued to do from the first separation to the present. I fear it is this characteristic of the true apostolical and historical church that is driving our anti-landmark brethren to the invention of a modernly organized church, suitable to modern liberalistic views. But I am for the scriptural and historical church, even if it is landmark, so-called.

CHAPTER X.

FIFTH, SIXTH AND SEVENTH CENTURIES.

We now enter the fifth century. The apostasy makes further changes, and the bishops grasp at augmented power.

Page 118: "Several causes contributed to bring about a change in the external form of ecclesiastical government. The power of the bishops, particularly those of the first order, was sometimes augmented and sometimes diminished, according as the times and occasions offered. . . ." In the following we see the two eggs out of which hatched the Roman and Greek hierarchies, though the first was about two hundred and the other about six hundred years hatching.

"In this century, they grasped at still further accessions of power; so that not only the whole eastern part of Illyricum was added to their former acquisitions, but they were also exalted to the highest summit of ecclesiastical authority; for, by the 28th canon of the council holden at Chalcedon in 451, it was resolved that the same rights and honors which had been conferred upon the bishops of Rome, were due to the bishop of Constantinople, on account of the equal dignity and lustre of the two cities, in which these prelates exercised their authority. The same council confirmed also, by a solemn act, the bishop of Constantinople in the spiritual government of those provinces over which he had ambitiously usurped the jurisdiction." But while the apostasy was still apostatizing, by continued changes for the worse, both in doctrine and in morals, where was the true church? Had God left himself without witnesses in the growing corruptions? No one to reprove and rebuke, and to contend for the faith. Read and see.

Page 122: "We shall confine ourselves to an account of the Donatists and Arians, who were the pest of the preceding century. The Donatists had hitherto maintained themselves with a successful obstinacy, and their affairs were in a good state. But, about the beginning of this century, the face of things changed, much to their disadvantage, by the means of St. Augustine, bishop of Hippo. The Catholic bishops of Africa, animated by the exhortations, and conducted by the cousels of this zealous prelate, exerted themselves with the utmost vigor in the destruction of those seditious sectaries, whom they justly looked upon, not only as troublesome to the church by their obstinacy, but also as a nuisance to the state. . . . " These Protestant historians call the true witnesses "pests," "seditious sectaries," "trouble to the church," and a "nuisance to the state," and they pronounced their punishment just. So we see which side they were on. "The Donatists denied that they belonged to the heretical tribe. . . . The first step that the emperor took was to impose a fine upon all the Donatists who refused to return into the bosom of the church and to send their bishops and doctors into banishment. . . . " What a travesty to call these murderers and robbers the church of Jesus Christ and the followers of the meek and lowly Jesus. It is the church being persecuted and soon to be driven into the wilderness, instead of into the bosom of iniquity. "The Donatists faction, though much broken by these repeated shocks, was yet far from being totally extinguished. . . . " That is right. "Far from being totally extinguished." The fact is, the gates of hades shall not prevail against it. "Marcellinus held, at Carthage, in 411, a solemn conference, in which he examined the cause with much attention, heard the contending parties during three days, and then pronounced sentence in favor of the Catholics."

Here is a significant marginal note for the fifth century, showing there was no pope up to that time. "It appears, therefore, from this event, that the notion of a supreme spiritual judge of controversy and ruler of the church, appointed by Christ, had not yet entered into any one's head, since we see the African bishops appealing to the emperor in the present religious question." Preachers on both sides were still called bishops.

Page 122: "The Catholic bishops who were present at this conference, were 286 in number, and those of the Donatists 279. The latter, upon their defeat, appealed to the emperor, but without effect. The glory of their defeat was due to Augustine, who bore the principal part in this controversy, and who, indeed, by his writings, counsels and admonitions, governed almost the whole African church, and also the principal and most illustrious heads of that extensive province. This conference greatly weakened the party of the Donatists; nor could they ever get the better of this terrible shock, though the face of affairs changed afterward in a manner that seemed to revive their hopes. . . . " Our historians called that a glorious defeat. They justified the cruel proceedings, and doing so, they took upon themselves the guilt of those robbers and murderers of the true church of Christ. They made themselves partakers of those wicked men's sins. "Fines, banishment, confiscation of goods, were the ordinary punishments of the obstinate Donatists; and even the pain of death was inflicted upon such as surpassed the rest in perverseness, and were the seditious ring-leaders of that stubborn faction. Some avoided these penalties by flight, others by concealing themselves, and some were so desperate as to seek deliverance by self-murder, to which the Donatists had a shocking propensity."

Page 143. Sixth century. " The Donatists enjoyed the sweets of freedom and tranquility as long as the vandals reigned in Africa; but the scene was greatly changed, with respect to them, when the empire of these barbarians was overturned in 534. They, however, still remained in a separate body, and not only held their church, but toward the conclusion of this century, and particularly from the year 591, defended themselves with new degrees of animosity and vigor, and were bold enough to attempt the multiplication of their sect. Gregory, the Roman pontiff, opposed these efforts with great spirit and assiduity; and, as appears from his epistles, tried various methods of depressing this faction, which was pluming its wings anew and aiming at the revival of those lamentable divisions which it had formerly excited in the church."

Tho persecuted they were not forsaken, for he had said: "All power in heaven and earth is given unto me, and lo, I am with you alway, even to the end of the age."

Now, notice the beginning of the papacy, with the true witnesses already in the valleys of Piedmont.

Page 151. Seventh century. "The disputes about pre-eminence that had so long subsisted between the bishops of Rome and Constantinople, proceeded, in this century, to such violent lengths, as laid the foundation of that deplorable schism, which afterwards separated the Greek and Latin churches. The most learned writers, and those who are most remarkable for their knowledge of antiquity, are generally agreed that Boniface III engaged Phocas, that abominable tyrant, who waded to the imperial throne through the blood of the emperor Mauritius, to take from the bishop of Constantinople the title of ecumenical or universal bishop, and to confer it upon the Roman pontiff. . . . For, when the bishop of Constantinople maintained that their church was not only equal in dignity and authority to that of Rome, but also the head of all the Christian churches, this tyrant opposed their pretensions and granted the pre-eminence to the church of Rome; and thus was the papal supremacy first introduced. The Roman pontiff used all sorts of methods to maintain and enlarge the authority and pre-eminence which they had acquired by a grant from the most odious tyrant that ever disgraced the annals of history. We find, however, in the most authentic account of the transactions of this century, that not only several emperors and princes, but also whole nations opposed the ambitious views of the bishops of Rome." . . . "Multitudes of private persons expressed publicly and without the least hesitation, their abhorrence of the vices and particularly of the lordly ambition of the Roman pontiffs; and it is highly probable that the Valdenses or Vandois had already, in this century, retired into the valleys of Piedmont, that they might be more at liberty to oppose the tyranny of those imperious prelates."

Notice the words: "And thus was the papal supremacy first introduced."

CHAPTER XI.

THE MEETING POINT.

There was no papal supremacy before the seventh century. There were metropolitan bishops clamoring for supremacy, of which we have given sufficient account. Before the wicked, imperial Phocas decided in favor of Rome, the Waldenses had taken the wings of eagles and fled to the valleys of Piedmont, that they might better "oppose the tyranny of these imperial prelates." The Waldenses of the twelfth century were accorded an existence "many ages before Peter Waldus," even making "their antiquity remount to the apostolic age." The Catharists of the twelfth century were mentioned also in the third century. So the Novatians of the third century were said to have continued till the Reformation, and even to the seventeenth century. And so of others. Thus the gulf is spanned, and there is an account of an anti-Catholic, and that means Baptist people, from the origin of Catholicism till now. The same people were also called Paulicians. Dr. Mosheim gives their history in the seventh century, in the ninth, and also in the eleventh centuries. And thus the bridge is crossed again. Read the following account of them in the ninth century, and see how bitterly they were persecuted.

Page 202. Ninth century. "The Greeks, during the greatest part of this century, were engaged in a most bitter controversy, or, to speak more properly, in a bloody and barbarous war with the Paulicians, a sect that may be considered as a branch of the Manichæans, and which resided principally in Armenia. . . . A certain zealot, called Constantine, revived, in the seventh century, under the government of Constans, this drooping faction, which had suffered deeply from the violence of its adversaries, and was ready to expire under the severity of the imperial edicts and of those penal laws which were executed against its adherents with the utmost rigor. Constans, Justinian II and Leo the Isansian, exerted their zeal against the Paulicians with a peculiar degree of bitterness and fury, left no method of oppression unemployed, and neglected no means of accomplishing their ruin; but their efforts were ineffectual, nor could all their power, or all their barbarity, exhaust the patience or conquer the obstinacy of that inflexible people who, with a fortitude worthy of a better cause, seemed to despise the calamities to which their erroneous doctrine exposed them. The face of things changed, however, to their advantage toward the commencement of this century, and their affairs wore a more prosperous aspect under the protection of the emperor Nicephorus, who favored them in a particular manner, and restored to them their civil privileges as well as their religious liberty. Their tranquility, however, was but of short duration; it was a transient scene that was soon to be succeeded by yet more dreadful sufferings than they had hitherto experienced. The cruel rage of persecution which had for some years been suspended, broke forth with redoubled violence under the reigns of Michael Curopalates and Leo the Armenian, who caused the strictest search to be made after the Paulicians, in all the provinces of the Grecian empire, and inflicted capital punishment upon such of them as refused to return to the bosom of the church. . . . But the most dreadful scene of persecution that was exhibited against these wretched heretics, arose from the furious and inconsiderate zeal of the empress Theodora. This impetuous woman, who was regent of the empire during the minority of her son, issued out a decree, which placed the Paulicians in the perplexing alternative either of abandoning their principles or of perishing by fire and sword. The decree was severe; but the cruelty with which it was put in execution by those who were sent into Armenia for that purpose, was horrible beyond expression; for these ministers of wrath, after confiscating the goods of above a hundred thousand of that miserable people, put their possessors to death in the most barbarous manner, and made them expire slowly in a variety of the most exquisite tortures. Such as escaped destruction fled for protection and refuge to the Saracens, who received them with compassion and humanity, and permitted them to build a city for their residence, which was called Tibrica. . . . Some Paulicians, toward the conclusion of the century, spread abroad among the Bulgarians their pestilential doctrines, which were received with docility, and took root speedily, as might naturally be expected among a barbarous people recently converted to the Christian faith. . . . They had not, like the Manichæaens, an ecclesiastical government, administered by bishops, priests and deacons; they had no sacred order of men distinguished by their manner of life, their habit, or any other circumstance, from the rest of the assembly; nor had councils, synods, or the like institutions any place in their religious polity. They had certain doctors whom they called Syneedemi, i. e., companions in the journey of life, and also Noratii. Among these there reigned a perfect equality; and they had no peculiar rights or privileges nor any external mark of dignity to distinguish them from the people. . . . They, moreover, recommended to the people, without exception, with the most affecting and ardent zeal, the constant and assiduous perusal of the Scriptures, and expressed the utmost indignation against the Greeks, who allowed the priest alone an access to these sacred fountains of divine knowledge. . . . The Greek writers, instead of giving a complete view of the Paulician system, which was undoubtedly composed of a great variety of tenets, content themselves with mentioning six monstrous errors, which, in their estimation, rendered the Paulicians unworthy of enjoying either the comforts of this world or the happiness of the next. These errors are as follows: . . . They treated contemptuously the Virgin Mary; that is to say, according to the manner of speaking usual among the Greeks, they refused to adore and worship her."

But here is where we began. This is a part of the first quotation we made. We have traced a people from the apostles to the present. Let us close with this very appropriate note:

Marginal note. Page 203: " It is not improbable that there are yet, in Thrace and Bulgaria, Paulicians, or Paulicans as they are called by some. It appears at least certain that in the seventeenth century some of that sect still subsisted. . . . The Paulicians seemed to have . . . been very numerous and diversified; and though persecuted and oppressed from age to age in the most rigorous manner by many emperors, they could never be entirely suppressed or extirpated." In other words: "The gates of hell shall not prevail against it." I am jealous for the veracity of Christ. If he did not fulfill his promise, it was either because he could not or would not, and in either case he will not do to trust. If he failed to keep his church, who knows but that he will fail to keep his people. If the enemy prevailed, then he forsook his bride in her greatest faithfulness and distress. He said he had all power, and that he would be with her in all the days even to the end of the age. He came to betroth a bride, and went away to abide the time for marriage. When he comes, will he marry another? Has the bridegroom at any time been without a bride? Has the head at any time been without a body? Did the body of Christ die? Did it die with the Novatians? Paulicians? Waldenses? When? Where? How? Skulk, ye dumb traducers of our Lord.

Waddington's Church History Epitomized.

[Waddington was an Episcopalian—Fellow of Trinity College, Cambridge. The agreement of so many unfriendly witnesses is an eye-opener, and ought to be a mouth-stopper. I must submit "two or three witnesses" on the Historical and several on the Conclusive.]

Page 43: "Of most of the apostolical churches, the first bishops were appointed by the apostles; of those not apostolical, the first presidents were probably the missionaries who founded them; but, on their death, the choice of a successor devolved on the members of the society. In this selection, the people had an equal share with the presbyters and inferior clergy, without exception or distinction; and it is clear that their right in this matter was not barely testimonial, but judicial and elective. In the management of its internal affairs, every church was essentially independent of every other.

"The churches, thus constituted and regulated, formed a sort of federative body of independent religious communities, dispersed through the greater part of the empire, in continual communication, and in constant harmony with each other. It is towards the middle of the second century that the first change is perhaps perceptible; as the numbers of the believers and the limits of the faith were extended, some diversities in doctrine or discipline would naturally grow up, which it was not found easy to reconcile except by some description of general assembly. (WERE THESE BAPTISTS OR CATHOLICS?)

Margin.—"This is made very clear, from the comparison of much contradictory evidence, by Bingham, Ch. Hist., b. iv. ch. 2, 3, 4, etc.

"'There is a great concurrence of evidence to show that no bishop was ever obtruded on an orthodox people without their consent. Mosheim (c. i. p. ii. ch. 2) attributes a great extent of general power to the people, not only in the election of their teachers, but in control of their conduct, and even extends it to decisions on controverted points and excommunication of unworthy members.''

Page 44: We believe the view of Mosheim, upon this subject, to be very nearly correct. C. 1. p. i. ch. 2." (BAPTISTS OR CATHOLICS?)

Page 46: "The sacraments of the primitive church were two—those of Baptism and the Lord's Supper. The ceremony of immersion (the name of the oldest form of baptism) was performed in the name of the three Persons of the Trinity. . . . Since the Church was then scrupulous to admit none among its members excepting those whose sincere repentance gave promise of a holy life to the administration of that sacrament, was in some sense accompanied by the remission, not only of the sin from Adam, but of all sin that had been previously committed by the proselyte—that is to say, such absolution was given to the repentance necessary for admission into Christ's Church. In after ages, by an error common in the growth of superstition, the efficacy inherent in the repentance was attributed to the ceremony. . . . But this double delusion gained very little ground during the two first centuries."

Page 53: "The original simplicity of the office of baptism had already undergone some corruption. The symbol had been gradually exalted at the expense of the thing signified, and the spirit of the ceremony was beginning to be lost in its form. Hence, a belief was gaining ground among the converts, and was inculcated among the heathen, that the act of baptism gave remission of all sins committed previously to it."

Page 54: "About the same time, and from causes connected with this misapprehension of the real nature of baptism, and the division of the converts, a vague and mysterious veneration began to attach itself to the other Sacrament; its nature and merits were exaggerated by those who administered and partook of it; it was regarded with superstition by those to whom it was refused; and reports were already propagated of the miraculous efficacy of the consecrated elements."

This was in the third century, when the ordinances begun to be turned into sacraments of salvation.

Page 79: *Novatians.*—"We may conclude with some notice of the sect of the Novatians, who were stigmatized at the time, both as schismatics and heretics."

Margin.— . . . "As to the latter charge, even their adversaries do not advance any point of doctrine on which they deviated from the Church."

"They arose at Rome about the year A.D. 250, and subsisted unti the fifth century throughout every part of Christendom.

"He considered the Christian Church as a society, where virtue and innocence reigned universally, and refused any longer to acknowledge, as members of it, those who had once degenerated into unrighteousness. This endeavor to revive the spotless moral purity of the primitive faith was found inconsistent with the corruptions even of that early age, and was regarded with suspicion by the leading prelates as a vain and visionary scheme; and those rigid principles, which had characterized and sanctified the church in the first century, were abandoned to the profession of schismatic sectaries in the third.

"From a review of what has been written on this subject, some truths may be derived of considerable historical importance; the following are among them: 1. In the midst of perpetual dissent and occasional controversy, a steady and distinguishable line, both in doctrine and practice, was maintained by the early Church, and its efforts against those whom it called Heretics, were zealous and persevering, and, for the most part, consistent. Its contests were fought with the 'sword of the Spirit,' with the arms of reason and eloquence; and, as they were always unattended by personal oppression, so were they most effectually successful—successful, not in establishing a nominal unity, nor silencing the expression of private opinion, but in maintaining the purity of the faith, in preserving the attachment of the great majority of the believers, and in consigning, either to immediate disrepute, or early neglect, all the unscriptural doctrines which were successively arrayed against it."

Margin.— . . . "His followers called themselves Cathari—Puritans."

Margin.— . . . "It should be mentioned that Cornelius, bishop of Rome, the principal opponent of Novatian, had motives for personal enmity against that "Ecclesiastic."

Page 85: *Constitution of the Church.*—We have already described the free and independent constitution of the primitive Church; the bishops and teachers were chosen by the clergy and people; the bishop managed the ecclesiastical affairs of his diocese, in council with the Presbyters, and 'with a due regard to the suffrages of the whole assembly of the people."

Page 86: "Constantine found the Church an independent body, a kind of self-constituted commonwealth, which might sometimes be at peace, and sometimes at variance with the civil government, but which was never acknowledged as any part of the whole body politic; it had a separate administration, separate laws, and frequently (through the perversity of its persecutors) separate interests also. The Christian, as a citizen of the empire, was subject, of course, to the universal statutes of the empire—as a member of the Church, he owed a distinct allegiance to the spiritual directors of the Church."

Page 153: "*Conference held at Carthage in* 411.—The tribune Marcellinus was sent into Africa by the Emperor Honorius, with full power to terminate the controversy; he convoked an assembly of the heads of both parties, and two hundred and eighty-six Catholic, and about two hundred and seventy-nine Donatist bishops, presented themselves in defense of their respective opinions. The most solemn preparations were made to give weight and dignity to this meeting, and its deliberations were watched with profound anxiety by the people of Africa. For three days the Tribune listened with respectful attention to the arguments advanced by both parties, and then proceeded to confirm the decisions of the former century, by pronouncing in favor of the Catholics. Augustin has deserved the glory of this spiritual triumph—and, that no means might be wanting to make it decisive, it was vigorously pursued by the myrmidons of civil authority, who inflicted almost every punishment on the contumacious, excepting the last."

You see, Waddington was in sympathy with

the Catholics in their first persecution. This was 300 years before there was any pope or hierarchy.

"The survivors took breath under the government of the Vandals, who conquered that part of Africa from the Romans about the year 427; and when it was recovered by Belisarius, more than a hundred years afterwards, the sect of the Donatists was still found to exist there as a separate communion. It was again exposed to the jealousy of the Catholics, and particularly attracted the hostility of Gregory the Great; but we do not learn that it suffered further persecution. We are told it dwindled into insignificance about the end of the sixth century; but it is not improbable that the Saracen invaders of Numidia found them, some years later, the remnant of a sect not ill-disposed to favor any invader, nor unmindful of the sufferings of their ancestors.

"The Donatists have never been charged, with the slightest show of truth, with any error of doctrine, or any defect in Church government or discipline, or any depravity of moral practice; they agreed in every respect with their adversaries, except in one—they did not acknowledge as legitimate the ministry of the African Church, but considered their own body to be the true, uncorrupted, universal Church. It is quite clear that they pushed their schisms to very great extremities—even to that of rejecting the communion of all who were in communion with the Church which they called false; but this was the extent of their spiritual offense, even from the assertion of their enemies."

We now make a long skip, as the historian is taken up with the Roman and Greek schism. But we strike our line further on.

THE PETROBRUSSIANS.

Page 287: "About the year 1110, a preacher, named Pierre de Bruys, began to declaim against the corruption of the Church, and the vices of its ministers. The principal field of his exertions was the south of France, Provence and Languedoc, and he continued, for about twenty years, to disseminate his opinions with success, and, what may seem more strange, with impunity. Those opinions may probably have contained much that was erroneous; but they are known to us only through the representations of his adversaries. In a Letter or Treatise, composed against his followers, thence called Petrobrussians, they are charged with a variety of offences, which the writer reduces under five heads—(1) The rejection of infant baptism. (2) The contempt of churches and altars, as unnecessary for the service of a spiritual and omnipresent Being. (3) The destruction of crucifixes, on the same principle as instruments of superstition. (4) The disparagement of the holy sacrifice of the Eucharist, in asserting that the body and blood were not really consecrated by the priests. (5) Disbelief in the efficacy of the oblations, prayers and good works of the living for the salvation of the dead. These errors, howsoever various in magnitude, are controverted with equal warmth by Peter the Abbot; but that which appears to have been most dangerous to the heretic, was the third; at least we learn, that in the year 1130, the Catholic inhabitants of St. Giles, in Languedoc, were roused by their priests to holy indignation against that sacrilege; and consigned the offender to those flames which his own hand had so frequently fed with the images of Christ.

"THE HENRICIANS. One of these, named Henry, an Italian by birth, obtained a place in the contemporary records, and gave an appellation to a sect, from him called Henricians. This enthusiast traversed the south of France, from Lausanne to Bourdeaux, preceded by two disciples, who carried, like himself, long staffs, surmounted with crosses, and were habited as Penitents. His stature was lofty, his eyes rolling and restless; his powerful voice, his rapid and uneasy gait, his naked feet and neglected apparel, attracted an attention, which was fixed by the fame of his learning and his sanctity. These qualities gave additional force to his eloquence; and as it was not uncommonly directed against the unpopular vices of the clergy, he gained many proselytes, and excited some commotions. Eugenius III. sent forth, for the suppression of this evil, a legate named Alberic; but it appears that his mission would have been attended with but little success, had he not prevailed on St. Bernard to share with him the labor and the glory of the enterprise. Henry was then in the domain of Alfonso, Count of St. Giles and Toulouse; and St. Bernard wrote to prepare that prince for his arrival and to signify his motives."

Margin.— . . . "Finding that they made no impression, they desired that a day might be appointed for them, on which they might bring their teachers to a conference, promising to return to the Church provided they found their masters unable to answer the arguments of their opponents; but that, otherwise, they would rather die than depart from their judgment. Upon this declaration, having been admonished to repent for three days, they were seized by the people in the excess of zeal, and burnt to death. And what is amazing, they came to the stake, and bore the pain, not only with patience, but even with joy."

Page 288: "The opposition of these heretics seems to have been more particularly directed against the wealth and temporal power of the Catholic clergy—but at the same time they rejected infant baptism, the intercession of saints, purgatory—and professed, in fact, to receive only those truths which were positively delivered by Christ or his apostles.

"HERESY of the CATHARI and PAULICIANS. Another religious faction had at that time considerable prevalence, which, under the various names of Cathari (or Catharists—Puritans), Gazari, Paterini, Paulicians, Bulgari or Bugari, . . . was more particularly charged with Manichæan opinions. The origin of these heretics has been the subject of much controversy; for, while some suppose their errors to have been indigenous in Europe, there are others who derive them in a direct line from the heart of Asia. It is certain that a very powerful sect named Paulicians, and tainted, though they might affect to disclaim it, with the absurdities of Manes, spread very widely throughout the Greek provinces of Asia during the eighth century. It is equally true, that after merciless persecution of about 150 years, their remnant still numerous, was permitted to settle in Bulgaria and Thrace. Thence, as is believed by Muratoni, Mosheim and Gibbon, they gradually migrated towards the West. . . . So early as the middle of the eleventh century many of their colonies were established in Italy, Sicily, Lombardy, Insubria, and principally at Milan; others in France, Germany and other countries; and they everywhere attracted attention by their pious looks and austere demeanor, the admiration and respect of the multitude. We are far removed from an opinion that would refer the origin of all the earliest Western sects to the emigrants from the East—that would consider, not only the Cathari, but the Petrobrussians,

Henricians, and even the Vaudois themselves, as descendants from the family of Manes—it is equally unreasonable to contend that this wild opinion had no existence in the West of Europe; or even to dispute their perpetuation through parties of Paulicians, who, from time to time, may have migrated into Sicily or Italy. It is, indeed, unquestionable that such was the case; and it is not impossible that they may have formed, even after their dispersion throughout Europe, a distinct and characteristic sect. But it would be absurd to ascribe to their influence the formation of sects, of which the leading principles were wholly distinct, if not entirely at variance with those of the Asiatics."

Page 289: THE VAUDOIS. We must again consider the Vaudois, or Waldenses, as a separate race among these latter—that we may not fall into the error of Mosheim, who ascribes the origin of that sect to an individual named Waldus. (Imagine the following quotations in large caps.)

Page 290: "There are some who believe the Vaudois to have enjoyed the uninterrupted integrity of the faith even from the apostolic ages; at least, it may be pronounced with great certainty, that they had been long in existence before the visit of the Lyonnese reformer. A Dominican, named Rainer Saccho, who was first a member and afterwards a persecutor of their communion, described them, in a treatise which he wrote against them, to the following purpose: 'There is no sect so dangerous as the Leonists, for three reasons: first, it is the most ancient—some say that as old as Sylvester, others as old as the apostles themselves. Secondly, it is very generally disseminated; there is no country where it has not gained some footing. Thirdly, while other sects are profane and blasphemous, this retains the utmost show of piety; they live justly before men, and believe nothing respecting God which is not good; only they blaspheme against the Roman church and the clergy, and thus gain many followers.' The author of this passage lived about the middle of the following century; and if the sect against which he was writing had really originated from the preaching of Peter, some eighty years before, the Dominican would scarcely have conceded to it the claim of high and unascertained antiquity. Says, again, St. Bernard, in one place, in substance, that there is a sect which calls itself after no man's name, which pretends to be in the line of apostolical succession; and which, rustic and unlearned though it is, contends that the church is wrong, and that itself alone is right. It must derive its origin from the devil, since there is no other extraction which we can assign to it."

"Nevertheless, as its origin was confessedly immemorial in the thirteenth century, and as there has not, perhaps, existed in the history of heresy any other sect to which some origin has not been expressly ascribed, we have just reason to infer the very high antiquity of the Vaudois.

"Many will think it more important to learn their doctrines than to speculate on their origin. On almost all material points they were those of the Reformation. In their discipline they endeavored to attain the rigid simplicity of the primitive Christians, and in that endeavor, perhaps they exceeded it.

"The persecution of Peter Waldensis, and the dispersion of his followers, occasioned, as in so many similar instances, the dissemination of the opinions; and, notwithstanding some partial sufferings which were inflicted in Picardy by Philippe Auguste, they were a numerous and flourishing sect at the conclusion of the twelfth century."

Page 291: THE ALBIGEOIS. It appears

that, at a synod held at Orleans, in the year 1017, under the reign of Robert, a number of persons, of no mean condition or character, were accused of heretical opinions. Manicheism was the frightful term employed to express their delinquency; but it is more probable that their real offense was the adoption of certain mystical notions, proceeding, indeed, from feelings of the most earnest piety, but too spiritual to be tolerated in that age and that church. It is said that they despised all external forms of worship, and rejected the rites, the ceremonies, and even the sacraments of the church, that they valued none save the religion within, the abstracted contemplation of the Diety, and the internal aspirations of the soul after things celestial. Accordingly, they were accused and convicted of heresy; and, as they firmly persisted in their errors, and, as the king had no repugnance to enforce the sentence, they were finally consigned to the flames."

Margin.—The Synod of Orleans charged the Albijois with a disbelief in the efficacy of baptism, in the change wrought by consecration of the eucharistical elements, and in the meritoriousness of prayers to martyrs and confessors. . . . And when the prelate, sitting in judgement on them, laid down the orthodox doctrine respecting some of those points, the heretics replied: You may tell such tales as those to men whose wisdom is of this world, and who believe the fictions of carnal men, . . . but to us, who have a law inscribed on the inward man by the Holy Spirit, and who have no other wisdom than that we have learnt from God, the creator of all things, you preach superfluous vanities deviating from real holiness. Wherefore cease your discourse, and do what you will with us. Already we do behold our King reigning in the heavens, who exalts us with his right hand to immortal triumphs, and to joys which are above. We should recollect that this account (like almost every other in which any heretical opinions are described) comes to us from the pen of an enemy."

Page 292: "EDICTS OF ALEXANDER III. That Pope, in a council held at Tours, in 1163, published a decree to this effect: 'Whereas a damnable heresy has for some time lifted its head in the parts about Toulouse, and has already spread its infection through Gascony and other provinces, concealing itself like a serpent within its own folds; as soon as its followers shall have been discovered, let no man afford them a refuge on his estates; neither let there be any communication with them in buying or selling; so that, being deprived of the solace of human conversation, they may be compelled to return from error to wisdom.'

"PERSECUTION of the ALBIGEOIS.—When the torch of persecution was transmitted to Innocent, the two principal seats of religious disaffection were the valleys of Piedmont and the cities of Languedoc; with this difference, however, that the Vaudois flourished in comparative and perhaps despised security, while the latter, more particularly denominated Albigeois, were rendered more notorious, as well as more dangerous, by the protection publicly afforded them by Raymond VI, Earle of Toulouse. Against these, therefore, the Pope's earnest and most assiduous efforts were directed.

"This expedition lasted six or seven years; and, at the end of that time, the spiritual missionaries engaged in it were generally known by the title of Inquisitors—a name, not indeed honorable or innocent even in its origin, but not yet associated with horror and infamy. Still matters did not proceed with the rapidity desired by the pontiff. . . .

"At length, in the year 1207, Innocent at once addressed himself to the arms of Philippe Auguste. He easily exhorted that monarch to march into the heretical provinces, and extirpate the spiritual rebels by fire and sword."

Page 293: "The Pope immediately launched the bolt of excommunication. They proclaimed a general campaign of all nations against the Albegois, and at the same time promised a general grant of indulgences and dispensations to all who should take arms in that holy cause. Having thus reduced those dissenting Christians to the same level, in a religious estimation, with the Turk and the Saracen, they let loose an infuriated multitude of fanatics against them; and the word 'Crusade,' which had hitherto signified only religious madness, was now extended to the more deliberate atrocity of sectarian persecution."

We now skip about 250 pages, taken up with Monachism, Mendicant Orders, Nuns, Popes from 1216 to 1305, the Greek Church, then a little on the Hussites and Wickliffites, which I would like to quote from, but our limits are reached. On pages 552-4, he shows the vain attempt of the Protests of the 16th century to tie on to this pure line of heretics. Read what follows about this.

Page 552: "*Attempts to trace the Continuity of the Protestant Opinions to the Apostolical Times.—* Several learned and pious Protestants have attempted to trace the uninterrupted descent of their doctrines, or, at least, of some essential portion of them, even from the apostolic times. Great ingenuity and research have been employed for this purpose, partly to make it thus manifest, that the Almighty, while he permitted so much iniquity to be perpetrated in his name, did still nourish in secret his true and perpetual Church.

. . .

"Very much has been written about the 'Lutheranism which was prevalent before Luther;' the unbroken series of 'Witnesses of the truth;' the unceasing protestations which have been silently breathed in all ages against the abuses of Rome."

Margin.— . . . This subject has been treated by Bossuet, in the eleventh chapter of his VARIATIONS, and, of course, not impartially; and thus, while he has unquestionably established many of his positions, he has advanced others which are untenable. (1) Respecting the ALBEGOIS. He has failed in proving their Manichæan origin—still more their Manichæan doctrines. . . . For the same reason he has failed in confounding them (the Manichæans) with the Catharists, Bulgari, etc., who were the real descendants of the Paulicians. (2) Respecting the Vaudois. He shows . . . that they were the same with the LEONISTS and the INSABBATES. But he does not establish his assertion, that they were founded by Peter Waldo of Lyons. . . . In the meantime, we must admit that he has, in our opinion, established his two leading positions: viz., that the Protestants fail in their attempts to prove an uninterrupted succession; and that those whom they claim as their ancestors differed from them in numerous points of doctrine.

Page 553: "It is unquestionable, that as early as the twelfth century, some of the Protestant opinions were openly professed and atoned for by death. And it is equally certain that, from the preaching of Peter de Bruis to that of Luther, there have subsisted, in some quarter or other of the Western community, various bodies of sectaries, who were at open or secret variance with the Church of Rome—who rejected . . . in part, or in the whole, her tenets, or her ceremonies or her ministry. It may be doubted whether the Albegois, in spite of the crusades of the Innocent, and the Inquisition of Toulouse, were ever extirpated. The Vaudois were certainly preserved through the perils of four centuries of oppression. The ashes of Wickliffe were not lost in their rough descent into the ocean; and the spirit which rose out of the funeral flames of Huss, survived to expand in the bosoms of compatriots. The spiritual Franciscans, who questioned the omnipotence of the Pope, and denounced the corruptions no less than the wealth of the clergy, are placed by Mosheim among the forerunners of the Reformation. At least it is certain that their continued insubordination, combined with such high pretensions to sanctity, had its effect in preparing the downfall of the Papacy; thus they may properly be numbered among the instruments appointed to divide its strength, and betray its fortress by intense discord to the foe without.

"Again, among the sects which we have mentioned as the more genuine precursors of Luther and Zwinglius, . . . there were points on which they differed both from the Roman Catholics and the Protestants. . . . Such were the sects from which the Protestants claim their descent, and to which they are justly grateful for having prepared their path, and set the example of non-conformity."

(The historian, here, in a marginal note, disclaims using the words sect or heresy in their usual opprobrious sense, and without any reference to the nature of their opinions. So did Mosheim in his appendix.)

Page 554: THE VAUDOIS.—In our journey back towards the apostolical times, these separatists conduct us as far as the beginning of the twelfth century. . . . Their origin is not ascertained by any authentic record; and, being immemorial, it may have been coeval with the introduction of christianity. Among their own traditions, there is one which agrees well with their original and favorite tenet, which objects to the possession of property by ecclesiastics. It is this—that their earliest fathers, offended at the liberality with which Constantine endowed the Church of Rome, and at the worldiness with which Pope Sylvester accepted those endowments, seceded into the Alpine solitudes; that they there lay concealed and secure for many ages through their insignificance and their innocence. This may have been so—it is not even improbable that it was not so. . . . It is sufficient to prove that they had an earlier existence than the twelfth century. (The historian is unconsciously writing the Perpetuity of the Baptists *as*, but not *of* the Protestants.)

Margin.—"Nevertheless, we are disposed to consider it as very probable then, on the sides and under the brows of those desolate mountains there may have existed, in every age, a few obscure peasants whom all the innovations of Rome have never reached. . . . It is proper to mention what those opinions really were which were condemned at Arros in 1005. . . . It was asserted that the sacrament of baptism was useless and of no efficacy to salvation. That the sacrament of the Lord's Supper was equally unnecessary. . . . That the sacred orders of the ministry were not of divine institution. That church rites of sepulture are to be ascribed to the avarice of the clergy. That penance was altogether inefficacious. This seems to have been an inference from their denial of the efficacy of baptism. . . . That the cross is not an object of worship; nor the Savior's image on the cross, nor any other image, etc."

Pages 554-5: THE ALBEGOIS.—When we turn to the history of the Albegois, we find there still less to flatter our hopes or encourage our pursuit. . . . If we should identify those Dissenters, as some have done with the Cathari, the Gazari, Paterni, Publicani, and others of the same age, who were collateral branches of the Paulician family, we are not any longer indeed at a loss to trace the succession to a very high antiquity. It is also true that the contempt of images, the disbelief in transubstantiation and some other Protestant principles, were faithfully perpetuated in that heretical race. . . . Upon the whole then, it seems impossible to establish, on historical ground, the theory of an uninterrupted transmission of the original faith from the primitive times to those of Luther. Indications of its occasional existence may be discovered, but no proof of its continuity. Yet it is no disparagement of those faithful witnesses, who were called into existence in the iron days of the church. They bequeathed to their fortunate successors their principle and their example. Nor were they, in their own time, without influence, nor even without peril to the pontifical predominances. Innocent III did not despise their infancy; he beheld it, on the contrary, with such anxious apprehension as to divert the engine with which he was armed for other purposes, to their destruction. . . . In the lineaments of that little cloud which raised its prophetic hand in the horizon of heresy, he read the denunciation of future wrath, and heard the distant murmur of advancing reason."

Page 556: "The ecclesiastical and civil authorities, legally and systematically, co-operated in the destruction of many bold and virtuous spirits, who, for three successive centuries, asserted, under different forms and names, the private right of reading and interpreting the Gospel."

. . .

Page 557: "It was not against the results of thought, but against the liberty of thinking, that the bolts were now really leveled. The rebellion was more detestable than the heresy; and the wretches who dared to place their Bible against the Church, were marked out, not for conversion, but for massacre."

Margin.—"Everything that fraud and calumny could invent seems to have been practiced on them. In 1487 and 1488 fresh bulls were issued, followed by military violence."

Now, reader, I have given you a little here and there of Waddington's history of the Baptists—not that name, for that name had not yet been accorded and adopted by the Baptists—but he has helped Mosheim to trace our history under some of the other names by which Baptists have been called. Waddington aimed to give the history: "From the Earliest Ages to the Reformation." He admits that the Protestants of the Reformation can not connect on to this line of faithful witnesses, but he contended for such a line, and his part of the line is that we are anxious to establish. We will let others hitch the Baptists on to this line when we come to the last division of this subjet: "IT IS CONCLUSIVE." The chain will be welded so that it can't be broken. We must comply with the Divine rule, in getting "two or three witnesses" under each head, so that "every word may be established."

Another History Epitomized.

The Religious Tract Society, of London, published six volumes, the title of which is, THE HISTORY OF THE CHURCH OF CHRIST PREVIOUS TO THE REFORMATION.

After diligent research, it vindicates the ancient-hated sects from the flood of foul aspersions heaped on them by Catholics, and even Protestants. The following is taken from Vol. 3, embracing from the sixth to the twelfth century. This is the period we are trying to bridge. Here is proof abundant to establish the doctrines of the "'CATHARI" and "WALDENSES," and clearly puts them in the line of Baptist Succession. Read, and let your heart leap for joy at the wonderful providence of God in preserving his witnesses through these dark ages of fire and blood. These Pedobaptist writers deserve the thanks of all Baptists, though their aim was to establish a succession of Protestant churches outside of Rome. These Protestant churches never came out of Rome, and never failed to protest against all of her abominations. I begin with "concerning the Cathari."

Page 274: "But Everninus goes on:—' Their heresy is this: they say, that the Church is only among themselves, because they alone of all men follow the steps of Christ, and imitate the apostles, not seeking secular gains, possessing no property, following the pattern of Christ, who was himself perfectly poor, and did not allow his disciples to possess anything.' Doubtless they carried this point too far, for rich Christians are charged to be rich in good works, willing to distribute, apt to communicate."—Tim. 6:17, 18.

"Everninus proceeds: . . . "Their own condition in the world they represent in such terms as these: 'We, the poor of Christ, who have no certain abode, fleeing from one city to another, like sheep in the midst of wolves, do endure persecution with the apostles and martyrs; though our lives are strict, abstemious, devout and holy, and though we seek only what is necessary for the support of the body, and live as men who are not of the world. But ye, lovers of the world, have peace with the world, because ye are of it. False apostles, who adulterate the word of Christ, seeking their own, have misled you and your ancestors; whereas, we and our fathers, being born and bred up in the apostolical religion, have continued in the grace of Christ, and shall continue so to the end of the world."

Page 278: "They are armed," says the same Egbert, "with all those passages of Holy Scripture which, in any degree, seem to favor their views; with these they know how to defend themselves, and to oppose the Catholic truth." . . .

"They are increased to great multitudes throughout all countries—their words eat like a canker. In Germany we call them Cathari; in Flanders they call them Piphles; in French, Tisserands, because many of them are of that occupation. . . ."

"They were a plain, unassuming, harmless and industrious race of Christians, condemning, by their doctrine and manners, the whole apparatus of the reigning idolatry and superstition, placing true religion in the faith and love of Christ, and retaining a supreme regard for the divine word."

CENTURY XIII—PETER WALDO.

Page 316 : "The reader will recollect the account which has been given of the Cathari, who were evidently a people of God in the former part of the last century. In the latter part of the same century they received a great accession of members from the learned labors and godly zeal of Peter Waldo. In the century before us they were gloriously distinguished by a dreadful series of persecutions, and exhibited a spectacle to the world, both of the power of divine grace, and of the malice and enmity of the world against the real Gospel of Jesus Christ."

Page 316: "A mistake arose from the similarity of names, that Peter Valdo, or Waldo, was the first founder of these churches, for the names Vallenses being easily changed into Waldenses, the Romanists improved this very easy and natural mistake into an argument against the antiquity of these churches, and denied that they had any existence till the appearance of Waldo."

"But from a just account of the subject, it appeared that the real Protestant doctrines existed during the dark ages of the church even long before Waldo's time."

Page 321: "So far was Waldo from being the founder of the Churches of the Vallies, that it does not appear that he ever was in Piedmont at all."

Page 322: "Everything relating to the Waldenses resembled the scenes of the primitive Church. Numbers died praising God, and in confident assurance of a blessed resurrection; whence the blood of the martyrs again became the seed of the Church.

"These things show the mutual connection of the Waldensian churches, and prove the superior antiquity of those of the Vallies, the severity of the persecution, and the important services of Peter Waldo. A very extraordinary personage! resembling, in many respects, the immediate successors of the Apostles themselves! But his piety, endowments and labors have met with no historian capable of doing them justice."

"CHAPTER II."
"THE REAL CHARACTER OF THE WALDENSES."

Page 323: "Nothing can exceed the calumnies of their adversaries. In this respect they had the honor to bear the cross of the first Christians. They were called poor men of Lyons and dogs; were called cut-purses in Italy, because they observed not the appointed festivals; and, resting from their ordinary occupations only on Sundays, they were called Insabathas—that is, regardless of sabbaths. In Germany they were called Gazares, a term expressive of everything flagitously wicked. In Flanders . . . they were often obliged to dwell in the woods and deserts. And, because they denied the consecrated host to be God, they were accused of Arianism, as if they had denied the divinity of Christ."

Page 328: "We have now seen the fullest testimony to the holiness of the Waldenses; and we shall see shortly that the doctrines which they held were no other than those, which, under the Divine influence, we have all along observed to be the constant root of virtue in the world.

"Claude, bishop of Turin, wrote a treatise against their doctrines, in which he candidly owns that they themselves were blameless, without reproach among men, and that they observed the divine commands with all their might."

Page 332: "How marvelous are the ways of God! How faithful his promise in supporting and maintaining a church, even in the darkest times! But her livery is often sackcloth, and her external bread is that of affliction, while she sojourns on earth."

Page 335: "The confession of the Bohemian Waldenses, published in the former part of the sixteenth century, is very explicit on these articles. They say, that men ought to acknowledge themselves born in sin, and to be burdened with the weight of sin; that they ought to acknowledge, that for this depravity, and for the sins springing up from this root of bitterness, utter perdition deservedly hangs over their heads, and that all should own that they can no way justify themselves by any works or endeavors, nor have anything to trust to but Christ alone. They hold that by faith in Christ, men are, through mercy, freely justified, and attain salvation by Christ, without human help or merit. They hold that all confidence is to be fixed in him alone, and all our care to be cast upon him; and that, for his sake only, God is pacified, and adopts us to be his children. They teach also, that no man can have this faith by his own power, will or pleasure; that it is the gift of God, who, where it pleaseth him, worketh it in man by his Spirit. They teach also the doctrine of good works as fruits and evidences of a lively faith." (Good, pure, simple Baptist doctrine.)

"The Waldenses, in general, express their firm belief that there is no other Mediator than Jesus Christ; they speak with great respect of the Virgin Mary, as holy, humble and full of grace; at the same time that they totally discountenance that senseless and extravagant admiration in which she had been held for ages. They assert that all who have been and shall be saved, have been elected of God before the foundation of the world; and that whosoever upholds free-will absolutely denies predestination and the grace of God.

" What they meant by an upholder of free-will is not hard to be understood—namely, one who maintains that there are resources in the nature of man sufficient to enable him to live to God as he ought, without any need of the renewal of his nature by divine grace.

"We honor, say they, the secular powers with subjection, obedience, promptitude and payment of tribute. On this subject they are repeatedly explicit, and mention the example of our Lord, who refused not to pay tribute, not taking upon himself any jurisdiction of temporal power."

" They give a practical view of the doctrine of the Holy Trinity, perfectly agreeable to the faith of the orthodox in all ages. Let it suffice to mention what they say of the Holy Ghost. We believe that he is our Comforter, proceeding from the Father and from the Son; by whose inspiration we pray, being renewed by him who formeth all good works within us, and by him we have knowledge of all truth."

" It is remarkable that an ancient confession of faith, copied out of certain manuscripts, bearing date 1120, that is, forty years before Peter Waldo, contains the same articles in substance, and, in many particulars, in the same words as those, an abridgement of which has been given.

"This conclusion from this fact is, that though Waldo was a most considerable benefactor to the Waldensian churches by his translation of the Scriptures, his other writings, his preaching, and his sufferings, he was not properly their founder. Their plan of doctrine and their establishment, particularly in Piedmont, was of prior date."

Page 338: Or, a dead faith is, to believe that there is a God, and to believe those things which relate to God, and not believe in him."

"They then proceed to show that the real Church of God consists of the elect of God from the beginning to the end of the world, by the grace of God, through the merit of Christ, gathered together by the Holy Spirit, and foreordained to eternal life."

Page 344: "In ecclesiastical correction, they were directed by our Lord's rule, in first reproving a brother in private; secondly, in the presence of two or three brethren; and, last of all, and not till other methods failed, in proceeding to excommunication. Private correction, they observe, is sufficient for faults not made known to many; but in the case of open sins, they followed the apostolical rule.

"Against the disorders of taverns, and the mischiefs of dancing, they are exceedingly severe. Remark one sentence: They who deck and adorn their daughters are like those who put dry wood to the fire, to the end that it may burn the better. A tavern is the fountain of sin, and the school of Satan."

Page 345: "There is also a book concerning Anti-christ in an old manuscript, which contains many sermons of the pastors; it is dated 1120, and therefore was written before the time of Waldo. The existence, therefore, of these churches is still further proved to have taken place before the days of that reformer."

Page 346: "The Albigenses, however, a branch of the Waldenses, in the year 1200, were so exceedingly numerous, that they then formed a distinct church, and were openly separated from the whole Roman system."

Page 348: "How happened it that they should possess so sound a portion of evangelical truth, so ably and judiciously confute established errors, so boldly maintain the truth as it is in Jesus, so patiently suffer for it, live so singularly distinct from the world, and so nobly superior to all around them; while princes, dignitaries, universities, and all that was looked on as great, splendid and wise among men, wandered in miserable darkness? It was of the Lord, who is wonderful in cousel and excellent in work; and his preservation of a godly seed in the earth, in such circumstances, is a pledge that he never will forsake his Church, and that the gates of hell shall never prevail against it."

Page 350: "All these were called, in general, Albigenses, and, in doctrine and manners, were not at all distinct from the Waldenses."

Page 352: "If the author before us had read, with the least attention, the Waldensian records, he would never have asserted that the Waldenses were legitimate descendants of the sect of Manes.

"The beginning of the thirteenth centry saw thousands of persons hanged or burned by these diabolical devices, whose sole crime was that they trusted only in Jesus Christ for salvation, and renounced all the vain hopes of self-righteous idolatry and superstition."

Page 354: "So true is it, that the blood of the martyrs is the seed of the Church, that, in the year 1530, there were in Europe above eight hundred thousand who professed the religion of the Waldenses."

Page 358: "A certain abbot undertook to preach to those who were found in the castle, and to exhort them to acknowledge the pope. But they interrupted his discourse, declaring that his labor was to no purpose. Earl Simon and the legate then caused a great fire to be kindled; and they burned a hundred and forty persons of both sexes.

"These martyrs died in triumph, praising God that he had counted them worthy to suffer for the sake of Christ. They opposed the legate to his face"

Page 369: "Then followed an account of their

articles of faith, particularly as to the Trinity, the incarnation and divinity of Christ and redemption. Sacraments they held to be only visible signs of an invisible grace—beneficial to the faithful, but not essential to salvation."

BOHEMIA—AUSTRIA.

Page 371: "The murders, rapes and desolations were horrible beyond all description. In particular, a number of women were shut up in a barn full of straw, which was set on fire; and a soldier, moved with compassion; having opened a place for them, that they might escape, these helpless victims of papal rage were driven back into the flames by pikes and halberts. Other cruelties were practiced on this occasion, so horrid, that they might seem to exceed belief, were not the authenticity of the accounts unquestionable."

Page 374: "Thus largely did the 'King of Saints' provide for the instruction of his Church in the darkness of the middle ages. The Waldenses are the middle link, which connects the primitive Christians and Fathers with the reformed; and, by their means, the proof is completely established, that salvation, by the grace of Christ, felt in the heart, and expressed in the life, by the power of the Holy Ghost, has ever existed from the time of the apostles till this day."

Page 382: "The acts of the inquisition of Toulouse preserve some of the accusations againt the Albigenses, whose identity with the Waldenses has already been shown. A brief extract may be given in this place.

"In the year 1283, William of Manuhaco was brought before the inquisitors; there was no accusation against his moral character, and the principal points recorded, as held by him, were, that neither the pope nor any man could be head of the Church of Christ—that the pope and his prelates had not the power of forgiving sins—and that the ceremony of baptism did not convey remission of sins. The newly-devised sacraments of the Church of Rome he declared to be of no use."

Marginal note.— . . . It is acknowledged by Gretzer and other Romish authors. See Allix's remarks upon the Albigenses, pp. 170, 172. Perrin also says, "The Albigenses of whom I treat differed not from the Waldenses as to their faith, only being called Albigenses, from the country of Albi, in which they dwelt. The popes, legates and inquisitors condemned, made war upon them, and accused them as Waldenses."

Page 401: It will, no doubt, gratify the reader to become acquainted with the doctrines of the Waldenses on these important points. They form, as already observed, a connecting link between the primitive and the reformed churches. They stood between the living and the dead till the plague was stayed, and it is most interesting to perceive the uniformity with which the leading vital truths were set forth in the different ages of the Church, though often in a very imperfect manner."

Page 405: "The Waldensian confessions of faith have been already noticed, but a few extracts may be added from the most ancient, which has been preserved, and which bears the date of 1120—more than a century previous to Waldo of Lyons. (Omitting five, all sound to the letter, we come to the sixth.)

Page 406: "*Of the sacraments.* We believe that the sacraments are the signs or the visible forms of holy things, holding it to be good that the faithful, at times, use these signs or visible forms if they are able to do so. But we believe, nevertheless, that the faithful may be saved who have not received the signs. We have not known any other sacraments than baptism and the eucharist."

"The writings of the Waldenses are consistent throughout; the same spirit appears in every part."

(Reader, imagine the rest printed in large caps.)

Page 407: "Nor can anyone be pointed out as the first reformer or establisher of these churches; while their writings expressly speak of never having believed the errors which they combat; and the assertions which assign their origin to Waldo, or even to Claudius, will not bear examination. In no historical document of any authority is there reference made to a change in the doctrinal principles of the inhabitants of these valleys. Though persecuted by the Romish Church for many successive ages, that church can not show that they ever were within her pale. Surely this is strong evidence that they possessed 'the faith as delivered to the saints.'"

Page 408: "Should it be asked, where was the true Church of Christ to be found after so many heresies were avowed by the Roman hierarchy; the answer is, it was to be found in the churches of the valleys of Piedmont."—Gilly, p. 253.

Page 413: "We have seen in what a remarkable manner God was pleased to preserve the light of his truth in these valleys during the dark ages of superstition, so that 'the gates of hell were not suffered to prevail' against this portion of the Church of Christ."

Page 415: "In these valleys the Waldenses still reside, the undoubted descendants of a race of men who never bowed to the Church of Rome, and never were enveloped in its darkness and superstitions."

Page 416: "The Most High showed that he would not suffer even the gates of hell finally to prevail against his Church."—Gilly, p. 242.

Page 418: "The present character of the Vaudois Church is still sound and scriptural. It was one of the chief objects of my excursions to these valleys, that I might ascertain the continued orthodoxy of this ancient Christian people, and I do not scruple to affirm, that the pastors maintain, with one single exception, the doctrines of the ever-blessed Trinity, the incarnation of its second person—JUSTIFICATION TO SINFUL MAN BY FAITH ALONE IN THE BLOOD AND RIGHTEOUSNESS OF CHRIST—the corruption and depravity of human nature, and an absolute need of the regenerating and sanctifying influences of the Holy Gospel, and subsequently to walk in the way of its commandments."

These are just a few sweet samples of this volume. It is Baptist History and Baptist Doctrine. They clearly make out the Succession, or Perpetuity, I am contending for. Why will Baptists try to hide or deny or ridicule the doctrine or the fact of Perpetuity? Why don't they want to believe it? WHY? O WHY? And echo answers, WHY? MYSTERY! HIDDEN MYSTERY! And it looks like the Mystery of Iniquity. There is so much in this and other histories I would like to copy for the reader. All this proves not only that the church was preserved from destruction, but also from corruption. I verily believe that the faith was kept purer in those days when corruption was charged, than in other days, when commonly credited with a better creed. This is confirmed by the testimony of both God and man. For God's testimony see such Scriptures as Rev. 12:11, 17; 14:4, 12, etc. I don't believe one of the charges made against the Lord, if they did crucify him and put him to an open shame; and he said they would do thus to his followers. The wicked world has always slandered both Him and them.

Butler's Ecclesiastical History Epitomized.

The author of this history, C. M. Butler, D.D., was Professor of Ecclesiastical History in the Divinity School of the Protestant Episcopal Church, Philadelphia. As this history is from the first to the thirteenth century, he does not connect the Baptists on to the Waldenses, but he clearly shows that the Waldenses were Baptists in doctrine, and that they were in the line of succession from the Apostles. We will let others hitch the Baptists on to this pure line of Baptist churches. My epitomy of this history can not be used here, as my limits forbid. Only one quotation can be used:

Page 566: (7) *Doctrines of the Waldenses.*—
"The Waldenses were entirely free from Manichæan errors. Even their enemies admitted that they were sound in the faith. In the south of France they sometimes aided the ignorant clergy in the defense of the faith against Manichæism. Their first principle was that the Scriptures are the only source of religious knowledge, and the only rule of faith; they denounced the Pope as the Anti-Christ, and the Church as the Apocalyptic beast and the whore of Babylon. Like the *Cathari*, they rejected the whole Ritual system

of the Church. They declared that no other laws than those of the Scriptures were needful. *They denied the necessity of baptism to salvation*, and the transubstantiation of the elements in the Eucharist. The penitential system of the Church and the doctrine of purgatory were also rejected by them."

Marginal note.—"The history and doctrines of the Waldenses have been the subject of much controversy and contention. It has always been the policy of the Romish writers to identify them with the Manichæan sects. Others have identified them with the Albigenses . . . who were not Manichæan, but held the same Scriptural system as the Waldenses. They also contend that the name was not derived from Waldo, but from the Valleys of Piedmont, in which they subsisted long before they were joined by the like-minded followers of Peter Waldo. It is claimed by them that the Waldenses have existed as a distinct body from the time of Silvester I (who died 855), and that an unbroken chain of witnesses to gospel truth . . . have been maintained. This position is connected with the interpretation of the two witnesses prophesying in sackcloth (Rev. xi:3), which finds its fulfillment in the preservation of a pure church in the darkest days of the Papal apostasy. The doctrines of the Waldenses are learned from two authentic productions of the early period of their existence—the tract on Anti-Christ, and a poem called "The Noble Lesson," a beautiful monument of pure Christian truth in the midst of the prevailing gross superstitions." (See Neander IV: 615-16; Alix, The Churches of Piedmont, chap. 18; Robertson; III:198-99; Elliot's Horac Apocalypticae, Vol. I-I:04.)

How unconsciously these Pedobaptist historians wrote Baptist history.

Page 561, chap. 83: *Peter of Bruis*.—"He vehemently attacked the system of the Church in doctrine and government, and professed to restore Christianity to its original purity and simplicity. . . . He contended that infants should not be baptized—nor the Eucharist regarded as a sacrifice—nor the Cross revered—nor the Churches consecrated—and that prayers, alms and masses were unavailing for the dead. His preaching produced great effects. Multitudes baptized in infancy were rebaptized. He was at length burned to death."

I insert here what Bishop Bossuet, the great Catholic controversialist, complaining of Calvin's party for claiming apostolic succession, said: "You adopt Henry and Peter Bruys among your predecessors, and everybody knows they were Anabaptists."—Benedict's History, p. 68.

Pages 562-3: (4) "THE CATHARI.—Their doctrines. Their connection with and derivation from the East—from the Euchites, and Bogamiles, and Paulicians—is too plain to be mistaken." (Notice the connecting words—"connection with" and "derivation from.")

"The whole prevailing system of ritual, images, bells, crosses, light, incense, vestments, chanting, holy water, relics, pilgrimages, unction, purgatory, prayer and masses for the dead, festal and saints' days, was utterly condemned and abolished; the Pope they regarded as Anti-Christ, and the Church as the harlot of the Apocalypse."

Marginal note.—"The names of these widely-extended sects, whose general system was the same, were numerous. Among them were Publicani or Poplicani, which seems to point to a connection with the Paulicians—Patarini, a name formally applied to the opponents of clerical marriage in Italy; Apostolici, from their pretensions to an Apostolic manner of life; Bonhommes, Bulgari (which connects them with Bulgaria);

Tisserand, because many were weavers, and, at a later date, the more celebrated name of the Albigenses."—(Robertson 3-182.)

Dr. Thos. O. Summers (Methodist), in his book *The Inquisition*, p. 10, says: "The first chapter of the history of truth always begins with the small voice in the desert; and deeply as the so-called Church of Christ had fallen from its original piety and purity, and degraded as it had become by corrupt and pernicious influences, there was not yet wanting a small minority who, "faithful among the faithless," and contending with every conceivable disadvantage and oppression, yet represented the simplicity and devotedness of the primitive disciples. Such were the Waldenses—a people singularly interesting; the pioneers of a later reformation; the spiritual isthmus which binds Protestantism to primitive Christianity; and the first who, in modern times, ventured to cut the tangled underwood of a false Christianity. Peter Waldus, a native of Lyons, who lived towards the close of the twelfth century, tormented and roused by the corruptions he witnessed around him, caused portions of the Scriptures to be translated into the current language; and, though originally a layman, formed around him a church to which he preached and expounded. Waldus's little band became afterwards associated with another body of humble disciples, the *descendants* of the *ancient* Paulicians, who inhabited the valleys of Piedmont, and were designated Vaudois (in French), Waldenses (in Latin), and Valleymen (in English), names which afterwards became affixed to the united community. These Christians cultivated the utmost simplicity of dress and manners. Unambitious of wealth, they abjured all unfair and dishonest means of acquiring gain; they observed the strictest temperance and chastity, and denied themselves, with true moral sublimity, even those innocent enjoyments which might appear to identify them with their ungodly neighbors. As many followed the occupation of traveling merchants or peddlers, answering in many respects to the *colporteurs* of modern days, they availed themselves of all favorable opportunities to instruct their customers in the doctrines of vital religion, not failing to exhibit the truth in marked and effective contrast to the corrupt and venal religionism of their day. It is admitted that their interpretation of sacred truth was conjoined with much that was defective and even puerile; but the Waldenses were true spiritual reformers, exhibiting, though in a yet more gloomy age, the leading views which afterwards distinguished the transition-period of Luther and his followers. A *section* of these primitive Christians was designated *Albigenses*, probably deriving their name from Albi, a city in Languedoc. As corruption and calumny are ever allies, they were branded by their enemies with every crime of which human nature is capable—with atheism, blasphemy, the worship of two gods, (in other words, Manichæism,) and with the most contemptuous ridicule of all sacred things. Their real crime, in the eyes of their accusers, was the superior purity of their lives, and the steady opposition they offered to the contemptible or corrupt practices of the Romish Church. So long as they freely disseminated their tenets, Popery felt itself no longer safe."

Dr. John Dick, in his *Theology*, p. 304, speaking of the organization of the Church, by Christ, says: "A church was formed which, notwithstanding powerful opposition and cruel persecution, subsists at the present hour."

Theodore Beza, the successor of John Calvin, *History of the Christian Church*, by Jones, p. 353, says: "As for the Waldenses, I may be permitted to call them the very seed of the primitive and pure Christian Church, since they are those that have been upheld, as is abundantly manifest, by the wonderful providence of God, so those horrible persecutions which have been expressly raised agains them, were ever able so far to prevail as to make them bend, or yield a voluntary subjection to the Roman tyranny and idolatry."

John Wesley, in his notes on Rev. 13: 7, says: "*And it was given him*—That is, God permitted him, *to make war with the saints*—with the Waldenses and Albigenses. It is a vulgar mistake, that the Waldenses were so called from Peter Waldo, of Lyons. They were *much more* ancient than him; and their true name was Vallenses, or Vaudois, from their inhabiting the valleys of Lucerne and Angrogne. This name, Vallenses, after Waldo appeared, about the year 1160, was changed by the Papists into Waldenses, on purpose to represent them as of modern origin. The Albigenses were originally people of Albigeois, part of Upper Languedoc, where they considerably prevailed, and possessed several towns in the year 1200. Against these, many of the popes made open war. Till now the blood of Christians had been shed only by the heathens or Arians; from this time by scarce any but the papacy. In the year 1208, Innocent III proclaimed a crusade against them. In June, 1209, the army assembled at Thoulouse; from which time abundance of blood was shed, and the second army of martyrs began to be added to the first, who had cried from beneath the altar. And ever since the beast has been warring against the saints, and shedding their blood like water. *And authority was given him over every tribe and people*—particularly in Europe. And when a way was found by sea into the East Indies and the West, these also were brought under his authority."

On Rev. 19:24, he says: "And what immense quantities of blood have been shed by her agents!

Charles IX, of France, in his letter to Gregory XIII, boasts that in, and not long after the massacre of Paris, he had destroyed seventy thousand Huguenots. Some have computed, that from the year 1518 to 1548, *fifteen millions* of Protesttants have perished by war and the inquisition! This may be overcharged; but certainly the number of them in those thirty years, as well as since, is almost incredible. To these we may add innumerable martyrs, in ancient, middle and late ages, in Bohemia, Germany, Holland, France, England, Ireland, and many other parts of Europe, Africa and Asia."

Oliver Cromwell, the Dictator of England, (Jones, p. 530), says to the Prince of Switzerland, in behalf of the suffering Waldenses: "Next to the help of God, it seems to devolve on you to provide that the most ancient stock of pure religion may not be destroyed in this remnant of its ancient professors. Here Cromwell calls the Waldenses 'the most ancient stock of pure religion;' not only ancient, but in the superlative, the most ancient.' This, then, must go back to the very beginning."

Dr. D'Anvers, in his work on baptism, page 341, lays in the claim of the Waldenses to apostolic origin as follows: "In the preface to the French Bible, and the first that ever was printed, they say that they have always had the full enjoyment of that heavenly truth contained in the Holy Scriptures ever since they were enriched with the same by the apostles themselves, having, in fair manuscripts, preserved the entire Bible in their native tongues, from generation to generation."

Notice here, that in this Waldensean record, we have two very important historic facts stated: 1. That the Waldenses claimed a regular succession from the apostles. 2. That they preserved the entire Bible, in manuscripts, all the time from the apostolic age. This flatly contradicts the presumptuous claim of the Roman Catholics, that if it had not been for them the Bible would have been lost. Thus, by Beza, Cromwell, and the Waldenses themselves, do I prove my proposition, that the Waldenses came from the apostles.

The following is from *The Texas Baptist Standard*, and is rich reading. Try it. Thanks to Bro. O. L. Hailey.

PRESIDENT GREGG AND THE WALDENSES.

President Gregg is a Presbyterian. He labored for many years in Boston. When Dr. T. L. Cuyler gave up his work as pastor of Lafayette Avenue Presbyterian Church, in Brooklyn, Dr. Gregg was his brilliant successor. He later became president of Western Theological Seminary, at Allegheny, Pa., which position he now fills. He is spending the winter in the South, on account of imperfect health.

While he was pastor in Brooklyn, his church sent him on a long vacation abroad. And when he came back he brought them greetings from many churches in the old world. When he reaches Rome, he gives them a greeting from the Waldensians. And it is in this connection that he uses the following words, which will make very charming reading to many Baptists, as well as many Presbyterians. These are his words:

"We have now reached Rome. But, allow me to say, our letter is not from the Church of Rome (so called). It is from a church in Rome; but a church older than the church of the Papacy. It is a letter from the Waldensian Church. The story of this church which comes straight from the Apostles, is the most moving story in all ecclesiastical literature. This is its story in brief: Missionaries sent from Rome, in the apostolic days, planted churches in the valleys of the Alps. These became the Waldensian churches. When others yielded to the Roman See, these spurned the yoke of the church of the Seven Hills, and kept their apostolicity intact. They were never subject to Rome. Rome changed, not they. Rome was guilty of apostacy, not they. If they are ancient, Rome is new. They are Rome's condemnation. This is the reason Rome has persecuted them, and again and again decreed their extermination. If it had not been that the towering Alps were their fortresses, they would have been speedily crushed; but they were the children of the mountains, and knew the fastnesses thereof and the narrow defiles, through which to escape. The mountains built their granite into them. They drank in glory and manhood and eternal fidelity from the snowy crests and thunder-riven peaks, and from the Alpine sky, which was all silver and gold. Once the Roman hierarchy captured this whole nation of God's people. The Roman Pontiff lied to them, and broke faith with them, and took them by guile. He slew them all but three hundred or so. These three hundred he banished. He drove them forth into the cold world, penniless. Geneva, the city of Calvin, opened its gates to these exiles, and rescued them. But the exiles of the Alps were homesick in Geneva. Out there beyond the lake was Mont Blanc, in its sunset glory, every day calling them home. Rather than die of homesickness, they planned to return home, or die in the attempt. The story of their return has no parallel for daring and success. How they made the Alps echo with their thanksgiving to God for bringing them back! Out of this nucleus the Waldensian churches were again grown. Friends from abroad helped them; Cromwell helped them, and so did Felix Neff and

General Beckwith. These latter brought themselves and their fortunes to them, and cast in their lot with the Waldenses, and by their wealth gave them temples and gave them schools. These were the men who kept the love of liberty alive in Italy until the day that Garibaldi and Victor Emmanuel championed the cause of liberty and made Italy free. It was they who raised the slogan cry: 'A free church in a free state.' When Victor Emmanuel bored his way into the city of Rome through the thick walls thereof, and smote into the dust the temporal power of the Pope, the Waldensians were in the front ranks of his army. One of the Waldensian soldiers was a colporter, and in his knapsack he carried a bundle of Bibles into the Eternal City, and made the day not only a victory for Emmanuel and Garibaldi, but a victory for God's Word. Prior to that, no Bible was allowed in the city of Rome. Since that, the Bible has been there as a free book."

Dr. D. N. Lord, (Presbyterian) says: "They have dwelt in the Cotti Alps from the commencement of the 1260 years, or from the beginning of the fourth century."

Hase, a great Lutheran historian, says: "They have a tradition, according to which, their origin is to be traced to primitive, and even apostolic times."

Dr. Alexis Masstin says, "the Vaudois of the Alps (Waldenses) are, in our view, primitive Christians, or inheritors of the primitive church, who have been preserved in these valleys, and it is not they who separated from Catholicism, but Catholicism from them."

Reinerius, a Popish inquisitor, charges the Waldenses with the following: "They declare themselves to be the apostle's successors, to have apostolic authority, and the keys of binding and loosing." Reinerius traces their history back to

Sylvester, 327, and says: "Some say they are descendents from the apostles."

And the learned Dr. Allix, in his history of the churches of Piedmont, gives this account: "that for 300 years or more the bishop of Rome attempted to subjugate the church of Milan, and rather than to accede to Rome's doctrines, they fled to the valleys of Lucerne and Angrogne, and thence were called wanderers, or the people of the valleys. Here is the bride in the wilderness."

IT IS CONCLUSIVE.

"In the mouth of two or three witnesses shall every word be established." This is the divine rule in settling disputed questions, and I propose to abide by it, and conform to it. Our witnesses are The Scriptures, Reason and Anology, The General Belief of the Proposition, more than two or three Historians who can not be suspected of religious bias, all to the effect that, according to the Scriptures, there has been a line of churches from the apostles to the Reformation, holding more tenaciously than to life, the true faith once for all delivered to the saints. This is not only Credible, but, from the great amount of Historic evidence, it is Conclusive. Now, for the conclusive evidence, to the effect that the Baptists of today are credited with the honor of constituting this end of the line. Those who read page 233 of this book can see, that the first end of the line, beyond question, is the history of churches, just like the Baptists of today, and like no others, yea, unlike all others, and especially unlike the Catholic Hierarchy. They also testify that those kind of churches were driven into the hiding-places prepared for them by Him who made the world and all that therein is. That these were the people that were so bitterly persecuted for 1260 years, according to the prophecy, and that these were the people that came out of the wilderness at the time of the Reformation, and that these same people were persecuted by Catholics, Calvinists, Lutherans and Episcopalians, see page 216.

Now, are there more than two or three witnesses that will testify that the Baptists constitute the continuity? Do they tie the Baptists on to the Waldenses, and the others, and thus give them the right of way back to the apostles? Come into court, ye honest and faithful witnesses for Christ, and tell us if the Baptists are right in claiming this continuity from the apostles.

Those of Mr. Campbell's school, who have given faitful testimony on another part of the subject, will they now help us out on this? Here is what Mr. Campbell himself said, in his debate with Bishop Percell, page 77: "The disciples of Christ are the same race, call them Christians, Nazarenes, Gallileans, Novatians, Donatists, Paulicians, Waldenses, Albigenses, Protestants, or what you please. A variety of designation affects not the fact which we allege; we can find an unbroken series of Protestants—a regular succession of those who protested against the corruptions of the Roman church, and endeavored to hold fast the faith once delivered to the saints, from the first schism in the year 250 A. D. to the present day; and you may apply to them what description or designation you please."

I now quote from Mr. Alexander Campbell, in his debate with McCalla. On page 65, he says: "We can show that, from the earliest times, there has existed a people, whom no man can number, that have earnestly and consistently contended for the true faith once delivered to the saints." On page 378 he says: "From the apostolic age to the present time, the sentiments of Baptists and their practice of baptism have had a continued chain of advocates, and public monuments of their existence in every century can be produced."

Mr. Campbell, writing to one of his disciples—Dr. Thomas, when Thomas had commenced re-immersing some of his own disciples that had come to him from the Baptists, see (Mil. Harb., vol. 7, page 57), says: "This (that there are some worthy Baptists) exactly accords with the views of some of our brethren long since expressed—that as it was with the Jews in the times of the Messiah and his apostles, so it is now with the Baptists. The nation, as such, continued to be the kingdom of God, until they rejected the offered salvation; so the present kingdom of God was found amongst those who plead for faith, repentance and baptism, as necessary to the admission into the kingdom of grace, until the present call upon them to reformation."

See the testimony of Mr. Burnett, editor of the *Christian Messenger*, Dallas, Texas. "Christ founded his Church upon a rock, and it has been there ever since. In the days of A. Campbell, it was wearing the name, 'Baptist Church.' With Alexander Campbell we say, the kingdom was with the Baptists before he and his co-adjutors started the reformation."

"There is nothing more congenial to civil liberty than to enjoy an unrestrained, unembargoed liberty of exercising the conscience freely upon all subjects respecting religion. Hence it is that the Baptist denomination, in all ages and in all centuries, has been, as a body, the constant asserters of the rights of man and of liberty of conscience." (Campbell on Baptism, 409.)

Mr. Campbell, in his debate with Walker, page 262, says: "The Baptists can trace their origin to the apostolic times, and produce unequivocal testimony of their existence in every century down to the present time."

Mr. Campbell said these things in the days of his greatest glory. His subsequent exclusion from the Baptists for heresy concerning the design of baptism, did not alter a single ancient historical fact. He knew the fact of Baptist Church Perpetuity, and said he could prove it, and he never afterward denied it; only he tried to hitch his new man-made church on to this Perpetuity. He and his tried hard to graft on in some way the broken-off branch on to the old olive tree, that it might partake of its root and fatness. But the branch from this wild olive tree can only be connected as a water-sprout, doomed for the knife when the ecclesiastical pruning time shall come.

(These Conclusive Concessions, as first prepared, were more numerous than here given, but were lost in the mail, and some of the concessions can't be reproduced in the short time allotted me.)

Read what others say.

We wish now to look into the character of these Waldenses, or Valenses, which is their true name, as many testify, and if the Baptists can claim them in their line of continuity. We will begin with this clipping from *The Southern Messenger*, the Catholic paper of Texas. Replying to a query of *The Baptist Standard*, it said, in its issue of July 1st, 1897: "If we speak of Baptists, we mean that sect known nowadays as Baptists with their present teachings and practices. But if by Baptists are understood all those sects of past ages which have, under various names, been opposed to the Catholic Church, and which may have had one or the other teaching or practice in common with the present Baptists, then, of course, the Baptist sect may be traced back to Apostolic times, as sects there always have been."

In 1819, the King of Holland appointed Dr. Ypeij, Professor of Theology in the University of Groningen, and Rev. J. J. Dermot, Chaplain to the King, both learned men and members of the Dutch Reformed Church, to prepare a history of their church. In the authentic volume which they prepared and published at Breda, they devote one chapter to the Baptists, in which they make the following statement: "We have now seen that the Baptists, who were formerly called Anabaptists, and in later times, Mennonites, were the original Waldenses, and who, long in the history of the church, received the honor of that origin.

"On this account the Baptists may be considered as the only Christian community which has stood since the apostles, and, as a Christian society, has preserved pure the doctrine of the gospel through all ages.

"The perfectly correct, external and internal economy of the Baptist denomination tends to confirm the truth disputed by the Romish church, that the Reformation, brought about in the sixteenth century, was in the highest degree necessary; and, at the same time, goes to refute the erroneous notion of the Catholics, that their communion is the most ancient."

"Let it be remembered," says Dr. Wheaton Smith, "that these learned men were not Baptists, that they proclaimed the result of their diligent research in the ear of a king, who listened unwillingly to their conclusions.

"Let it be remembered that, as a result of their investigation, the Government of Holland offered to the Baptist churches in the kingdom support of the State; and, true to their principles, they declined it."

Sir Isaac Newton says, as quoted in Appleton's Encyclopedia: "The Baptists are the only body of Christians that has not symbolized with the church of Rome."

This testimony is of the highest order, and refutes the assertion sometimes made by men who, no doubt, are sincere, but lacking in information, that Baptists originated at Munster in 1534.

The Munster rioters were composed of Romanists and many non-professors, and a few who repudiated Infant Baptism. Menno, the greatest Baptist of those times, denounced their conduct as "against the spirit and word and example of Christ." Again Menno says: "I warned every man against the Munster abominations in regard to a king, to polygamy, to a wordly kingdom, to a sword, etc., most faithfully."

In the language of Dr. Brown: "It is now too late in the day to confound this primitive people with the Munster sect, because both were called by their enemies Anabaptists. As well confound the Baptists of the United States with the Mormons of Salt Lake. I thought it proper to note this; although no man of intelligence and candor believes that Baptists so originated. The Baptists had been in existence full fifteen hundred years when Bockold, Mathys and their frantic followers commenced their career of folly."

Kellar, the historian of Germany, says the

Anabaptists and the Waldenses were the same people.

Dr. A. H. Newman, in *Western Recorder*, says: "As regards Kellar's position, the editor and the readers of this paper and my book can not fail to see that I am entirely in agreement with him (Kellar) as regards the continuity of evangelical life during the mediæval time, the historical connection of the Waldenses and the Anabaptists, and that of the latter and modern Baptists. I do not always regard Kellar's arguments from individual cases as conclusive; but I believe that his main position has been abundantly established."

Zwingle, the Swiss reformer and contemporary of Luther, says: "The institution of Anabaptists is no novelty, but for thirteen hundred years has caused great trouble to the church."

As Zwingle died in 1531, his accusation would show that the Baptists date as far back as two hundred years after the death of Christ. We have, however, a better testimony than this.

This, you will observe, is not Baptist testimony, but Reformed Dutch and Swiss and German. It is as true as it is manly and generous. Put this testimony with Mosheim, that their origin is *hid in the depths of antiquity*, and you have established, as thoroughly as any fact of history can be established from this style of testimony, that the Baptists can successfully trace their genealogy far back toward the apostolic age.

Of the German Baptists, Bancroft, the great American historian, himself not a Baptist, has made a noble record. He says: "With a greater consistency than Luther they applied the doctrines of the reformation to the social positions of life, and threatened an end to priestcraft and kingcraft, spiritual domination and vassalage. They were trodden under foot with foul reproaches and most arrogant scorn; and their history is written in the blood of thousands of the German peasantry; but their principles . . . witness that naturally the paths of the Baptists are not paths of freedom, pleasantness and peace."

Cardinal Hosius, a learned Catholic, who was chairman of the Council of Trent, speaking of the Baptists, says: "If the truth of religion were to be judged of by the readiness and cheerfulness which a man of any sect shows in suffering, then the opinions and persuasions of *no sect can be truer or surer than those of the Anabaptists*, since there have been none for *these twelve hundred years past* that have been more grievously punished." Mark the fact that *for twelve hundred years prior to* 1570 *the Baptists* had suffered. The most of this suffering was on account of *rejecting alien immersion and denouncing infant* baptism. Cardinal Hosius traces them back to 350 A. D. In the preface to the French Bible, the first ever printed, the Waldenses claim to have been enriched by the Holy Scriptures, given to them by the apostles, and to have preserved the Holy Scriptures from generation to generation."

Dr. D. M. Evans, in his *Landmarks of Truth:* "A concise view of all Religions" ties the Baptists to the Waldensian line. On page 54 he says: "The Baptists, as a sect, may be said to have existed *from* the time of Peter Waldo, who commenced his agitations in 1180; and established churches *among* the Waldenses. His doctrines were the impropriety of infant baptism, and the necessity of immersion to the validity of any baptism. This sect was established in England by Walter Lollard in 1338. His followers were called after him, Lollards; but the name gradually gave place to that of Baptists."

Dr. Evans ties the Baptists tight enough to the Waldenses, but he mistook the origin of that people, as all others testify. But as a half-loaf is better than no bread, we let him tie us on. He says, Waldo and his followers "formed an association with other pious people." That is, they joined the Baptists, "who were older than Waldo."

Rev. William Cecil Duncan, professor of the Greek and Latin Languages in the University of Louisiana, says: "Baptists do not, as do most Protestant denominations, date their origin from the Reformation of 1520. By means of that great religious movement, indeed, they were brought forth from comparative obscurity into prominent notice, and through it a new and powerful impulse was given to their principles and practices in all those countries which had renounced allegiance to the Pope of Rome. They did not, however, originate with the Reformation, for, long before Luther lived, nay, long before the Roman Catholic Church herself was known, Baptists and Baptist churches existed and flourished in Europe, in Asia and in Africa."

Wall, p. 20, says: "The Anabaptists are a pernicious sect, of which kind the Waldensian brethren seem to have been. Nor is this heresy a modern thing, for it existed in time of Austin." That takes them back to at least A. D. 354.

And I want your attention to the testimony of a very learned historian—a Catholic—Louis Cormenin. In his history of the Popes, part 2, p. 197, he says: "In Germany it was still worse; the reformed, moved by religious fanaticism, pursued the sect of the Anabaptists with the utmost rigor, and exercised such frightful cruelties toward them, that the hair rises on the head when we read the recitals that historians have given us. Instead of being intimidated by tortures, these new martyrs surrendered themselves to their executioners; they were seen mounting the funeral piles, singing the praises of God; the most delicate females sought the most cruel torments, to give proof of their faith; young virgins walked to punishment more gaily than to the nuptial ceremony; the men evinced not the least signs of fear, when contemplating the terrible instruments of torture; they sang psalms while the executioners were tearing off their flesh with red-hot pincers. Even when their bodies were half consumed by the fire, their members broken, and the skin, torn from their skulls, was hanging about their shoulders, they exhorted the assistants to become converts to their doctrine. Never had any sect shown such extraordinary constancy in persecutions; thus, the admiration which their courage inspired drew a great number of Catholics and Lutherans into their ranks. If the excellency of a religion could be proved by the testimony and number of its martyrs (as the Catholic priests maintain), the sect of the Anabaptists would, doubless, be superior to any other, since it had, in less than a year, more than a hundred and fifty thousand martyrs, which is more than the martyrologists count during the long persecutions of the Pagan emperors." Here, then, is the authority of a learned Catholic writer, and he puts the Anabaptists or Baptists in the line of Rev. 12: "And the dragon was wroth with the woman, and went to make war with the remnant of her seed, which keep the commandments of God, and have the testimony of Jesus Christ."

By what *means* the punishments of these Baptists were inflicted, I here submit, from *Dr. Chandler's History of Persecutions*, as given by Jones in his *History of the Christian Church*, page 120, the following: "They were publicly whipped, drawn by the heels through the streets of cities, racked till every bone in their body was disjointed, had their teeth beat out, their noses, hands and ears cut off, sharp-pointed spears run under their nails, were tortured with melted lead thrown on their naked bodies, had their eyes dug out, their limbs cut off, were condemned to the mines, ground between stones, stoned to death, burnt alive, thrown headlong from the high buildings, beheaded, smothered in burning lime kilns, run through the body with sharp spears, destroyed with hunger, thirst and cold, thrown to the wild beasts, broiled on gridirons with slow fires, cast by heaps into the sea, crucified, scraped to death with sharp shells, torn in pieces by the boughs of trees, and, in a word, destroyed by all the various methods that the most diabolical subtlety and malice could devise." These persecutions of Christians—Baptists—members of the true Churches of Christ, for the first three centuries, were carried on principally by Jews and Heathens. These persecutions were permitted and appointed to the true Church, which honor is conceded by all as falling to the Baptists. Her persecutions prove her Pepetuity.

The following is a clipping from *The Religious Herald*, some 25 years ago. The author's name is lost. It is a fine summing up, and as such I adopt it.

"The early Baptists of the United States came hither from the old world—for the most part, from Wales. The first Baptist churches in New England, New Jersey and Pennsylvania—the first in the order of time in the country—were largely of Cambrian or Welsh extraction, embracing alike their ministers and private members. The Welsh Baptists claim their origin direct from the Apostles, and their claim has never been successfully controverted. They maintain that the light of a pure Christianity has been preserved among her people during all the 'dark ages.' They were a pastoral people, dwelling in their mountain homes. They were subjected to almost constant persecution, and therefore sought to conceal themselves in their mountain recesses, that have been so appropriately styled the 'Piedmont of Britain.' And yet the fact of their early existence is placed beyond peradventure or doubt. They attracted the attention of the Romish church, and as early as the year 597 a monk visited them, by the name of Austin, and sought to win them to his views. They met him in a great convocation of twelve hundred pastors and delegates, when he laid before them three distinct propositions, all of which they rejected. The first related to the observance of Easter, the second required their submission to Austin, as prelate of the church which he represented; and the third demanded that they should give 'Christendom,' that is, infant baptism, to their children. These conditions very clearly define the position of those to whom they were addressed and by whom they were rejected. They would not administer infant baptism; they would not yield to the demands of the English or Romish church; they would not observe a festal day appointed by that church. And you will observe the date of this occurrence. It was in the year 597—now 1310 years ago.

The English Baptists are able to trace their principles and practices with great distinctness through a period of more than five hundred years. They are now, and have long been, a power in that land. The late Dr. Chalmers pronounced them, 'for their number, the most intellectual body in England.' Their annals are adorned by such names as Hall, Riland, Fuller, Carey, Marshman and Ward, etc.; in earlier times, by the names of Wicliffe, Bunyan and Milton.

But, leaving the Baptists of England, we pass over to Continental Europe. And here we first meet the Dutch Baptists in Holland. That they are a very ancient people, we have the highest proofs of history.

Following the line of Baptist history, we must pass over the Alps into the vales and among the rocky fastnesses of Piedmont; for, from the testimony of Drs. Dermont and Ypeij, the Baptists were 'the original Waldenses, and have long, in the history of the church, received the honor of that origin.' That people have been known under different names: Waldenses, Albigenses, Cathari, Poor Men of Lyons and Vaudois; but, during the long, dark ages of the church, they held fast the faith, and preserved the ordinances as they were delivered to the saints. They have been appropriately styled 'the burning bush' of the Christian dispensation. The fires of persecution have raged around them, heated to the intensity of Nebuchadnezzar's furnace, but they have not been consumed.

Beyond this people we find the Paulicians, of whom the Empress Theodora caused not less than one hundred thousand to be put to death, and whom Robinson, the historian, calls 'Trinitarian Baptists.' They first began to attract attention in the seventh century. In the fourth century the Donatists arose, holding the same general views; and in the third the Novatians.

"But I need proceed no further in this direction. These statements sufficiently indicate the line of inquiry, by which we undertake to show that gospel churches, such as were planted by the Saviour and his apostles, have been preserved through all the succeeding ages.

"This glance at Baptist history is sufficient to establish several important propositions; as for example, that the Baptists did not come out of the church of Rome, either at the time of the reformation, or at any other time—and for the best of all reasons—they were never in that church.

"Again, the history of the Baptists shows that they have always been the firm and consistent advocates of religious liberty. This has ever been a cardinal feature in their faith and polity, and, by their maintenance of it, they have made the Christian world greatly their debtors. Upon this point, were it needed, there could be given an array of testimony, of which the following is a sample.

"Said the late Judge Story, when speaking of the Baptists: ' In the code of laws established by them in Rhode Island, we read for the first time since Christianity ascended the throne of the Cæsars, the declaration that conscience should be free, and that men should not be punished for worshipping God in the way they were persuaded he requires.'

"Nor is this all. The Baptists, in holding fast this principle of religious liberty, have always yielded to others what they have claimed for themselves. While they have suffered untold persecutions for the truth's sake, they have never persecuted in return; while they have freely given their blood as martyrs for the truth, the blood of martyrs is not found upon their garments."

And Bancroft, the great American historian, said: "Freedom of conscience, unlimited freedom of mind, was from the first the trophy of the Baptists."

Herbert S. Skeats, author of the History of the Free Churches of England, who takes pains to remind us that he is not a Baptist, says: "It is the singular and distinguished honor of the Baptists to have repudiated from their earliest history all coercive power over the consciences of men with reference to religion. No sentence can be found in all their writings inconsistent with these principles of Christian liberty."

But it may be said that the best Baptist scholars

repudiate this theory of church succession, and therefore my own people are against me. That Dr. Whitsitt said that the Baptists had their origin in 1610, and that the English Baptists invented immersion in 1641. Well, Dr. Whitsitt, like the rest of us, has been misunderstood. He said some unfortunate things, perhaps, for which he has suffered severely. In 1885 I was editor of the *Baptist Gleaner*, in which a report came that Dr. Whitsitt said, the Presbyterians were older than the Baptists. This brought on a correspondence with Dr. Whitsitt, also with Dr. T. T. Eaton, then his pastor. This correspondence appeared in the *Gleaner*, from which I quote what Dr. Eaton said, as I am anxious that the Baptists shall be better understood, and that they should the better understand each other. Dr. Eaton said: "I have heard Dr. Whitsitt's entire course of lectures on Church History and on Polemics, and I never heard him express an idea at variance with the faith of the denomination in the South, although those are the very subjects on which it was 'reported' he was not sound. Since the appearance of the paragraph above mentioned, I have talked with Dr. Whitsitt about it—he being a member of my church and an intimate personal friend. He does not recall ever having said what is charged against him, is sure he did not say it, because such is not his belief. To say that 'Pedobaptist churches are true churches of Christ' conveys the idea that they fulfill the New Testament conditions of a church, when the fact is, they are in error on the fundamental question as to the material of which a church should be composed. Dr. Whitsitt says that he often uses the term 'church' in referring to Pedobaptist bodies, not meaning that they fulfill the Scriptural conditions, but simply using language as it is commonly used. Everybody does the same thing. It is simply calling organizations by the names by which they are known to the world.

"While in this line, let me say a word as to Professor Whitsitt's teaching on 'Baptist Succession.' After listening to one of his lectures on Baptist history, I remember stating to him my own belief on the subject, and he added heartily, 'That's my belief exactly.' My statement was in substance as follows: Baptist principles are clearly taught in the New Testament, and the promise is given that they shall never be destroyed, but shall finally dominate the world. God would not leave himself without a witness on the earth to principles of such importance, and especially so after the promises he has made. We are, therefore, authorized, aside from all historical evidence, to believe that at no time since John the Baptist has the world been without men adhering to Baptist principles—witnesses for the truth. How well we can trace any line of succession, will depend upon how well old records have been preserved. When we remember that, in many ages and lands, it was all a man's life was worth to be known as believing Baptist doctrines, and bear in mind that the very existence (humanly speaking) of such people depended on their successfully concealing themselves it is unreasonable to expect that anything like a regular line of succession can be made out at this day. I added that this fact compels us to build upon the Bible, instead of building upon history, which is to be used simply to confirm what we learn from the Scriptures. The argument we can make from history, however, is as strong as in the nature of the case could be reasonably expected.

Many of the old documents in existence have never been carefully studied, and I, for one, would favor the sending of some competent man to Europe, and supporting him while he studied the documents which remain, and gather material for the most thorough Baptist history that can now be written. Many documents have perished, and many of the facts were never committed to writing at all. We owe it to ourselves and to the world to learn all that is to be known concerning our history."

Dr. Whitsitt never said that the Baptists invented immersion in 1641, though he has often been thus quoted by Pedobaptists. He says, on the first page of his book, that immersion begun with John the Baptist, and has continued till now, and is essential to Christian baptism. A better understanding of each other would give us a better standing with each other. We all do wrong and say wrong, and there ought to be that forgiveness for each other that we ask of God for ourselves. When Dr. W. P. Harvey delivered that great sermon on Baptist History, in the Fourth and Walnut Street Church, Louisville, Ky., the church, in requesting it for publication, appointed Dr. Whitsitt or the committee, to secure its publication. The sermon was on Church Perpetuity. Dr. Whitsitt may have said some unfortunate things, and in many things was doubtless misunderstood, but the contention, I trust, is closed, with books on both sides, and the Baptists are at peace again on that subject. But did not the Southern Baptist Convention endorse and have published Dr. J. B. Hawthorn's attack on

Church Succession? No, indeed. The great majority deplored that part of the speech, but there was so much good in the speech, and so much regard for the old faithful servant of God, that they ordered it published, in spite of that defect. The great address of E. W. Stephens, L.L.D., President of the Southern Baptist Convention, on "The Place of Baptists in History, is published by the Sunday-school Board of the Southern Baptist Convention. I wish I could make some extracts, but my limits now forbid. I have before me that great address of Dr. Geo. W. Lasher, editor of the *Journal and Messenger*, of Cincinnati, on "Indebtedness of the World to Baptists for the Maintenance of a Pure Gospel." I have many places marked for quotation here, but must forgo it. It is sound through and through.

I have also that great address of Dr. A. E. Dickinson, editor of *Religious Herald*, Richmond, Va., on "What Baptist Principles are Worth to the World." I make one quotation from page 22.

"If Baptists could have been overthrown, it would have been done long ago. Almost every weapon has been tried against them, and with what result? Since our Lord bade us go into the world and disciple all nations, baptizing them into the name of the Father, Son and Holy Ghost, there has never dawned a day when the prospect for the Baptists was brighter than it is this day, and the morrow will be for them brighter still. These principles of ours are yet to be laurel-crowned. To use the words of a celebrated Baptist martyr, "Divine truth is immortal. It may be scourged, crucified, and for a season entombed, but on the third day it will rise again victorious, and rule triumphant forever."

Perhaps I have a dozen histories of the Baptists, written by Baptists. I wish I had a hundred more, and I hope that 100 more will be written during this generation. That would result in a more extended reading, as each author has his circle and circumscribed influence, and no author can reach all Baptists. The greatest injury we are now suffering most from is ignorance of Baptist history, and this ignorance is greatly due to the ponderous books, filled with confusions—worse confounded of all the isms, that we have no use for, and ought to have no knowledge of. I have tried to cull what we want and need, and NO MORE, and to extend the quotations to "the two or three witnesses" that settle all disputes. I have others marked, but this is enough to show how they all run. I have aimed to give the right idea of Baptist Church History. I have proved what sort of a church he built, and have shown that it was that kind of a church that the gates of destruction raged against, and that kind of a church has been doing the business of the kingdom ever since; that, therefore, his promise has been kept, so that we can, with unspeakable gratitude and confidence in God, say: Now unto him that is able to do exceeding abundantly above all that we ask or think, according to the power that worketh within us, unto him *be* the glory in the church and in Christ Jesus unto all generations forever and ever. Amen.

THE END

A Biographical Sketch of Joseph Burnley Moody (1838-1931)

BY

John Franklin Jones

A Biographical Sketch of Joseph Burnley Moody (1838-1931)

Joseph Burnley Moody—pastor, author, editor—was born in Clarksville, Virginia June 24, 1838, the son of William A. and Emily Royster Moody. Brought up on a farm, Moody taught and merchandised in young adulthood (*ESB*).

He professed faith in Christ and was baptized into the Bethel Church, Christian County, Kentucky, in July 1855. He was ordained September 11, 1876 by Pewee Valley Church, Oldham County, Kentucky. Educated at Bethel College, Kentucky, he received a D.D. degree in 1891 (*ESB*).

Moody served as the pastor of several churches in Kentucky, Tennessee, Arkansas, Texas, and Florida. The churches included Pewee Valley, Kentucky (1876-80); Lagrange, Kentucky (1877- 80) (*ESB*); Ell Creek, Kentucky (1877-80) (Lasher); Harrod's Creek, Kentucky (1879-80); Paducah, Kentucky (1880-82) (*ESB*); Trezavant, Round Lick, Shop Springs and Martin, Tennessee (1883-86); P. Gilead and S. Central, Memphis, Tennessee (l888) (Lasher); Gilead and Bagdad, Kentucky (1889) (Grimes); Overton, Kentucky (1890-92) (*ESB*); Hot Springs, Arkansas (1893-94); Sunset Church, San Antonio, Texas (1895-96) (Grime); Tampa, Florida (1897-98); and Hot Springs, Arkansas (1899-1902) (*ESB*).

JOHN FRANKLIN JONES

He was editor of *Baptist Gleaner* (1882-86), *The Baptist* (1886-89), and *The Baptist and Reflector* (1889) (*ESB*). Moody wrote prolifically. Among his published works are the following books: *Debate on Baptism, and the Work of the Holy Spirit: in Which the Place of Baptism in the Gospel Economy, Its Design, and the Work of the Holy Spirit in Conversion Are Considered* (1889); *Baptist, Why and Why Not* (1900); *The Distinguishing Doctrines of Baptist* (1901); *The Twelve W's of Baptism* (1906); *My Church, Its Character and Perpetuity* (1908); *My Church* (1908?); *After Death* (1910); *Rights and Restrictions of Women in the Churches; or, Paul Harmonized with the Law and the Gospel* (1910); *The Perfect Gospel* (1922); and *The Exceeding Riches of the Manifold Grace of God* (n.d.) (Starr).

Many of his pamphlets, articles, and sermons are extant. They include: "The Nashville Debate Between Moody and Harding" (1899) (Lasher), "The Name Christian" (1883-85); "Baptist Authors Vindicated," (1889); "Vindication Concerning and Containing the Anderson Letters" (1894); "The Culpability of Ignorance, An Address on 1 Cor. 15:38" (1894); "Baccalaureate Sermon Preached at Ouachita College June 3, 1894" (n.d.); "The Two Covenants" (1896); "The Barren Fig Tree, The Fruitless Christian" (1910); "Church Government," in *The Baptist and Reflector* (1901): 131-206; "Co-operation of Churches: Speeches Nov. 16, 1901, Little Rock, Arkansas" (1902); "The Seven Sabbaths" (1910?); "Address to Gospel Mission Brethren" (1910); "Baptismal Regeneration" (1910); "Baptism and Remission" (1912); "Atheism; Immoral and Irrational" (lectures delivered over eight states, urged for publication) (n.d.); "Sin, Salvation, and Service" (n.d.); "To the Gospel Mission Baptists" (n.d.); "The New-free Woman" (n.d.); "Valid Baptism" (supplemental to "The Twelve W's of Baptism," considered the baptism of anti-missionaries) (n.d.); and "Why Baptist? Why the Church? Why a Baptist?" (n.d.) (Starr).

Moody married Jennie L. Jones December 22, 1895. The marriage was blessed by four children (Grimes). He died in Jacksonville, Florida September 8, 1931 (*ESB*).

BIBLIOGRAPHY

Encyclopedia of Southern Baptists. S.v. "Moody, Joseph Burnley," by Leo. T. Crismon and James Brewer.

Starr, Edward C., ed., *A Baptist Bibliography Being a Register of Printed Material By and About Baptists; Including Works Written Against the Baptists*. 24 vols. Chester, PN: American Baptist Historical Society, 1953. S.v. "Moody, Joseph Burnley, 1838-1931."

Grime, J. H. *History of Middle Tennessee Baptists with Special Reference to Salem, New Salem, Enon and Wiseman Associations*. Cave City, KY: N.p., 1902.

Lasher, George W., ed. *The Ministerial Directory of the Baptist Churches...* Oxford, OH: Ministerial Directory Co., 1899.

BY JOHN FRANKLIN JONES
CORDOVA, TENNESSEE
JULY 2006

THE BAPTIST STANDARD BEARER, INC.

a non-profit, tax-exempt corporation
committed to the Publication & Preservation
of the Baptist Heritage.

CURRENT TITLES AVAILABLE IN
THE BAPTIST *DISTINCTIVES* SERIES

KIFFIN, WILLIAM	A Sober Discourse of Right to Church-Communion. Wherein is proved by Scripture, the Example of the Primitive Times, and the Practice of All that have Professed the Christian Religion: That no Unbaptized person may be Regularly admitted to the Lord's Supper. (London: George Larkin, 1681).
KINGHORN, JOSEPH	Baptism, A Term of Communion. (Norwich: Bacon, Kinnebrook, and Co., 1816)
KINGHORN, JOSEPH	A Defense of "Baptism, A Term of Communion". In Answer To Robert Hall's Reply. (Norwich: Wilkin and Youngman, 1820).
GILL, JOHN	Gospel Baptism. A Collection of Sermons, Tracts, etc., on Scriptural Authority, the Nature of the New Testament Church and the Ordinance of Baptism by John Gill. (Paris, AR: The Baptist Standard Bearer, Inc., 2006).

CARSON, ALEXANDER	Ecclesiastical Polity of the New Testament. (Dublin: William Carson, 1856).
BOOTH, ABRAHAM	A Defense of the Baptists. A Declaration and Vindication of Three Historically Distinctive Baptist Principles. Compiled and Set Forth in the Republication of Three Books. Revised edition. (Paris, AR: The Baptist Standard Bearer, Inc., 2006).
BOOTH, ABRAHAM	Paedobaptism Examined on the Principles, Concessions, and Reasonings of the Most Learned Paedobaptists. With Replies to the Arguments and Objections of Dr. Williams and Mr. Peter Edwards. 3 volumes. (London: Ebenezer Palmer, 1829).
CARROLL, B. H.	*Ecclesia* - The Church. With an Appendix. (Louisville: Baptist Book Concern, 1903).
CHRISTIAN, JOHN T.	Immersion, The Act of Christian Baptism. (Louisville: Baptist Book Concern, 1891).
FROST, J. M.	Pedobaptism: Is It From Heaven Or Of Men? (Philadelphia: American Baptist Publication Society, 1875).
FULLER, RICHARD	Baptism, and the Terms of Communion; An Argument. (Charleston, SC: Southern Baptist Publication Society, 1854).
GRAVES, J. R.	Tri-Lemma: or, Death By Three Horns. The Presbyterian General Assembly Not Able To Decide This Question: "Is Baptism In The Romish Church Valid?" 1st Edition.

	(Nashville: Southwestern Publishing House, 1861).
MELL, P.H.	Baptism In Its Mode and Subjects. (Charleston, SC: Southern Baptist Publications Society, 1853).
JETER, JEREMIAH B.	Baptist Principles Reset. Consisting of Articles on Distinctive Baptist Principles by Various Authors. With an Appendix. (Richmond: The Religious Herald Co., 1902).
PENDLETON, J.M.	Distinctive Principles of Baptists. (Philadelphia: American Baptist Publication Society, 1882).
THOMAS, JESSE B.	The Church and the Kingdom. A New Testament Study. (Louisville: Baptist Book Concern, 1914).
WALLER, JOHN L.	Open Communion Shown to be Unscriptural & Deleterious. With an introductory essay by Dr. D. R. Campbell and an Appendix. (Louisville: Baptist Book Concern, 1859).

For a complete list of current authors/titles, visit our internet site at:
www.standardbearer.org
or write us at:

he Baptist Standard Bearer, Inc.

NUMBER ONE IRON OAKS DRIVE • PARIS, ARKANSAS 72855

TEL # 479-963-3831   *FAX # 479-963-8083*
EMAIL: Baptist@centurytel.net   *http://www.standardbearer.org*

Thou hast given a standard to them that fear thee; that it may be displayed because of the truth. — Psalm 60:4

www.ingramcontent.com/pod-product-compliance
Lightning Source LLC
Chambersburg PA
CBHW021135230426
43667CB00005B/123